Praise for *Journey from Head to Heart*

"What separates this book from the majority of self-help manuals is the author's awareness that many people in today's world neglect to acknowledge the importance of personal faith and spirituality in the growth process, and in turn, are unable to integrate their actions with their beliefs."
                                                    —Lisa Heidle, *Rebecca's Reads*

"For beginners on a spiritual voyage, as well as for experienced travelers, *Journey from Head to Heart* is very powerful. I couldn't put it down. Its stories, told with clarity and simplicity, make it a treasure."
                                         —Dr. Linda O'Neal, Executive Director,
                                                    Southwest Education Alliance

"This book is for people struggling with work/life balance, for entrepreneurs, for those seeking their authentic purpose in life and work. It lays out a plan to get ego out of the way, lead with humility, and communicate so that others are attracted to your cause."
                                                    —Dick Moeller, President
                                     St. David's Community Health Foundation

"I wish every teacher would read this, as well as anybody who works with people. It should be required reading for school administrators. The subject is heavy, but the book is easy to read. It has good rhythm and balance. The first few sentences will grab you. Once I started reading, I couldn't put it down."

                                                    —Dr. Donna Nicholson
                                         Superintendent, Trinity Charter Schools

"[She] has written a very honest book about speaking the truth in love and in writing this work she has effectively so mediated the Spirit that most, if not all, her readers will be inspired to consider growing toward becoming a living expression of the truth she models in her reflection upon her own life and in her keen articulation of her research and its assimilation. It's an excellent and powerful work. Moreover, it's a gift."
                                                    —Dr. Bob Lively, author
                                          A Walk with God through Forgiveness

"This is a book to not only read but to be digested and utilized. The tools presented are both practical and effective in bringing about a change in communication skills."   —Ron Mullen,
                                                    former mayor of Austin, TX

"*Journey from Head to Heart* provides critical insight for those who desire to find greater purpose and meaning in the journey of life. She has an amazing gift that she utilizes daily to help people find discover a more meaningful in the journey of life! A *must read* for anyone serious about enhancing their daily living."

—Paulette Schwartz, Minister of Pastoral Care
Riverbend Church, Austin

"One of the things a reader wants from a non-fiction book is illustration. Nancy's book is full of good examples of the life lessons she gives."

—Rev. Gordon Smith

"*Journey From Head to Heart* is profound, challenging our assumptions about what can and cannot be changed; and addresses not just interpersonal relationships, but changing corporate cultures in ways that call forth the best in employers and employees, producing productive, healthy, and happy members in the work place."

—Judith K. Johnson, MSE, MA

Journey from Head to Heart:
Living and Working Authentically

Nancy Oelklaus

First printing March 2008

Library of Congress Cataloging-in-Publication Data

Oelklaus, Nancy, 1943-
  Journey from head to heart : living and working authentically / Nancy Oelklaus.
      p. cm. -- (Spiritual dimensions series ; bk. #7)
  Includes bibliographical references and index.
  ISBN-13: 978-1-932690-43-9 (trade paper : alk. paper)
  ISBN-10: 1-932690-43-3 (trade paper : alk. paper)
  1. Self-actualization (Psychology) 2. Self-realization. 3. Authenticity (Philosophy) 4. Spiritual life. I. Title.
  BF637.S4O38 2007
  158--dc22
                          2007037851

Distributed by: Baker & Taylor, Ingram Book Group, Quality Books
Loving Healing Press
5145 Pontiac Trail
Ann Arbor, MI 48105
USA

http://www.LovingHealing.com or
info@LovingHealing.com
Fax +1 734 663 6861

Loving Healing Press

This book is dedicated to Lois Marie and Anne Marie,

from whom I learned my toughest lesson;

to Harlan, Brett, DeAnn, Todd, and Scotti,

from whom I learned the irresistible power of a forgiving heart;

and to Dad.

Table of Contents

Table of Figures...vi
Index of Poems..vii
Preface ix
Introduction.. xiii

Chapter 1 – Wayfaring to Wayfinding 1
   Transition from Wayfaring to Wayfinding.........................6
   Wayfinding 7
   Find Fellow Wayfinders...13
Chapter 2 – Leave the Pain 17
   The Energy Analysis®..21
   Energy in Systems: Neuronal Connections.................28
   The Impact of Leadership...30
Chapter 3 – Transforming Negative Energy 35
   What's the Whole Truth? 35
   The Whole Truth Letters 35
   Transform Defects to Shortcomings 38
Chapter 4 – Tune into the Voice 41
   A Heart That Watches and Receives.........................45
   What Happened to Me 48
   What Happened to Her 51
   A Letter from God 52
Chapter 5 – Draw Your Circle...57
   What People Truly Want: Wayfinding 59
   My Experiences with the Circle 61
   Prelude...69
Chapter 6 – A Different Kind of Fire.....................................69
   Failing with "As" 71
   Three Love Stories 72
   Igniting the Fire 76
   Transcendence 81
   Putting the Golden Rule to Work..............................82
   Conclusion 85
Chapter 7 – The Power of Speaking from the Heart 89
   Energy of Love 89
   Words from the Heart 90
   Divinity of the Heart 91
   What We Learn with Our Hearts, or Not at All............92

The Wisdom of Silence..98
We Don't Take Time to Solve Our Problems.................................100
Importance of the State of Relaxed Alertness.............................102
Say Only What Truly Needs to Be Said.......................................103

Chapter 8 – Practice Humility...111
How Ego Forms...111
What Happens When Ego Shatters...118
Role Models..119
Your Highest and Best—The Authentic Profile.............................123

Chapter 9 – Thread the Eye of the Needle 131
Workplaces Where People Thrive..132
From Victims/Victimizers to Learners..136
Acceptance and Willingness..138
Ego Forged Through Wayfaring...140
A Tool for Transcending Ego 141
The Missing Piece of Leadership...145
Conclusion 147

Chapter 10 – Throw away the Chart and Tune In 149
Intent Changes Attitude..150
Assumptions Lead to Expectations 152
The Authentic Self..155
The Place Where Truth Lives..156
Meeting Standards While Developing Potential............................156
A True Story about Ego's Domination 158
Tune in to What?..158

Chapter 11 – Set a Boundary and Set Yourself Free........161
The Problem 166
Setting a Boundary...168
Becoming Free..169
Another Way of Becoming Free 170
Rewrite of My First Five Years..178
Why We Must Rewrite the Story..179
Freedom 181

Chapter 12 – Use the Toolbox 183
Ask, Release, and Wait..183
Love Letter..185
Sayings That Steer My Course 186
Bibliography for My Life...187
Listen 188
Apply the Principle of Matching States..189
Affirmation 190

Precision in Language.. 191
The Circle: a Focusing Tool.. 192
Where, Within Me, is this Flaw?.. 193
Goal Setting with Blockage Removal 195
Accountability Partner for Goal Achievement 195
Shred It.. 196

Afterword **199**

Guide for Wayfinders' Meetings **201**

References **203**

Suggestions for Further Reading...........................**207**

Suggestions for Further Viewing **210**

About the Author..**211**

Index..**212**

Table of Figures

Fig. 2-1: Person on antidepressants 23

Fig. 2-2: Person on with major life stressors..24

Fig. 2-3: Linda's first analysis 25

Fig. 2-4: Linda showing increased capacity over time 26

Fig. 2-5: Janie after verbal attack..27

Fig. 2-6: Neuronal Connections...29

Fig. 2-9: Authentic Profile of Leader #1 31

Fig. 2-10: Energy Analysis of Leader #1 32

Fig. 2-11: Employees of Leader #1..32

Fig. 2-12: Employees of Leader #2..33

Fig. 3-1: Character Defects vs. Shortcomings 38

Fig. 4-1: What the Voice Said to Me 50

Fig. 5-1: The Circle 60

Fig. 6-1: Maslow's original 5-level pyramid..87

Fig. 6-2: Maslow's new 8-level pyramid 87

Fig. 8-3: Average Brain Weight by Age..112

Fig. 8-4a: Example of an Authentic Profile...126

Fig. 8-4b: Example of an Authentic Profile 127

Fig. 8-5: Construct the Timeline of Your Life 128

Fig. 9-1: Right-hand Column, Left-hand Column 142

Fig. 9-2: Threading the Needle 144

Fig. 11-1: How Neurons Make Connections..172

Index of Poems

Touch Me, Too xii

Junctures 2

Protection 3

Self-Deluded 3

Hitting Bottom 4

A Prayer for Transformation 5

A Meditation on Lightning 6

Sunset #1 6

Love, Not Adore 7

Silence 9

Possibilities 13

"The Tables Turned" 44

Communion 47

Child 117

"If" 121

I Know My Name 153

Free To Be Me 154

Gods 154

Spears 177

Bumper Car Words 178

Turn Into The Slide 180

Do It Anyway 186

Preface

It was my ego that stood one morning on the jagged rocks jutting into the Atlantic Ocean and prayed to the winds to let me work with the best, smartest people in the world. But it was God who answered my prayer and led me, head bowed, to a 28-day treatment program for addiction. I expected to land on a prestigious university campus, not in these remote hills. My books—even my journal—were checked at the door, and I began to experience the life-changing model developed by Liliane and Gilles Desjardins (www.higherpower.info). I'm not an alcoholic or a drug addict. Oh alright, for a two-year period I was overly dependent on painkillers and sedatives, but I was free from those drugs, as well as the debilitating migraines that had driven me to take them. I was not, however, free from the disease of alcoholism that had ravaged my family for generations. The manifestation of disease in my own life was workaholism and codependence, so I ended up in a residential treatment program, "invited" to attend by my husband, who loved me enough to tell me that I needed help and here is where I could get it. As I experienced the Desjardins' unconditional love, I found, for the first time in my life, the power of simple acceptance, which I described like this:

> "Rushing water is the only sound I hear, punctuated by the occasional call of the cardinal atop the tallest tree and the swish of light wind through the tall pines. My eyes follow the sound to the cantilevered boulders and terraced pools that guide the water's path through this place that bridges mountain and valley. Cool droplets glance my shins as I jockey, positioning my body for the best view. But there is no best view, precisely why I feel so safe in this place.

> "Here, I know I will not be abused by someone's idea of what I need to do to be the best. My laurels don't matter. Neither do yours. No measuring. No comparing. No pertinent questions: 'Why don't you [do this]? Why can't you [do that]? Have you ever thought about...?' None of that. Just peace.

> "No leapfrogging or catapulting here. Every rock has its unique place in the water's glide and fall. Every tree. Every fallen leaf and insect. Every patch of sky and wispy cloud.

> "So I come here in silence, in reverence, and in the serenity that knows.

> "I am accepted.

> "Simply accepted."

To this point, my greatest handicap in life had been that I appeared attractive, smart, and strong. I looked as if I had it all together, so most people left me alone. But in this place, when I checked in, they discovered I had a hearing problem and had left my hearing aids at home because they needed cleaning. So, for the first class I was respectfully escorted to a seat with earphones wired to the ceiling. Someone gently placed them over my tired ears. What relief! I was so grateful I almost cried. Listening was easy. For the first time, I didn't have to strain to read the teacher's lips.

A few years later, an audiologist explained to me that the type of hearing loss I had, which she called a "cookie," was hereditary. I was born with it! The line graph she showed me revealed a normal pattern until the lines suddenly dropped, as if someone had taken a bite out of a cookie. For the first time, I understood why I read lips so well; why I am such an intent, focused listener; why I always sat near the front in my classes; why my parents used to say, "Do you hear me!?" when I didn't immediately obey.

As I yielded to the imperfection of a hearing impairment, I relaxed. Completely relaxed. Maybe for the first time in my life.

Growing up, what I had learned about love was very confusing. I had taken refuge in school and church. But even in these places I learned that to get approval I had to meet someone else's expectations, which I now realize was *conditional* love. (i.e. you meet my conditions, and I give you love.) In effect, I made those people and their beliefs my gods.

But in this beautiful, remote place, for 28 days, I lived in an environment in which no one was a favorite. It seemed that everyone was getting what he or she needed. For the first time in my life, the alcoholics were not getting more attention than I was. There was no one I needed to please. It was an amazing difference from what I had experienced out there in the real world. Yet, this new world was also real. I learned that if I didn't follow the rules, I would be corrected gently, with respect. But I *would* be corrected. I would not be overlooked.

Here, all my books, even my journal, were taken from me and locked up. For 28 days, I was not to exercise my mental faculties. Instead, I was to open more of my emotional and spiritual being. Long hikes were encouraged, and beautiful trails made them enjoyable.

I learned how dependent I had become on books. Some people might even call it an addiction. In a sense, books had also been my gods. If I had a problem, I went to the bookstore or library—not to the chapel to pray. But here I could learn simply by sitting and being quiet. I learned that I didn't have all the answers for other people, even when I thought I did. I learned that I suffer from the "halo effect", the notion that I have to be better than everyone else, making a god of my own image of myself. I learned that all addictions grow from four roots: control, security, suffering, and sensation. I learned about "process addictions," like addiction to work, exercise, relationships, Internet—even books! I experienced the miracle of witnessing someone (my roommate) finding God for the first time.

Based on watching what areas of the brain activate when stimulated by spiritual language and images, neuroscientists have identified what some call the "God spot." It's in the right hemisphere, the same part of the brain that wordlessly appreciates art and creation. As one of my clients put it, "Once that God spot lights up, then I can see the tiny lights along the trail leading me forward." Some say we are "hard-wired" for a relationship with God. Frankly, I don't care about scientific or religious debate that attempts to establish what God is, where God is, who is going to heaven, or who is right. What I care about is living my life as fully as possible. Within me is the capacity, if fleetingly, to leave my ego and be one with God. Those are moments of grace. When they occur, I am at my best. People come. They want me to teach them. As I teach them, I learn and my life continuously improves. This book contains many of their stories. The names I've used are fictitious, to preserve anonymity. As I live out my life, I want to spend more and more moments in a state of grace. That is all.

Touch Me, Too

The sunrise hour
I spend with me.

Waft of newborn air,
Constancy of trees,
And fresh bird calls—

From a distance.

Gradually the light of day
Enfolds the slumberous hill
And gentles it to
Awakening.

Then it comes alive—
Moves.

I rise from my
White, warm piles,
Walk boldly to the edge,
And say to the sun,

"Touch me, too."

Introduction

Contact (1997), a movie adaption of Carl Sagan's 1985 novel of the same name, announced a new frontier for explorers. In the movie, Jodie Foster plays the role of an astronomer named Ellie who receives significant funding to erect huge satellite dishes, like stethoscopes, to "tune in" to deep space and listen for signs of life. The central question of the movie asks if there is other intelligent life in the universe, and a refrain goes, "If it's just us, it seems like an awful waste of space." After an agonizingly long period the sounds begin to come, like a heartbeat, and scientists put the pieces of the puzzle together. In the aggregate, these signals give instructions for building a spacecraft for one person to travel to the heart of the universe. With federal funding the spacecraft is built, and ultimately Ellie is selected as its pilot. Along the way she has fallen in love with Palmer, an author and theologian played by Matthew McConaughey. While she has faith in the pursuit of truth through science, he has faith in the pursuit of truth through God.

At the launch the movie focuses on what happens to Ellie. She is shaken, catapulted, rattled, and hurtled through fantastic light shows with dramatic speed. The compass locket that Palmer has given her is shaken loose and she extricates herself from the chair to retrieve it, symbolically choosing love over her own personal safety. She loses consciousness, and when she awakens she has landed on a calm, perfect beach with white, white sands, lapping blue water, and gentle breezes. Through the plasma-like substance that surrounds her walks her father, as she remembers him from childhood when her love affair with space began as together they tuned into faraway voices on his ham radio. Ever the skeptical scientist, Ellie realizes he isn't real, to which he answers, "We thought it would be easier for you this way." When she asks, "Are there others?" her dad replies, "Many others."

"Why did you contact us?" is her next question.

"We didn't contact you; you contacted us," was his reply. His bottom-line message to her: "In all our searching, the only thing we find that makes things bearable is each other... This was just a step. When you're ready, you'll take another. Make small moves. The most important thing is to keep searching for your own answers."

When she alights from the spacecraft with only a small facial wound, Ellie finds a dismayed crowd of witnesses who tell her the spacecraft never took off; instead, it crashed into the ocean. Moreover, they said her trip had lasted only a fraction of a second while her estimate of time elapsed was eighteen hours.

Of course, since the project was federally funded there was a Congressional hearing, with Ellie caught in a dilemma. On the one hand, she was a skeptical scientist. On the other hand, "I had an experience I can't explain. It was real. It changed me forever. It made me realize how tiny, insignificant, great, and precious we are. We are not alone. I experienced awe, humility, hope." As a scientist, she believed that everything could be explained without the existence of God, but through this experience she had stepped into a spiritual dimension unlike anything she had ever known. She was torn between what she knew from academic, scientific discipline, and what she knew in her heart as true. Thus conflicted, and in the face of no tangible evidence, she is discredited using the argument of Occam's Razor, a medieval scientific principle that affirms that, all things being equal, the simplest explanation has to be the right one. The simplest explanation said this space journey was a hoax.

Palmer, man of faith, is the only person on Capitol Hill who believes her. Her experience aligned with what he knew to be real. He said, "As a person of faith, I'm bound by a different covenant, but my goal is the same—the pursuit of truth." At the end of the movie, the two of them drive off together—perhaps a symbolic marriage of science and faith—as a crowd representing the 80-95% of people in the U.S. who believe in God look on.

Bruce Lipton (2005) is another person who found God through science—the science of cellular biology. It startled him to realize that it was the environment, not the genetics, of the cell that controls it.

> "The nature of the cell's membrane that was 'downloaded' into my awareness.... convinced me that we are immortal, spiritual beings who exist separately from our bodies. I had heard an undeniable inner voice informing me that I was leading a life based not only on the false premise that genes control biology, but also on the false premise that we end when our physical bodies die... At that astounding moment [I] came to realize that the protein 'switches' that control life are primarily turned on and off by signals from the environment... the universe" (p. 184).

God is Truth. God is Love. God is Light. God is the Great "I AM". The Dalai Lama has affirmed that the new frontier is the journey within, and that assertion is echoed by the enormously successful DVD, *The Secret* (2006). The chorus for transcendence is growing larger and louder.

Rabbi Michael Lerner (2006) avows that the so-called Red States are not Far Right strongholds; rather, they are the voice of the heartland calling out for meaning, which the Far Left has not given for fear of casting their lot with the right-wingers.

Increasing numbers believe that it may be possible to "slip the surly bonds of earth," in the words of John Gillespie Magie, Jr. in his poem *High Flight,* "…and touch the face of God."

How does one make this journey? How does one know where to start? How to steer? What to take along?

This book is a guide for the journey.

> "Someday, after we have mastered the winds, the waves, and gravity, mankind will harness for God the energy of love. Then, for the second time in the history of the world, we will have discovered fire."
>
> Teilhard de Chardin

1 Wayfaring to Wayfinding:

From Measuring Up to Accepting Grace

Wayfaring

Grandmother used to give me graham crackers to munch on in church to keep me quiet. In her church—or any other at that time—there wasn't much to interest children. But I was a fairly calm child so I did a lot of listening, especially to the hymns. I remember one that went, "I am a poor, wayfaring stranger, traveling through this world of woe." The idea is that here on earth we walk dusty roads as wayfarers, lost from our homes. Around us is sin, woe, and all manner of unpleasant experiences. But if we'll just hang in there eventually we'll get to a different place—heaven presumably, although the word is never mentioned— where we'll see our deceased loved ones and then we'll be "...over Jordan... home." When we find that heaven, we will be dead according to this hymn.

Well, I've done my share of wayfaring. That is I've learned what is needed for success in this world, as I define success. First, I learned to walk, feed myself, dress myself, talk, and then read and write. Along the way I learned how to keep myself reasonably safe and get along with other people reasonably well. Also, I made reasonably good grades in school and completed advanced degrees. I've held responsible positions without ever getting fired and have led efforts for change. People familiar with Maslow's Hierarchy of Needs (see p. 87) might say I reached the level of Self Actualization, or becoming all that I could be.

At one time—not too long ago—I read as many as five books a week in a quest to know more. At other times I became very confused about which road to take. In my darkest time, I woke up living a life I hated—violating even my own principles, values, and standards for living. I had gotten lost while wayfaring. I had read the "signs" incorrectly.

The idea of having to die before I can reach anything resembling a state of joy and peace isn't very attractive to me. I began to feel very strongly that there must be more I could do right here on *terra firma* to improve my state of mind and find a more meaningful purpose for my life. So I took stock of myself.

Junctures

Junctures—that's what they are—
The intersections of life
With no street names
And no road numbers—

Or different road numbers.
Is this A2?
Or is it N11?
Or are they the same?

And where the hell am I,
Anyway?

At a juncture—
On the roadway of life.

Do I go on?
Or turn back?

I was a performer. If people wanted to get something done, they asked me. Do you know what people do for performers? They applaud them. So I had received much positive reinforcement for doing what other people wanted me to do—so much so that those other people had, in effect, become my gods.

My life was out of balance. According to Loehr and Schwartz (2003), the human system has four sources of energy: physical (including health, food, exercise, rest), mental (where I had overdosed), emotional, and spiritual. I discovered that I had "shut down" my emotional system many years before in order to avoid pain. I have learned that the emotional center of the brain doesn't have "switches" for every emotion. Instead, it has one master switch labeled "emotion." So when I unwittingly told my brain to turn off pain, it heard, "Turn off emotion." I even used to take pride in the fact that people could not hurt my feelings.

Some people say we change only out of pain. This was true for me. As I look back at the poetry that flowed so freely at the time, I remember the pain.

Protectio

Pins can't penetrate my
Not even for beauty's '
Sharp Lines
Dr. Executive
No Adornment
Everything Perf'
Business Suit .
From Pain.

4

Journey
Why don't more
have been fewer
tion, transposec
makes cowards
to fly to othe
Shakespear
what it has

Years after I wrote this poem, when
clothes but unable to find anything in the
what I already had, I hired a wardrobe consulta.
was to interview me about what I did in every part c
well as professionally. Then we went to my closet to fin.
fit my needs. After a morning of sorting, I discovered I had
wardrobe that was suitable for relaxation and recreation. Thre.
tic lawn bags of excess professional clothing went to Goodw.
afternoon I returned to my office and began returning telephone call.
the middle of one call I was overcome with nausea and felt that I migh.
faint. At that moment, I recognized the symptoms of withdrawal and realized that I had overdosed on my addiction to clothing. Unable to find the
sensation or "high" that I had previously reached from a new outfit, I had,
just as alcoholics do, "bottomed out." I just no longer got a kick out of going shopping as I had before.

Self-Deluded

How self-deluded can you be?
Sister, let me tell.

Anesthetize yourself with work
And get your kicks from migraines.

Insulate yourself from friends,
Pretending you don't need them.

Alienate as many as you can
So they don't get close.

OD on food or clothes or pills or sleep,
Pretending that you need them.

How self-deluded can you be?
Sister, let me tell.

people make needed change? Throughout history there
pioneers than settlers. Shakespeare offers this explana-
from Act III, Scene I of *Hamlet*: "Thus... [what we know]
of us all—and makes us rather bear the ills we have than
that we know not." A scientific term for the phenomenon
describes is inertia—the tendency of a body to keep on doing
been doing.

Hitting Bottom

I bottomed out.
I hit the wall.
And no one even knew.

My face was the same—
My hair—
My hands—

The work went on,
And I smiled.

Although I was very active in my church, even my spiritual life wasn't spiritual; it was superficially religious with the same intellectual approach that I had learned so well in school and that served me well in my career.

I began to realize I had to make a change when I drove into a parking space at 7:30 on the first morning of a new project. Early morning is my best time of day and I love new beginnings. Yet, on this morning when I normally would have been full of energy and excitement, I heard an inner voice say, "I am *so tired*." For the first time this voice got my attention.

The next time I "heard" my inner voice, I was driving home from work in the late afternoon. This time its message was more disturbing. "If you don't get out of here, you're going to die."

Simply stated, I had been living someone else's life. Whose life? The life of the woman I thought I ought to be based on some notion of what was acceptable to other people. But this woman I had concocted was not in alignment with what was in my soul, and some perceptive people saw the symptoms of my pain—allergies, debilitating migraines, workaholism. Increasingly, something inside told me things had to change. Granddaughter of one of the last pioneers who settled the territory that is now called Oklahoma, I felt the strong pull of my ancestry to leave that which was comfortable, secure, and safe to venture into the unknown.

A Prayer for Transformation

Freight trains are heavy, important, on track.
They're noisy and fearless and prompt.
They carry the freight that runs the world.
And they're indispensable.

They're hunched from stuffed cases;
Their planners are full.
Respected, revered, and admired.
You can count on them solid to get the job done.

Sailboats are open and friendly and free—
Flowing with current, catching the wind,
Eyes to horizon and on,
Gliding toward vast father sky.

A sailboat is what I aspire to be,
But can there be metamorphosis
From steel rail to white wind?
What cocoon—will do?

So I struggle on the banks,
Magnets in my pockets,
Pulling me toward important tasks.
But the sail in my soul wants the wind.

Beneath my pain, I was yearning for a better life for myself and those I loved. Love is the most powerful force in the universe. When our yearning grows from love, nothing can stop us. Pain may be an incentive or a by-product of breaking the barriers—but if we love, we are safe.

In a segment of *Family Ties*, the television show that catapulted Michael J. Fox to stardom during the 1980s, the character of Alex P. Keaton asked, "How do you know if you're good?" The clearest answer he got was, "You know if you're good from what other people tell you." But this answer is incomplete. Which other people? If people are giving you conflicting information, which ones do you listen to? And what about the danger of becoming dependent on other people to the detriment of listening to your own inner voice?

On a journey of self-discovery how do you know if you're on the right track? Out of all the self-help books, spiritual teachings, and conflicting religious beliefs, how do you know which ones are right for you?

Not through wayfaring, but through wayfinding.

A Meditation on Lightning

I drove out of the car lot
Onto rain-slick pavement,
Gently gliding that gray Lincoln
Toward almost-exhausted
Gray clouds.

It was our last dance,
And the skies
Threw silver streamers
At forked angles—
In celebration.

This was the car
I drove to freedom,
And I grasped—hard—
The padded, elegant wheel,
Wanting not to turn loose,

Knowing it was time
For us to part.

I needed You then,
And You were there.

Transition from Wayfaring to Wayfinding

To make the transition from wayfaring to wayfinding, I stopped looking to other people for affirmation. I stopped following prescribed courses of study or career paths. I started paying more attention to the voice within and sought the solace of nature.

Sunset #1

Soft, end-of-day light
Beyond the hills
Beckons my soul fully
To sense, feel, and know.

With the kind guidance of Mother Nature, I began to feel safe enough to release all the pent-up emotion that I had blocked for decades. It came out of me in cascades of grief and anger.

Love, Not Adore

Please don't adore me—
Not even admire
Or deign to call me "bright."

Now, I don't want scorned
Or rejected
Or dumb.

But "adore" is so distant.
"Admire" lacks warmth.
And bright? Well,

I'd rather be close,
Accepted, and loved.

Can I be bright
And be loved?

After I stopped being a wayfarer looking to people, work, places, and things for meaning, after I accepted the humanity of my own deep feelings, after I started observing Nature and listening to her voice, I became calm enough to become a wayfinder.

Wayfinding

The Hawaiian Islands rose from the ocean floor, through volcanic activity over a period of hundreds of thousands of years. When they appeared in the middle of the Pacific Ocean, of course, they were uninhabited. They were lava. They were more remote and isolated than any other archipelago on earth. Yet, by the time Captain James Cook arrived in 1731, people had been living on the islands for generations. Where did they come from? Their ancestors arrived in these islands long before they had the compasses or sextants that had aided Captain Cook and his crew. What tools, then, did they use, besides sheer courage?

The people who first found the Hawaiian Islands most likely came from Asia, Indonesia, and Africa, navigating unknown waters with paddles and canoes, using the ancient art of wayfinding that had been passed down through the generations. Simply stated, the wayfinder knew how to read the stars, the winds, the waves, and the behavior of such animals as dolphins and seabirds to determine where land was. They knew the time of year and the time of day when the winds would be most favorable for sea travel—and the direction in which they were blowing. Memorizing the star pattern in the sky at the time of their departure, they kept that pattern in mind to know how far and in what direction they had traveled. Uncertain of exactly what they would find, they envisioned an area where they most likely would find land, in much the same way that a golfer tries only to get onto the green before aiming directly at the flag. Similarly, once they got close to land, from the behavior of birds and the nature of the water, wayfinders could find the land.

Similarly, the wayfinder on a journey of self-discovery also learns to receive feedback that lets her know whether or not she is staying on course to reach her goal. Following are the feedback sources I learned to trust:

Insight from Contemplation and Journaling. When I began the practice of contemplation, I called it "meditation," not knowing the difference between the two. The practice I have today has evolved. In the beginning, I was terrified to look so deeply within, so at the suggestion of a friend, I followed Steinbrecher (1988). I remember the Saturday morning vividly, when I finally found the courage to try the technique suggested in the book. As I remember, the method was something like this: Close my eyes. Imagine I am going into a cave. I turn slightly to the right, then make a "hard left." Go through the door that is there and wait for a guide to come and lead me. Expecting the worst, I entered the cave of my mind, turned slightly to the right, then made a hard left and slowly, hesitantly, went through the opening that was there. In my mind, I opened my eyes. In reality, my eyes were closed, but as the eyes of my heart opened, tears coursed down my face. I was looking at the most beautiful beach I had ever seen—blue waters, blue sky, gentle breeze, pristine sand. Looking down, I immediately spotted my guide—a happy, chattering crab, scurrying toward me, smiling at me, and beckoning me to follow.

That was how I began the practice of meditation. My experience was beautiful and peaceful. I realized the innermost part of me was sheer joy. For the first time in my life, I knew that the universe is a friendly place.

Since that time, my practice has changed as I have changed. What I do today technically is not meditation, which is meditating on a scripture or a phrase. Instead, I practice contemplation, which is emptying myself to be in the presence of God, alternatively writing and listening. Today, I simply sit quietly and let my mind settle. I "listen" to my inner "guidance system," known variously as the "still, small voice" or "soul" or "Holy Spirit." Some mornings, it has nothing to say. Other mornings, it does. I journal what my inner voice says. I trust it. I act on it.

Silence

I extinguish all the voices.
I turn out all the lights.
I lie down and listen to the silent silence.
I hear the silent drip of raindrops,
The silent call of wind.
The silent course of teardrops.
The silence of the void.
Then from the silent silence, I hear a silent voice.

Readings. In earlier times, I read as many as five books a week in an effort to stay current. I no longer do that. Instead, I read when directed by my inner voice. I consider carefully what other people—even people I admire—tell me I "must read." Instead, I'm more likely to pick up a book after contemplation and open it randomly. Or, after seeing a book often referred to, I consider that it might be something I want to learn about. After I've seen the reference three times, I buy it. Now I am reading books about people I would like to become more like. When certain passages *resonate* within me, or stir my heart, I know they are teaching me what I need to learn at that moment. This same voice informs me concerning other media—movies, television shows, plays, musical performances. But I'm also free to turn off the voice and simply enjoy anything I choose.

People I Trust. Fortunately, there are a few people who want the best for me, who understand my life's path and goals, and who act as a mirror for me when I need a reality check. Often, I simply tell them what has happened and ask them to tell me what they heard. If I'm acting out of anger, they tell me. If they hear sadness or despair, they tell me. If I am violating my own principles, they tell me so. I heed what they say. As I learn and change, I accept new advisors who have experienced what I want or something close to it. If you choose to become a wayfinder, find others to go on the journey with you. Become each other's trusted advisors.

Art. The art I am attracted to often shows me where I am on the path. For example, early on my journey, I was on the highway, traveling back to where I live. I was driving west, into the sunset, which is sheer beauty and delight for me. But on this day, my inner voice said, "I want to go *home*. But I don't even know where *home* is." Not too long later, visiting the Museum of Modern Art in New York City, the painting I was most drawn to was *Christina's World* by pre-Raphaelite artist Andrew Wyeth. This painting shows a girl on the ground, crawling and reaching toward a house that is still some distance away. This experience let me know I was still pretty early in the journey.

Nature. In a sense nature, like art, has exactly the right lesson for me. My job is to sit, look, listen, experience, and pay attention to what my heart is doing. Often, my inner voice delivers the message from the experience I'm having, as illustrated by this story, which appeared in *The Systems Thinker* (2006):

> "This morning as I sat on the deck, sipping a mug of coffee, listening to morning sounds and delighting in the coolness that promises summer won't last forever, I spotted two wrens in the tree between our neighbor's deck and ours. For some unexplained reason, this tree has shed leaves throughout the summer; now, only the tips of the branches are green.
>
> "Before I see the two birds, I hear them. First a melodic, ten-note song. Then a shorter, monotone trill. My eyes follow my ears, searching the bare branches for the source, which turns out to be two small wrens. The wren on the tree's right sings. The wren on the tree's left emits the monotone trill. They repeat their duet. Then again. And again. Over and over again.
>
> "Same species. Two completely different sounds, but clearly connected to each other. They continue for several minutes, their timing impeccable, as if flawlessly following a composer's invisible score. Then, after a long pause, they change the order of their songs. The second bird starts first, with its monotone trill, followed by the first bird's melodic, ten-note song. 'So,' I thought. They know their part, and they sing their part, only varying the order in which they do it.'
>
> "As they flew away, I realized that, since they are the same species, either bird can probably sing either part, depending on some unknown "signal." But they can't "sing the part" of cardinals, because they are wrens, limited and defined by a narrow set of characteristics and capabilities that are described in only 14 lines of print in Peterson's *Field Guide to the Birds of Texas.* Wrens follow patterns. That's all they can do."

Thinking, "There's a story in this," I went to my computer, intending to write it. But first, I checked e-mail and discovered there was more to the story than my experience with two wrens. This message from a client was in my inbox:

> "I've realized that I have lived most of my life feeling miserable, and I think I'm too comfortable with that. Comfortably uncomfortable. It's a pattern. The truth is, I don't want to be miserable—to create drama and crises. Every time I take steps

forward, I discover old footprints that reveal a little more about myself. Not pleasant, but good to be aware of so that I can step in a different place and not just keep retracing the old. I know that I want to be content, fulfilled, and peaceful. To get there, I have to make it simple. I'm stepping forward, slowly."

When we are young and impressionable, patterns form within us, from our experiences. As we grow older, we repeat those patterns, both the patterns we love and the patterns we hate. But within each of us is an Authentic Self—the person we are in our hearts—the Truth that transcends the patterns. When we choose to live, think, speak, and hear from our hearts, we transcend limiting patterns. Wrens can't do that, but people can.

The client who e-mailed me the message above has decided not to be defined by other people's actions and behaviors. She has decided to be the person who is in her heart. Her first steps are tentative, unsteady, as first steps always are. But the heart is the home of courage, so slowly, inexorably, she moves forward to live the life she truly wants.

If Alex P. Keaton asked me, "How do you know if you're good?" my answer would be that I don't focus on whether or not I'm "good." What's more important to me is this question, "Am I in alignment with the highest and best intent for my life? Where am I in my journey? What feedback am I getting?"

Feedback from Nature

My friend Jane told me the following story about feedback that came to her from nature, encouraging her not to give up and assuring her that, in the long run, everything would be alright.

Jane knew that all had not been well in the school district before she agreed to be superintendent, but she had no idea of the extent of the problem until six weeks after her arrival, when the business manager brought three fat portfolios to her office that implicated board members in illegal activity. Because the district desperately needed new school buildings, Jane decided to wait to act until after a bond election, which passed. She did, however, call the board president to inform him of what she intended to do, giving him time to think and the chance to turn himself in. Immediately after the successful bond election, she again called the board president to tell him she was on her way to the district attorney's office. This time, he told her she would be fired, adding, "The only way you can save your job is to sleep with me."

Jane realized, in addition to the legal issue already in front of her, she would also have to file a sexual harassment lawsuit, to add to the turmoil.

As if that weren't enough, her husband had suffered a closed head injury a few years earlier and now, disabled, was losing his sanity.

In the midst of the quagmire, Jane took solace walking the land she and her husband had bought in this breathtakingly beautiful part of the country that belied the corruption and difficulty she had found there. On an especially stressful day, she walked all the way to the back of the land, along a small creek swollen by a recent rain. She sat on a rock, looking at the rushing water, crying out to God, "Why am I in this mess? What am I supposed to learn from this awful experience?" When she opened her eyes, she saw something she had never seen in that little creek before—three minnows, swimming frantically in a small whirlpool. "They must have come from the waterfall created by the rains," she thought to herself, and they can't figure out how to get out of here." Then she turned her head, looking up to the wider creek just beyond the small whirlpool. At that moment, she heard a voice within. "Like these minnows," it said, "if you just stop fighting and go with the current, there's calm water ahead. You can't see it, but I can."

Ultimately, she was fired by the malfeasant board, despite the outcry of the community. But after that, through community petition, five board members were ousted from the school board. When community leaders asked her to return to the superintendency, Jane declined. The work she had come there to do was done. It was time to move on. Today, her husband deceased, she lives peacefully in that calmer water, in a different state, doing work that she loves with people she respects and who respect her. She is thriving.

The voice that Jane heard—the voice that I hear—is available to anyone who is willing to listen. Some people, like Annie Robinson, call it intuition. Annie Robinson came into my life late. In fact, I almost missed her. She taught the art and science of intuition to a devoted following. One of the stories told at her memorial service was this one, from her daughter. In her last days, Annie kept having dreams about digits that were all the same, like 111 and 555. These dreams kept recurring, night after night. It was only after her death that their meaning became clear. The time recorded on her death certificate was 5:55.

Right up to the end, her inner voice was telling her where she was on the journey. Eventually, she understood.

So it is with all of us. Our work is only to listen.

The *wayfinding* explorers memorized the star pattern of the night sky on the day of their departure. This memory gave them information about how far they had traveled. So it is with the wayfinder on this journey. But it isn't the stars that we remember—it's the people in our lives when we began the journey and the degree of pain we were feeling.

Most often, journeys of self-discovery begin with pain. It seems that someone is there to inflict the pain, and others are present to comfort you—even, perhaps, to guide you. At some point, you'll realize that a similar situation is happening and those same people are present. You'll also know, from the difference in how you are thinking, feeling, and behaving, that *you* are different. Your pain has lessened or disappeared altogether. You have changed. Compassion has replaced repugnance. Self-confidence has banished victimization. Love has uprooted hatred. Beauty has made ugliness disappear. Faith has overcome fear. Your world is bigger; your God is larger.

The ancient Hawaiians relied on star patterns to guide their way. Our stars are the constellations of people who help us gauge our progress. Who are your "markers"? Where are you on the journey?

Possibilities

Possibilities swirl like whirlpools or supernova.
I watch, puzzled, to know which frame to freeze or seize.

Then realization comes.

Jump in and ride the watery, starry rings through the spiral,
To find the point.

Find Fellow Wayfinders

Genuine success is creating and living a life that aligns with who you truly are. The purpose of this book is to provide a little information, awareness, and many tools that make success possible. People who choose to live the life that is truly theirs make a commitment to speak from their hearts, work the process with rigorous honesty and purity of intent, and be authentic.

Palmer (2000) writes about the importance of "inner work," noting,

> "If people skimp on their inner work, their outer work will suffer as well... We could spread the word that inner work, though it is a deeply *personal* matter, is not necessarily a *private* matter: inner work can be helped along in community... Left to our own devices, we may delude ourselves in ways that others can help us correct" (pp. 91-92).

Therefore, I suggest you find fellow wayfinders, each on his or her own journey of self-discovery. Go at your own pace to deepen the learning and increase the likelihood that you will actually release the parts of your life that aren't working and replace them with the life you truly want to live. Stay in touch with your fellow wayfinders as you live life from the new patterns you have chosen and use the tools for staying on course. You will use each other as a "sounding board" to help you refocus as difficult situations arise.

Recently one of my wayfinding friends called following a telephone conversation with her father that activated old memory. I said, "It's just chemistry—liquid sloshing around in your brain. Here are a couple of things that might change the chemicals." I offered one tool from this book [see Chapter 12 - Toolbox] along with a story from my own life that taught me a lesson.

Similarly, two clients who are partners in a small business have to deal with a third important person who frequently pulls one of them aside for his latest get-rich scheme that inevitably sidetracks them. I suggested, when this happens, that the person who has been pulled aside go immediately to the other partner and say, "I've been hijacked." Don't repeat what he said; that would only reinforce it. The other partner, upon hearing the word "hijacked," will refocus the partner on the mission and goals of the organization, the progress that has been made, and the next positive step they have agreed to. They will continue to talk until centered, with all vestiges of the hijacking having disappeared from mind.

These are examples of how we can help each other. Using this book as your guide, you will awaken your truthful *realization* of how your brain and memory system have developed, over time, and that, along the way, working with an underdeveloped brain, you might have stored memories that do not serve you well and that are actually blocking you from living the life you want. You will complete a process for *releasing* the patterns that don't work for you and *creating* new ones. You will establish a firm foundation for living your new life. Then you will use the tools for staying on course to sustain the changes you have made. You will have become a *Wayfinder.*

Chapter 1 Exercises

1-1. Have you had any experiences similar to those described in Chapter 1? What are they? How did they change you?

1-2. What spiritual work have you already done? How did it change you?

1-3. What's the next major learning in your journey that you want to acquire?

1-4(a). What feelings come up for you as you reflect on Chapter 1?

1-4(b). If your answer is fear, what is the source of that fear? How old is it? What do you want to do with it?

2   Leave the Pain

In the elegant office of the psychologist I had chosen from the *Yellow Pages*, I wrote my answers to the questions. When I read, "What is your goal for your counseling sessions?" my eyes filled with tears and pain pierced my heart. Without hesitation I wrote, "Relief from pain." I had reached my limit, and I was exhausted from the effort. I was ready to leave the pain, ready to learn how to live my life differently. What I hoped was that the psychologist would give me a few affirmations that, like a magic wand, would make all my difficulties go away. I wanted an easy answer and quick fix.

Like me, most people prefer to live life painlessly. Something hurts us, and we bounce back quickly, like a four-year-old saying, "That didn't hurt." Or we wail for a moment and then look for a Band-aid®, preferably one stamped with cartoon characters to help us cover a wound with make-believe fun. Like me, some people eventually feel a pain that no Band-aid® can cover. Then they decide to leave the pain. Unlike me, some people can keep up this denial for a lifetime, for the sake of appearance or personal expectation. In the great Greek tragedy *Oedipus Rex* by Sophocles, the chorus ends the play with these words, "Therefore, while our eyes wait to see the destined final day, we must call no one happy who is of mortal race, until he hath crossed life's border, free from pain!" Thus, happiness and pain seem detached opposites, either/or extremes, as if one person cannot experience both.

We want to be happy. In fact, in the U.S. the pursuit of happiness is part of our DNA.

> "We hold these truths to be self-evident that all men are created equal; that they are endowed by their Creator with certain inalienable rights; that among these are life, liberty, and the *pursuit of happiness*" (*Declaration of Independence*).

We go to great lengths to make ourselves and other people happy, including engaging in all manner of dysfunctional and addictive behaviors—flattery, deception, manipulation, abuse of alcohol or drugs, immersion in fantasy such as television, accumulation of material goods—anything that makes us look or feel good and thus numbs the pain we truly feel.

In Sophocles' words, "The keenest sorrow is to recognize ourselves as the sole cause of all our adversities," so we blame other people for our misfortunes because it takes the burden off of us and makes us feel better. Some of us continue to do this for a lifetime and thus deceive ourselves into believing we are free from pain. However, it is this very pride that prolongs our suffering. Nothing else. *Hubris,* the Greek word for pride, was most often the tragic flaw that brought heroes down. And it is pride that continues to bring us down. Every time we tell the story of how someone wronged us, we experience the pain again, one more time. It is only our pride that binds us to the wound.

There is only one way to leave the pain. Face it. Look it in the eye. Walk through it. Feel it intensely. Acknowledge your own role in bringing it on. Love yourself anyway. Grieve it. Accept it. Learn from it. Then let it go. With love, we are able to leave pride and embrace humility as the pathway to happiness. Even Sophocles recognized the power of love to relieve pain. "One word frees us of all the weight and pain of life: That word is love" (*Oedipus at Colonus*).

Leaving the Pain through Cataclysm

For many people, leaving the pain is cataclysmic. So it was for me. First, it meant leaving a familiar place. Then it meant divorce and my children's disapproval, which was the worst pain of all. Ultimately, it meant acknowledging my own shortcomings. It meant I had to stop running from that which made me unhappy and take a long, hard look at what I was running from. It meant years of a process that some refer to as "peeling the onion," as I gradually became aware of the neuronal connections, memories, and patterns of behavior that were not serving me well. For the first time I fully understood what Socrates meant when he said, "The unexamined life is not worth living."

Yet still I was intent on restoring my image of perfection until finally I submitted to someone who could see the exact nature of my wrongs and lift the veil for me. Only then did I begin to experience healing and freedom from pain. In the eighth chapter of the Gospel of John, Jesus explains that as long as people find their identity and meaning in life from worldly matters, they do not know God. But when they let go and open themselves to God, then as Peterson (1995) writes: "you will experience for yourselves the truth, and the truth will free you" (p. 208). The word "salvation" derives from the Latin root *salve* which means "healing." For my healing to occur, I had to let go of that which separated me from God, which was my own ego. On my own, I couldn't do it. I had a blind spot. I couldn't see what I couldn't see. That's how powerful my ego was. It had blinded me.

Leaving the Pain through Being Startled into Action

She had come to this place two weeks early, which meant she desperately needed treatment and a safe place to stay. Just days before the end of our 28-day program she stormed into our room, throwing things. I was sitting on the balcony watching the waters rush over the rocks in the nearby stream. I didn't know what to say, so I continued to do what I was doing, which was nothing. She came out to the balcony and said, "They say they might not let me leave." She had just come from a session with the psychiatrist.

"Why not?" I asked.

"They say I haven't found a Higher Power and I can't leave until I do."

I didn't know what to say, so I did not respond. Instead, I turned back to enjoy the serenity I had found on that balcony, feel the breeze, hear the birds, and be quiet.

There was a very, very long silence accompanied by the quiet swishing of the soft wind through the pines.

Then—quietly—with awe—she whispered, "That's it."

"That's what?" I asked.

"The stillness." Long, long pause. "Isn't there something in the Bible about being still?" she asked.

"Be still and know that I am God," I answered.

"That's... it," she said slowly, with real peace in her voice as she rose from her chair to go back to the psychiatrist's office. She had found a Higher Power. Ultimately, she was dismissed with the rest of us at the end of the 28 days.

Until that moment my roommate had been spinning through life like a top, never stopping until she dropped and then, after short rests, spinning again. For her, life was noisy and fast.

At that time I knew a little about the brain. I knew that our brains work best in a state of relaxed alertness. To my delight the curriculum in this place precisely fit what I knew about how the brain works, and I felt that if people could just get still, something inside their brains would tell them what to do next. This experience with my roommate taught me that, when we get still, we open to a voice we cannot hear in the normal din and clamor of modern life.

In that moment, my roommate left her pain, startled into the experience by the ultimatum she had received. Some of us need to be startled in order to be able to leave the pain.

Leaving the Pain through Steady, Sustained Personal Change

But what about those who experience neither cataclysm or surprise? How do they leave the pain? Or, after cataclysm or surprise, how does one sustain the change that has begun? After all, the neuronal patterns and cellular memories are still there. Whatever we learned, whether erroneously or not, in our early formative years stays with us as our "default" behavior. Can one cataclysmic event change that pattern for always?

Technically the answer is "Yes," but realistically it is "Probably not for always." Without reinforcement, learning fades. For example, can you write the Pythagorean theorem today even though you knew it perfectly in the tenth grade? Can you name all the prime numbers? Do you even remember what a prime number is? Can you diagram a sentence? Write a verb in the past perfect progressive tense? Recite Portia's "Mercy Speech" from *The Merchant of Venice*? Probably not. You learned all of these things in school after the age of 6.

Similarly, when as adults we make a decision to leave the pain, we must realize that our brains and bodily memory systems are holding patterns created when we were much younger and which will try to pull us back into old behaviors that we want to leave. This is why alcoholics are encouraged to make new friends to replace their drinking buddies. Simply being in the presence of people with whom they have drunk alcohol will likely trigger their own addictive patterns and pull them back into drinking. It's why members of Al-Anon are encouraged to form relationships with people who "have what they want."

If I have decided to leave the pain of not having enough money because my credit card debt is so high, then in my free time a good choice would be to take the dog for a walk or take a picnic to the park instead of going to the mall.

Then there are those people—the majority—whose lives aren't marked with addiction, whose jobs are not obsessions, whose friends engage in healthy activities, whose marriages are stable. What about them?

A Process That Works for Everyone

Just as our fairy tales don't reveal what "happily ever after" looks like, neither do our visions for ourselves or our children's futures go very much beyond college. What is needed is an understanding that, throughout the process of formal schooling, we are learning to gain control over our environment. We learn to talk, walk, feed ourselves, dress ourselves, get along with other people, behave in a mannerly way, make pleasing choices, follow a group's rules, do well in school, find something we're good at, choose a profession, take the courses that lead to success in that field, perhaps choose a suitable mate, graduate, get a job, go to work, earn enough money to support ourselves, get better at our jobs and rise to the level of someone's expectations—our own or those of others, as we understand them. We are Wayfarers finding our way through our physical world. As Wayfarers we're learning control. And control is one of the four core addictions that separate us from God and from our own authenticity.

Another way of saying this is that until we reach adulthood we are growing our egos, defined as "the division of the psyche that is conscious, most immediately controls thought and behavior, and is most in touch with external reality" (*American Heritage Dictionary*, 2004). All of us have an ego, which means we are susceptible to the flaw of pride as we exercise the control we have so carefully learned over external reality. In other words, ego "hooks" us to the external world.

But there comes a time in adulthood when we must align who we truly are with what we do and how we act. When it's time to become authentic— to realize our purpose in life, our heart's desire. When it's time to look at the 95% of our behavior that is coming out of our subconscious and make adjustments to any patterns that formed before the age of 6 that are not serving us well. In order to do this we have to put our egos aside and thus eliminate the barrier we have erected between ourselves and God during the time we were Wayfarers. And we have to have a process for doing this that is sustainable. A process that we can repeat with increasing richness of understanding. A process that will serve us for the rest of our lives. A process for "letting go" of our hard-earned Wayfaring lessons, with the realization that they have been mastered so we don't have to work on them any more. A process which opens a new phase in our lives, a movement from journey to journey, from pathways to flows. A process called Wayfinding.

The Energy Analysis®

Senge (1990) coined the term "mental models" to describe "…deeply held internal images of how the world works, images that limit us to familiar ways of thinking and acting." As a result of these mental models, Senge says, "New insights fail to get put into practice because they conflict with [our mental models]' (p. 174). He goes on to say that mental models "…shape how we act…" because they "…affect what we see." Pointing to the earlier work of Harvard's Chris Argyris, Senge asserts that:

> "…trapping ourselves in defensive routines that insulate our mental models from examination, we consequently develop as adult learners, who are highly skillful at protecting [our] selves

from pain and threat posed by learning situations, but consequently fail to learn how to produce the results [we] really want." (p. 182).

Unexamined mental models are blind spots. We can't see them, but most other people can. Our lack of awareness leaves us vulnerable to manipulation—both being manipulated and manipulating others. A client once told me that his grandmother had "...taught me how to hate." She taught him, instead of seeking vengeance, to put his anger "...in a locked box, on the shelf." He was not aware that this mental model had manacled his ability to be an effective leader. Repeatedly, he failed to address important issues among his employees that needed to be aired. His leadership decisions depended on other people's behavior, not his own inner guidance. He depended on the favor of his superiors to maintain his position. His pandering style had lost the respect of his employees. By the time I met him it was too late to reverse the damage he had done. As a leader he was ineffective. It was way past time for him to unlock that box of anger and hatred! The lessons we receive from those we love are very difficult to unlearn. Difficult, but not impossible.

One of the tools that may be used to bring subconscious mental models to conscious awareness is the Energy Analysis® an adaptation of the stock-and-flow-diagram created by Jay Forrester for the field of systems dynamics. From Forrester's work, as well as subsequent work by Barry Richmond, the Energy Analysis® "photographs" the human energy flow in the form of a graph derived from an individual's answers to questions about what's giving and depleting their energy on a scale of 1-10, with 10 being high.

Imagine that there is a "battery" powering your life, giving you the energy to accomplish your goals. Now ask yourself these questions:

- What's going into the battery that gives you energy?
- What's flowing out of the battery that's depleting your energy?

The supply of energy, represented by the battery, is healthy enough to allow us to accomplish our goals when it ranges from 300 to 850 on the vertical axis. Any more than 850 indicates excessive ego that is pushing too hard; any less than 300 means we'll move forward very slowly, if at all.

Once people see what has previously been hidden, they are better able to bring about the change they want. For example, Fig. 2-1 is the graph created by iThink® software for someone who has been taking prescribed antidepressants:

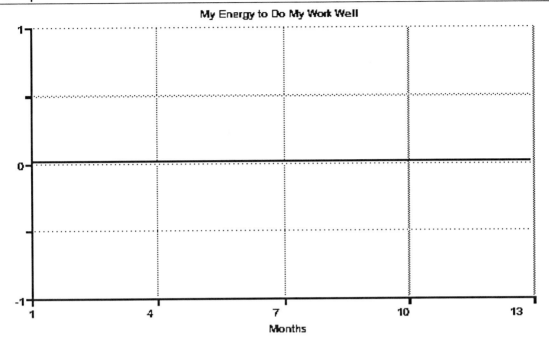

Fig. 2-1: Person on antidepressants

First, notice that the number at the top of the vertical axis, representing capacity, is far below the desirable minimum of 300.The flat, zeroed line mirrors the effect that antidepressants have on emotions—no highs, no lows—just an even, mellow existence. Stress at the office had led this person to take the antidepressant. Prior to that she had experienced several significant stress-related symptoms including hair loss.

Only one other time have I seen a graph like the one above—in a person who had learned from the experience of many years in therapy (including hypnosis), as well as having had a life-changing spiritual experience when a close friend was murdered. Through her study of near-death experiences, this person had found a place of perfect peace. Her experience had been so profound that she had learned to live without fear. When I told her that the only other graph I had seen like hers was from a person who was taking antidepressants, she laughed. "I've just learned that I had to let go of my ego," she said.

Fig. 2-2 is a graph created by iThink® software came from data collected from a person who, within the past six months, had experienced dramatic changes including divorce and change in job, two of life's leading stressors. The number at the top of the vertical axis is significant, representing capacity or available energy in one's "battery."

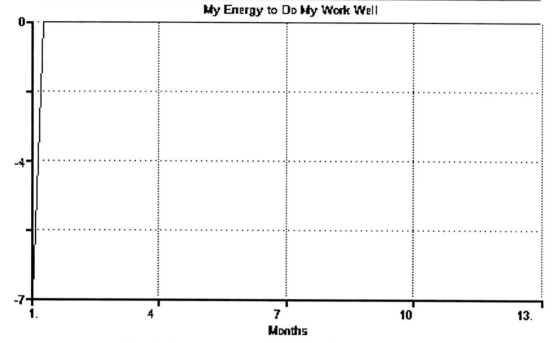

Fig. 2-2: Person on with major life stressors

The graph's vertical axis says this person's energy level is zero, representing a virtual standstill. She must replenish the energy supply before she will be able to move forward. Although she is in a high-profile job, she doesn't have energy available for any more major changes, at least for the time being and probably not for the next 13 months (horizontal axis).

A picture, as the saying goes, is worth a thousand words. When people see their data represented in this graphical form, they are often stunned to see what they had sensed but hoped wasn't true. Often they decide to make some change, however small, that serves to give them more positive energy. For example, in the second case, the person noted that it was time to see the doctor. For several days she had been suffering from a respiratory problem, putting off going to a physician because she didn't want to take the time away from work. Looking at reality via this graph piqued her desire for change. This person was also able to see very quickly some other positive steps that she could take to minimize the energy depletion. She named a few, then said, "These are things I had recommended that other people do, but I didn't realize I wasn't doing them myself until now." Thus, the Energy Analysis® allowed her to see what she previously could not see.

Some clients take one look at their graphs and exclaim, "This is not how I want to be." Their emotional reaction to the truth about their current state propels them to take immediate action. They suddenly find the energy they need to get where they want to be. According to Loehr and Schwartz

(2003), there are four sources for human energy: physical, mental, emotional, and spiritual. To make a change, people need only consider what is giving or depleting their energy and find where they are out of balance, thus discovering the leverage for change. The Energy Analysis® is a valuable tool, depicting graphically where we actually are.

Some clients return at intervals to gauge their progress and slowly, steadily make needed adjustments. Such was the case with someone I'll call Linda. Fig. 2-3 is the graph from her first Energy Analysis®,

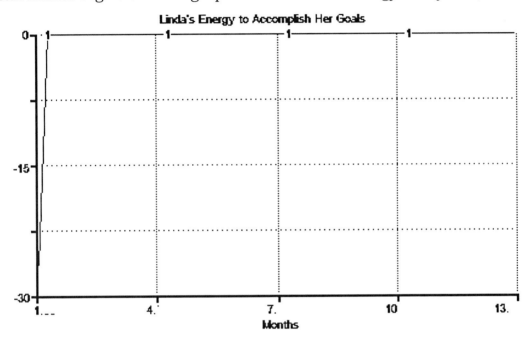

Fig. 2–3: Linda's first analysis

Like the previous client, Linda is at a virtual standstill. There is so much depletion in her system that she is very unlikely to reach the goals she longs for. But after extensive conversation that enhanced her understanding of what she was doing to herself, she made a decision to change. Within a little over a year, her picture had dramatically changed as shown in Fig. 2-4.

Her capacity had increased over time to a healthy level. She has enough energy to meet life's challenges successfully, and her life has become more enjoyable.

Unfortunately, many people become accustomed to the pain, to low-level anxiety or worry that actually increases over time in response to stress. They slowly adapt to their environment until calamity strikes.

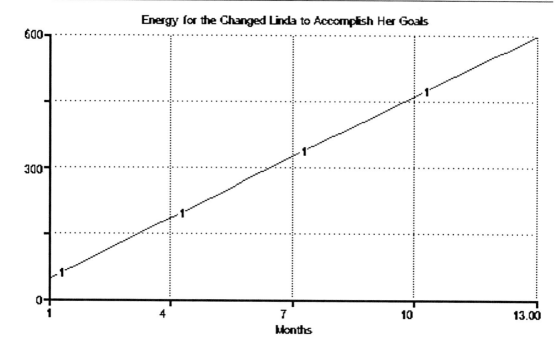

Fig. 2-4: Linda showing increased capacity over time

Our internal environment is controlled by chemicals. One of these chemicals, cortisol, is emitted with stress. Designed to be an effective response to keep us safe, when it is unremittingly released, it increases our anxiety to disproportionate levels and eventually starts breaking down the immune system. Schulkin (2003) writes,

> "Normal fear, unbridled by constraints, can turn into chronic anticipatory angst. In this context, the mechanisms of normal fear are over-expressed, resulting in pathological anxiety. All of this takes a toll on normal systemic bodily and neural function" (p. 99).

The External Environment Affects You

A mistake led me to realize how greatly one's energy level can be affected by external environment. A client sent me the data to create the energy graph for one of her direct reports. Forgetting that I had already done it, I interviewed the employee again by telephone, asking the same questions her boss had already asked her. Apparently she had forgotten the earlier experience, as well, because she didn't mention that she had already answered these questions. The data for the first graph had been collected from Angela while she was at a company retreat in a relaxed setting showed a very high score of 850. The second graph, from data collected during a telephone call in the workplace, showed Angela's energy "tank" to be significantly lower, although still in the acceptable range around 400.

The energies swirling around human beings from their external environment control their internal chemistry to a very great extent. It is a rare person who can rise above external pressures to maintain his or her chosen state of mind. Inappropriate or irrational behavior from colleagues or constituents can, in fact, impair one's state of mind, state of health, and most certainly performance.

Take the example of Janie. Shortly after starting a new job as an executive, she incurred the wrath of another executive in the form of a verbal attack. Shortly after her attack, Fig. 2-5 shows what Janie's graph looked like:

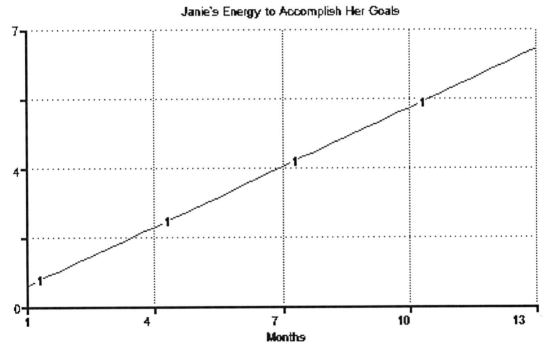

Fig. 2–5: Janie after verbal attack

Notice that the capacity in this "container" for Janie's energy is 7, which is well below the minimum 300 for acceptable performance. Within a few weeks, her physician prescribed antidepressants. During the first six months of coaching her, I received an e-mail from Janie that read, "What I experienced in my first few weeks in this job threw me off my game."

In fact, the Energy Analysis® revealed that all four of the people directly supervised by the verbal attacker had low capacity, with three of them at 0 and one, an older, experienced person who worked by choice, not because she had to, and was therefore less vulnerable to threat, scored only 200. *If anyone in a system is verbally attacked, threat is present for everyone.* Intuitively, people know that if it happened to someone else, it might happen to them. They become hyper-vigilant trying to appease the verbal attacker so that they themselves do not fall prey. At the same time, they start to play roles instead of fulfill responsibility as complete human beings with full voice. Potential dissipates. Everyone suffers. Often, people get sick. The system suffers. The whole organization suffers. The cost is high.

Energy in Systems: Neuronal Connections

Consider the dilemma of stress in the workplace: absenteeism, turnover, conflict. Consider the significance of employees' states of mind to these issues. Imagine, even, that a group of people might be able to boost the health of their organization and thus reduce their health care costs, when each person becomes aware of this invisible system and takes personal responsibility for his or her own state of mind.

The movie *Pay It Forward* (2000) tells the story of a junior high school boy who takes seriously his social studies teacher's assignment to come up with an idea that would change the world. His simple idea was that each person do or say something kind for three other people, asking each of them to "pay it forward" by finding three more people on whom to bestow acts of kindness. This child's idea worked, and the movie ends with people holding lighted candles as far as the eye can see, reminiscent of the lines in Perry Como's song *One Little Candle* (1952): "If everyone lit just one little candle, what a bright world this would be." As Williamson (1992) says,

> "As we let our own light shine, we unconsciously give other people permission to do the same. As we're liberated from our own fear, our presence automatically liberates others." (p. 191).

Systems are made up of people, each one with billions of neuronal connections and complex memory systems. Fig. 2-6 (on the next page) depicts only a tiny section of one person's neuronal connections in the brain. If you want a challenge, circle every neuronal connection you can find with a red pen!

This small sample is an intricate system of its own. Imagine, then, what happens with a team of people working together. Imagine the illustration above as becoming holographic, with the whole containing all parts and each part containing the whole. Through the power of mirror neurons, what this person says or does sparks brain activity in that person, and like boomerangs, the vibrations are continuously going out and coming back. This *is* the system.

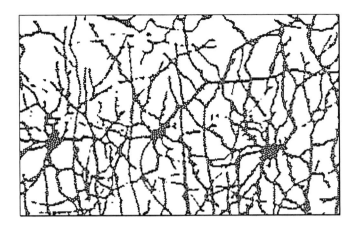

Fig. 2–6: Neuronal Connections[1]

Synergy, *as* defined by the *Oxford English Dictionary,* is the "correlated action of a group of bodily organs." When the intricate system within one person *attunes* to the intricate systems in other people, what results is "increased effectiveness or achievement produced as a result of combined action or cooperation" (OED). The *attuning* signal is one person's desirable state of mind, revealed by the voice. Just as a concert master takes the lead of an orchestra in tuning the instruments before a concert or rehearsal, so one person's *voice,* conveying words and state of mind, determines the climate for the whole group. And the most desirable voice, the one most readily followed, is *authentic.* It rings true.

We don't have a choice about whether we are emitting vibrations that are affecting other people. We do it all the time. We do have a choice about what we are sending out—our state of mind, especially our feelings, whether we express them or not. Within a working group, the system created by each person's vibrations and the interactions among all the people's vibrations collectively determine the energy that is available to the group for learning, change, and creation.

When she was in charge of Disney's employee recognition programs, Dee Hansford researched the effect of positive reinforcement on workers. When only affirmed for what they do well, employees improved their performance. They improved not only what they were already doing well, but they also improved what they were not doing well, without having it pointed out. The late Madeline Hunter, noted education expert, used to point out that the

---

[1] Small portion of figure 3.1 (p.41) from *The Neurobiology of Memory* (1989) by Dudai, Yadin (used with permission)

best climate for learning is a positive environment; second best is negative; the worst is neutral—no one cares.

You might test the notion that a system for getting back what we send out truly exists. The next time you're in heavy traffic with people trying to merge into your lane, allow not just one but three vehicles to get ahead of you. Then pay attention to how willing other drivers are to allow you to merge later on. You might dub these occurrences as coincidences. If so, start paying attention to these coincidences. How often do you receive kindness when you haven't given any? Keep a record. Find out for yourself.

The Impact of Leadership

By virtue of the position they hold, the vibrations emitted by leaders have greater impact. Leaders have the power to hire and fire people, determine who gets a bonus or promotion, who gets placed on what team, and who has access to growth opportunities. A leader's Authentic Profile is a snapshot of the best vibrations within them—the state of mind and direction that are likely to elicit the most positive aspirations in those whom they lead. Steps for creating your own Authentic Profile will be covered much later in this book (see p. 123). Fig. 2-9, for example, is the Authentic Profile of a principle-centered leader of a healthy team

The Energy Analyses® of this leader's team members attests to their system's overall health. Remember the number at the top of the vertical axis? It's a clue to the capacity of the team for learning, change, and creation. It is noteworthy that this leader has studied Stephen R. Covey's work and just before the Energy Analysis® had led her team in a study of Covey's (2004) work.

Fig 2-10 on p. 32 display's this leader's graph, with a very desirable capacity score of 750.

Fig. 2-11 depicts how the other members of her team scored. Keep in mind that the ideal range is 300-850.

Only three of the team of 12 (25%) have significantly depleted energy—those with scores of 200, 40, 0. One, with a score of 1050, is pushing very hard, ego-dominated.

Now consider what is happening in the next case, in which the leader's Authentic Profile© does not reveal such a strong principle-centered focus. In fact, my interviews with employees indicated that a significant number felt that he engaged in favoritism and retaliation, managing by personality, not principle.

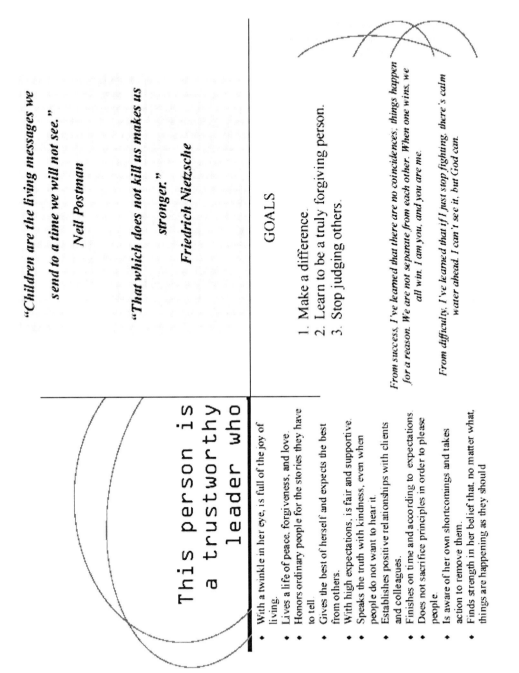

"Children are the living messages we send to a time we will not see."

Neil Postman

"That which does not kill us makes us stronger."

Friedrich Nietzsche

GOALS

1. Make a difference.
2. Learn to be a truly forgiving person.
3. Stop judging others.

From success, I've learned that there are no coincidences; things happen for a reason. We are not separate from each other. When one wins, we all win. I am you, and you are me.

From difficulty, I've learned that if I just stop fighting, there's calm water ahead. I can't see it, but God can.

This person is a trustworthy leader who

- With a twinkle in her eye, is full of the joy of living.
- Lives a life of peace, forgiveness, and love.
- Honors ordinary people for the stories they have to tell.
- Gives the best of herself and expects the best from others.
- With high expectations, is fair and supportive.
- Speaks the truth with kindness, even when people do not want to hear it.
- Establishes positive relationships with clients and colleagues.
- Finishes on time and according to expectations.
- Does not sacrifice principles in order to please people.
- Is aware of her own shortcomings and takes action to remove them.
- Finds strength in her belief that, no matter what, things are happening as they should

Fig. 2-9: Authentic Profile of Leader #1

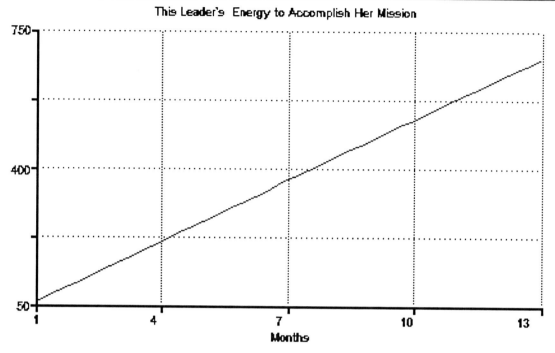

Fig. 2-10: Energy Analysis of Leader #1

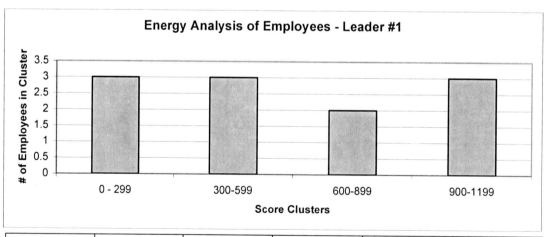

Mean	Median	Mode	Min	Max	Std. Dev
535	300	300	0	1050	413

Fig. 2-11: Employees of Leader #1

In my interview with him, he acknowledged that his leadership style is "I expect people to do their jobs," thus revealing a lack of understanding of the importance of empowerment and collaboration. Also, I noted that he knows only one way to learn—read about it—but he said he hadn't done much reading lately. He does not understand *experiential* learning and, although he had known for several years that his leadership wasn't working, he chose to do nothing differently. Fig. 2-12 shows the energy analysis of his employees. Although this leader's Energy Analysis® had a strong capacity score of 600, the scores of his staff were mostly low:

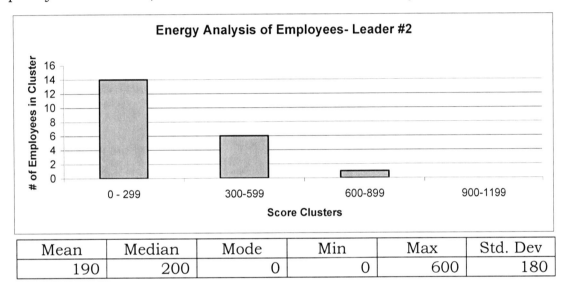

Mean	Median	Mode	Min	Max	Std. Dev
190	200	0	0	600	180

Fig. 2-12: Employees of Leader #2

Counting 300 as an acceptable score, 14 of the 23 members of this team (61%) have capacity scores that show depletion. The fact that 9 out of 23 rose above the conflicts at work to maintain a healthy energy level shows that it can be done. Thus it is clear that people, by remaining true to themselves and confident of their ability to succeed no matter what happens in their current job, can energize themselves, regardless of what the leader or anyone else is doing. But most people do not have this awareness and easily succumb to the energies swirling around them at work.

The manifestations in this case included excessive gossip, formal and informal complaints to the human resources department, isolating from others, and outright conflict, including outbursts of anger, profanity, and name-calling. The larger organization struggled with issues from this department for years.

The first order of business with this group is to change the leader, who clearly was looking out for himself but not his team. Then the group must rebuild capacity by learning how to manage emotional energy and deal with conflict at work. They also benefit from increased awareness of their own Authentic Profiles© and how to remain aligned with the highest and best within themselves throughout the day. Most people lack the ability, commitment, and accountability to give themselves the regular reinforcement required to stay with the process. If the change effort ends too soon, they easily lapse back into old behaviors. Every time such a lapse occurs, the length of time required for the next change effort increases.

The larger organization has a responsibility to provide a favorable climate for its employees. Just as companies have an obligation to keep employees safe from physical harm, so it is time to realize that the emotional climate must be suitable to allow human potential to develop and maximize productivity. After all, for most organizations, payroll is the biggest expense. It just makes sense to maximize return on that investment.

Enough. It's time to leave the pain. The Energy Analysis® is one place to start.

3 Transforming Negative Energy

What's the Whole Truth?

It is possible to transform negative energy into positive and to also get "stuck" energy to flow. In so doing, we consciously change the chemistry that flows through our brains and bodies. To do this, think about a current situation that is causing you some difficulty, discomfort, or pain. Something you're angry or in grief about. In a journal or on a sheet of blank paper, describe the situation. Then answer these questions:

Where in your body do you feel uncomfortable?

As you sit with this discomfort, can you think of other times in your life when you have felt like this? When? Describe what was going on at that time.

How is this present situation like what was happening the first time you had this feeling?

If the answer doesn't come right away, just sit with the question. The answer may come in a dream or in the early morning hours, as you are awakening. Keep your journal beside your bed. As soon as the answer comes, write it.

Once the original incident is remembered, then the brain and body memory systems have remarkable power to transform the original hurt and replace it with a new story about you—*the whole truth* story, minus the negative emotion. With your now fully developed brain, with compassion, you can more clearly see the truth and tell a more authentic story.

The Whole Truth Letters

A simple, easy way to get started is to write the *whole truth letters*, a process I learned in the treatment and renewal center designed by Liliane and Gilles Desjardins, creators of the Desjardins model of recovery (www.higherpower.info). Think back to any incident that upset you

- Any person, group or institution that made you angry or fearful during your whole life.
- Any person who disappointed you.
- Any teacher who discouraged you.

- Any parent who didn't give you what you needed or who abused you in any way.
- Any sibling who taunted or annoyed you.
- Any boyfriend/girlfriend who dumped you disrespectfully.
- Any ex-husband or ex-wife with whom issues have not been settled.
- Any church or institution that violated you in any way.
- Any employer who wrongfully treated you.
- Anything that is still unresolved.

Write a letter to that person or institution or group. Tell them what you really think and how you truly feel. Use profanity, if it comes up. Don't censor your words. Get the negative energy out. Write in letters that are five lines tall, if that helps. Use color or drawings, if you wish. These letters are for *your* healing—not to be sent. At the top of the first page, write these words: "God guides my hand to write what needs to be written by me now. God loves me now." Relying on that intent, write without guilt or self-judgment.

The purpose of the whole truth letters is to get the energy moving. It isn't the original incident itself that continues to hurt—it's the emotion that is bonded to the incident. This energy is stuck.

The beginning of transformation is to get this energy moving and stop remembering the old offense. Ruiz writes,

> "How many times do we make our spouse, our children, or our parents pay for the same mistake? Every time we remember the mistake, we blame them again and send them all the emotional poison we feel at the injustice, and then we make them pay again for the same mistake" (pp. 12-13).

We do the same thing to ourselves.

> "The human is the only animal on earth that pays a thousand times for the same mistake. The rest of the animals pay once... But not us. We have a powerful memory" (p. 12).

The *whole truth letters* are a solution. Not a once-only process, you can write a *whole truth letter* any time you're having difficulty. Remember that you have tens of billions of neurons in your brain alone, not to mention the neurons in other parts of your body. A single dendrite on one of those neurons might have more than 15,000 connections to other neurons. Do you remember this illustration? A small section of your system of neuronal connections was shown in Fig. 2-6.

So a single memory can be connected to this and that and the other, which is why some people describe this process as "peeling the onion." Remember that we have tens of billions of neurons. Each of those tens of billions of neurons has multiple dendrites, and just *one* of those dendrites might have 15,000 or more connections to other neurons. The complexity is mind-boggling, which is why it is fruitless to analyze other people's behavior. You won't live long enough to untangle that web! But you can accept this complexity and begin to untangle your own web—at least those memories that are causing the most pain and thereby the greatest blockage.

After you've written the whole truth letters, follow this process to transform negative energy:

1. Read the whole truth letters to a trusted person who is a good listener. This person's job is only to "bear witness" with kind acceptance.

2. Burn, shred, or tear the letters. Old thoughts are persistent. They want to hang around. So, when you think this thought again, remember, "I burned/shredded that. It's gone. It no longer exists." Or "I tore you into tiny, confetti-like pieces and threw you away." Actually, the act of tearing adds the value of body movement to push the energy out. Your body will help you remember. If you choose to shred the letters, remember the sound of the shredder as the words go through. The louder, the better! If these thoughts ever return again, simply remember the sound of the shredder and think, "Those words are gone."

3. Using the list in Fig. 3-1 as a prompt, name your own depleting energies as they were revealed in the letters you just read (resentment, fear, judgment, rejection of self or others, etc.). These depleting energies are blocking you from living the life you want. To move the energy, you must first name the blockage. Through transforming unwanted energy, you will have a "change of heart."

4. From your observation of what you wrote in the *whole truth letters*, list 1-3 predominant character defects.

5. Transform the defects you identified by asking for more of what you are "short" of (i.e., shortcoming). Name what you are "short" of and want more of.

Transform Defects to Shortcomings

CHARACTER DEFECTS	SHORTCOMINGS
Rejection of others	Acceptance of others
Rejection of self	Acceptance of self
Impatience	Patience
Impulsiveness	Maturity/ease/moderation
Envy	Rejoice in other's good
Jealousy	Live and let live
Inadequacy	Adequacy
Justification	Trust/faith
Over-sensitivity	Humility/humor
Procrastination	Action now
Dependence	Live and let live/faith
Worry	Trust divine order
Indecisiveness	Decision now
Isolation	Participation/love others
Self-pity	De-dramatize/laugh at self
Victim syndrome	Humility/honesty
Perfectionism	Acceptance of human nature
False pride	Humility
Guilt	Self forgiveness/acceptance
Resentment	Forgiveness/peace
Blame	Take own responsibility
Intolerance	Tolerance
Demand	Do for others/give of self
Rationalization	Reality/honesty
Vengeance	Forgiveness/understanding
Manipulation	Total honesty
Alibi (Lies)	Honesty/truth
Dishonesty	Honesty/reality
Selfishness	Sharing/gift to others
Egotism	Considerate of others
Egocentrism	Centered on others
Fear	Faith
Scarcity	Abundance/God is our source
Timidity	Boldness/move out in faith
Judgment	Live and let live

Fig. 3-1: Character Defects vs. Shortcomings

Used with permission from Liliane and Gilles Desjardins

6. As a daily practice, each morning identify 1-3 character defects that are active for you. Borrowing the seventh step prayer from Alcoholics Anonymous, write,

"My Creator, I am now willing that you should have all of me—good and bad. I pray that you now remove from me every single defect that stands in the way of my usefulness to you and my fellows. Remove from me _____, _____, _____. Grant me _____, _____, _____"

Then don't work at it. Let it go. Your subconscious brain will work on it, incrementally, and gradually create the reality you want. When I can't immediately identify the defect that is most active for me, I imagine a searchlight starting at the top of my head, bringing my defects "to light." Instantly, at least one "pops up."

7. Finally, read aloud these statements about forgiveness
   • "Forgiveness occurs when you systematically lay aside conclusions you have reached about other people and the motivations for their actions." (Nemeth, 1997)
   • "Forgiveness is not the approval of the wrongdoing. It is reclaiming my freedom of choice."
   • "Forgiveness is not weakness. It is strength of character. I have the courage to let go, turn the page, and start over. It is a statement that says, 'You have no more power over me.'"
   • "To forgive does not mean that I need to like you or approve of what you do. It means I understand your dis-ease. It means I don't hate you. I don't fear you. I am free. You can't hurt me any more. I have the wisdom and strength to make choices"
   • "Resentments and anger are self-punishment. Forgiveness is self-nurturing."
   • "The Spanish derivation for 'resent' is 'resentir,' which literally means "to feel again." So when we choose not to forgive, we choose to feel the original hurt again—and again—and again."

Within us at all times is unlimited possibility. Only our choices determine our limits. When you choose to stop resenting and start forgiving, you actually change the chemistry of your brain with your choices. Because of past conditioning, you must make this choice every day. This is a life-long, not a semester-long, course. Still, the choice is yours. And now you have a tool for doing it.

It's an exciting adventure to discover that we can, in the words of poet, author, consultant, and Director of the LBJ Library, Betty Sue Flowers, "tell a different story" about our experiences, processing through the negative emotions surrounding them. We can replace resentment with forgiveness and understanding. We can replace self-censorship with self-acceptance. Once begun, this is a recursive process. We keep coming back to it any time a negative emotion or experience arises or a situation reminds us of an earlier trauma. Instead of staying trapped in the memory, we process through and replace it with one that brings us peace.

My own transformation experience has lasted for over ten years, although the most intensive work is over. Now I use these tools the moment I realize I'm having difficulty. I no longer allow issues to go unaddressed or emotions ignored. Dealing with emotions in a healthy way has become a matter of daily practice using these tools. It's like anything else; you can choose to study for the test in small amounts, over time, or you can stay up all night cramming. You can clean the house once a week, or you can wait for a month and take twice as long. You can repaint the house when you see the first chips and smudges, or you can wait until the realtor says you have to do it if you expect to sell it. Would you rather do it the hard/expensive way? Or the easy/less expensive way? It's your choice.

Chapter 3 Exercises

1. To get started on your Whole Truth letters, begin writing, "I am really angry that..." Write until you get all of your anger out onto the paper. Then shred or burn what you have written.

2. Having done that, what are you ready to let go?

   Now write a forgiveness letter, first to yourself and then to everyone to whom you wrote an anger letter.

3. In the future, if your mind tries to return to this old way of thinking, what will you do? (Examples: Smell the smoke and remember "I burned those"; hear the shredder as the pages went through; feel and hear the tearing of the page as I ripped it up.)

4. What new thinking will replace the old?

4 Tune in to the Voice

But what if prayer were more about listening to God
In the silence of our hearts,
Than about bombarding God with our piety?

Imagine a glass of muddy water.
When you look into it,
you can see nothing through the cloudiness.
But if you leave the glass alone for a while,
And allow the water to become perfectly still,
You will see how the mud settles
And the water becomes clear.

Prayer time and prayer space can be like that water.
If we let ourselves come to rest,
To a state of physical and mental equilibrium,
The ocean within us will become calmer and clearer,
And we will be better able to pick up the still small voice
Which is God's whisper in our heart.

From: *The Gift of Prayer* by Margaret Silf

Voices

Our brains and memory systems are like that glass of muddy water—full of particles and waves holding information that contains our thoughts and controls our actions and behaviors. We have gathered this information from the world around us—what we read, what people said to us, what we saw and experienced. Without our conscious awareness, we have been programmed. This programming is our ego, our adaptation to the external world. From this programming come voices that say things like, "I'm too good for this" or "I'm not good enough for that." Thoughts, ideas, and images flow through our minds in stream-of-consciousness fashion, often without words. Some people describe this flow as "monkey mind," "the committee in my head" or "static between my ears." It's an unsettling, uneasy, albeit familiar, state of mind.

For example, payment from a client comes slowly; in the delay, your mind says, "They're not happy with me. They aren't planning to pay the bill. They will tell other people I'm no good, and I'll never get another client." Some people call this pattern of thinking a slippery slope because once you start down it, there's no stopping until you hit the bottom. Then, after you pick yourself up, you think, "Maybe if I had done this... or that... things would be different," thus continuing the self-flagellation in a somewhat different form. In other words, if something unexpected happens, you assume it is negative and you are to blame. The vacuum created by no communication is a strong attractor for those self-defeating voices within us to tell ourselves a story that fills the empty space and takes control. What we often don't realize is that *we have the power to choose the story that we tell.*

I felt myself going down that very slippery slope when a client's payment was past due. My anxiety had been heightened because the three-month project was halted after only a month with the explanation that the organization couldn't afford it. After the invoice became overdue, I left voice mail and e-mail messages that were not answered. All of this behavior was very unusual for this type of client, so I decided not to stay in limbo. I wrote a letter that said everything I truly needed to say, clearly and forthrightly. I respected both myself and the client, and I offered to lower the amount due in order to clear the matter. Within two days, the client called, apologized, explained the delay, and assured me I would receive the full amount right away. This telephone conversation gave me the opportunity to probe the true reason for the cessation of work, which was, in fact, financial. Moreover, the client assured me the approach I was taking was the one needed; they're just not able to pay what it costs.

When we make up stories about how people are or what they are thinking we close the opportunity to learn what's really going on. Without that learning we keep telling ourselves the same stories, over and over, which is Einstein's definition of insanity—"doing the same things, over and over, expecting different results."

Delays are invitations for the committee in our heads to begin the chatter, in much the same way as a lull in a meeting invites restlessness. To be content with stillness seems contrary to the norm for most people, but unless we learn it, we are controlled by voices in our heads that stifle our self-esteem, creativity, potential, and possibility. They keep us "stuck," unable to learn and change, and they keep us from being authentic.

Most of us have been compared to other people at some time, so one of the flows into that stream of voices gives us the idea that we have to be better than other people. Therefore, without our awareness, the competition begins, and we hear ourselves trying to "top" someone else's story, proving that our trip was bigger or better or more expensive than the one they are telling about. We find it difficult just to listen to appreciate. Instead, we listen to determine if we can tell a better story. If we can't, we change the subject until we find one where we *can* come out on top—or we move to another group. Thus our ego is strengthened and our Authentic Self neglected.

Those of us with a lot of schooling are very well trained in mental processes, so the stream in our heads carries standards by which we measure ourselves and everyone else. "Can I think of anything else that would make this better?" is our driving question. We have to make an "A," even when there is no test. Many of our interactions are based on proving who is right. A while ago, I was present for a birthday celebration for a young man in his mid-twenties. During dinner I turned to him and asked, "What do you remember as your happiest birthday?" He thought for a moment and then said, "When I was ten years old, I had a party with my friends at McDonald's…" In mid-sentence, his mother interrupted him. "No. That's not right. We went to Pizza Hut."

He looked at her. "I think it was McDonald's," he repeated.

"No, I'm certain it was Pizza Hut because I…." she went on to prove her point while I watched her son's shoulders sink and the energy for re-telling a happy memory go out of him. He never finished the story.

If I had asked this mother, point-blank, "Would you rather be right, or would you prefer to have your son feel free to express his feelings and tell his stories in your presence?" she would undoubtedly have said she wanted her son to be free to express himself. But without that question to bring her to conscious awareness of what she was doing, her default setting—to be right—activated to trounce her son. This mother's profession requires exactitude, and she has not yet come to the awareness that the skills that serve her so well in her work are not the skills that give life to relationships.

Having been a teacher, I know how difficult it is to leave that role at the front door of your home. I wasn't very successful at it, either. But now I wish when my children told me about problems at school, I had just taken them in my arms and said something like, "I am so sorry that happened to you." I wish I had not tried to fix or advise. I wish I had made grades less important and teachers less godlike. I wish I had known that what my children needed was an unconditionally loving parent who would just sit with them for awhile and honor their feelings.

Living life "by the books" is missing the mark. The poet William Wordsworth knew this and wrote about it in 1798.

"The Tables Turned"

UP! up! my Friend, and quit your books;
Or surely you'll grow double:
Up! up! my Friend, and clear your looks;
Why all this toil and trouble?

The sun, above the mountain's head,
A freshening lustre mellow
Through all the long green fields has spread,
His first sweet evening yellow.

Books! 'tis a dull and endless strife:
Come, hear the woodland linnet,
How sweet his music! on my life,
There's more of wisdom in it.

And hark! how blithe the throstle sings!
He, too, is no mean preacher:
Come forth into the light of things,
Let Nature.be your teacher

She has a world of ready wealth,
Our minds and hearts to bless—
Spontaneous wisdom breathed by health,
Truth breathed by cheerfulness.

One impulse from a vernal wood
May teach you more of man,
Of moral evil and of good,
Than all the sages can.

Sweet is the lore which Nature brings;
Our meddling intellect
Mis-shapes the beauteous forms of things:—
We murder to dissect.

Enough of Science and of Art;
Close up those barren leaves;
Come forth, and bring with you a <u>heart</u>
That watches and receives. (emphasis mine)

From Wayfaring to Wayfinding

In Wayfaring, we learn how to make our way through the world—how to feed and groom ourselves, how to manage our lives, how to stay healthy, how to make a living, how to get along with all kinds of people, how to act in social situations, even how to present the image we want to the world. But in Wayfinding, our goal is to find out who we *authentically* are and align our lives accordingly. To accomplish this, we must transcend the patterns developed through the years of Wayfaring and learn to live from our hearts, not our heads. Like me, you may have taken on an identity that is not authentic for you. If so, Wayfinding will make the correction. The course seems uniquely designed for each Wayfinder, so no one book, person, or experience will have all the answers you seek. Rather, you already have an inner guidance system—a presence—a voice that resolves unfinished business and tells you what to do next. Your job is to hear and honor this voice and follow, even when it seems contrary to what you have previously learned while Wayfaring.

A Heart That Watches and Receives

The voice for Wayfinding comes from the heart. In the human embryo the heart, which is the first organ to form, starts beating in the third week after conception. The heart is the last organ to stop functioning when we die.

According to research by The Institute of HeartMath®, a nonprofit founded in 1991 to conduct research and provide education about the power of the heart, "...the heart's electromagnetic field [is] by far the most powerful field produced by the body" (Childre and Martin, 1999, p. 34). Moreover,

- Information sent from the heart to the brain can have profound effects on our higher brain centers.
- Our heart rhythms affect the brain's ability to process information, make decisions, solve problems, and experience and express creativity.
- When subjects in research studies achieve entrainment of the brain with the heart, they report heightened intuitive clarity and a greater sense of well-being (p. 46).

For years I attended seminars, interviewed experts, and read books about the brain, especially the emotional brain. My search led me to the heart.

Soon after I began a practice of sitting in silence in the early morning, I began to experience a slight tingling, as if passageways were opening up. I felt this tingling especially in my fingertips. Then I became aware of it in my heart, located right behind my breastbone. It felt warm, shaped like my cupped hand, and oh-so-slightly gurgling, like the old-fashioned Christmas lights that bubble up from a colored base into a candle-shaped glass bulb. That was when I started listening to the voice of my heart. When I could feel my heart, I became able to hear its voice. HeartMath® research indicates (Childre & Martin, 1999),

> "When we're first learning to make the distinction between the head and the heart, it's easy to be fooled. But there's a big difference between emotions driven by the head and emotions of the true heart. To avoid confusion, we like to speak of emotions in terms of... 'higher' and 'lower' ... The lower [emotions] refer to those feelings that are colored by the attachments and conditions placed on them by the mind... The higher [emotions] ...don't hedge or barter. Instead of saying, 'I'll do this *if* you do that,' they express themselves authentically without expectation"

When I have difficulty distinguishing what's coming from my head or my heart, I start my sentence with: "What I *truly* need to say is..." Like a wedge, this phrase opens the door to my heart, and good results usually follow—maybe not in the short term, but always in the long term.

HeartMath® finds that the following "power tools" are at the "heart's core": sincerity, appreciation, nonjudgment, and forgiveness (Childre and Martin, 1999). But these are not the only energies that might be present in the heart. It's possible for people to "harden" their hearts by opening them to lower emotions. In Chapter 3 you learned how to make the transformation and thus transcend these lower emotions.

Peace is the prerequisite for Wayfinding, and joy is the result. Another result is enlightenment. Several years ago it became clear to me that, since God is Truth, God is Love, and God is Light, my job is only to speak the truth in love, then relax and let God take it from there. God brings Enlightenment. Often, I see people's countenances change when they open to Truth and Love and receive Enlightenment.

So the gateway to Wayfinding is through speaking the truth from love, then accepting the enlightenment that results. The prerequisite is peace, which is most easily found in silence. Trappist monk Father Thomas Keating says, "Silence is the language God speaks, and everything else is a bad translation." In the 13th century, Meister Eckhart wrote, "Nothing in all creation is so like God as stillness". A poem I wrote in my early stages of Wayfinding describes the exquisite experience of stillness and peace.

Communion

The spell of the deep snow
In the woods
Drew my sister and me
From the path of the road.

We found the tracks of the deer.
One, a small one,
Had scraped the white mounds
With his small belly.

We found Sacred Space,
Sat side by side on a log,
Listening
To Silence.

Truth came.
We spoke it
With Love.

I lifted my face to the falling
Snow, opened my mouth, and
Offered my tongue for
Divine Communion.

The process for Wayfinders works something like this:

1. Make a decision to hear the Voice and do what it says.
2. Sit still and listen.
3. Clear out the lower emotions that are the particles and waves of muddy water. Let them "settle" by settling old accounts, forgiving, accepting, and transforming lower emotions into their higher opposites (more about this in Chapter 7).
4. Increase awareness of the effect that your environment is having on your state of mind. Change what needs changing. Do it immediately. Taking 3 and 4 together reminds me of something one of my spiritual teachers said, "Change your attitude or change your address." Of course, changing your environment might not

mean changing your address. It might mean re-arranging furniture, painting, getting rid of objects that remind you of unpleasant experiences or addictions. It might mean changing the television programs you watch or the places you go. It might even mean changing the people you hang out with. It also might mean silencing the negative voices in your head and replacing them with kind, affirming words.

5.   Be at peace. Establish spiritual practices that enable you to return to peace whenever you feel the slightest ripple of uneasiness (sometimes referred to as dis-ease).

What Happened to Me

If I told all of the stories of how the Voice has worked with me over the years since I began the practice of sitting still in silence, this book would be so long that no one would read it. So I'll just say that sometimes I sense from within my heart what I truly need to do. Sometimes an insight will come through art, books, movies, or other media. A quick example of that: My husband and I had come dangerously close to the precipice of divorce. While in the throes of the struggle, we attended a local production of the Scott McPherson play, *Marvin's Room*, because a friend who had a part in the play had invited us. Near the end of the play, these lines roared at me: The scene is that two estranged sisters are reminiscing about the life of service one of them had led—service to a sick father and a mentally ill relative, both of whom lived with her. Brushing aside the sacrifice she had made, the serving sister said, "I've had so much love."

Her not-so-faithful sister responded, "Yes, they do love you very much," to which her serving sister replied, "Oh, no. It's not that they love me. It's how much *I* have loved *them*. That is the gift—how much I love them."

What became clear to me in that moment was that I needed to shift the focus to how much I loved my husband, not how he was behaving, which was, after all, a fleeting, transitory state. I had allowed his recent behavior to capture my focus, and resentment reigned within me. The gift of this play—the lesson—was to remind me to keep the focus on my love for him and let everything else go. This is an example of how the Voice works with me through media. It pierces the hardening process that has begun again in my heart and re-ignites Love.

The Voice also works with me through the words of other people and through my own experience. To hear it most clearly, I am open. No longer do I try to hide the fact that I'm struggling. I speak of the struggle and listen to what people have to say. This happened to me early in my Wayfinding experience as I worked with a group of educators at the Jakarta International School in Indonesia. I was there for a two-day workshop. On the morning of the first day, as I began, I realized that one of the participants—a tall, dark, handsome young man—was frowning. Not too far into the presentation, he raised his hand and said, "I'm experiencing some cognitive dissonance." I thought, "Omagosh. I'm in trouble!" I wasn't even sure what "cognitive dissonance" was, but from the look on his face, I could tell it wasn't good, so my mind began racing, sorting through everything I knew to try to make him happy.

It didn't work. By midday, two other people at his table were frowning, so I didn't go to lunch, preferring to stay and rework my design in an effort to bring him and his two friends on board. The result of my effort was that, by the end of the day, he had recruited his whole table, and my fear had increased to anxiety.

That evening, one of the principals—a gracious, kind woman—took me out to eat. During our meal, she said, "I think the workshop is just fabulous."

"Really?" I replied. "I think it's awful."

She looked shocked. "Why?"

"I can't really put my finger on it. I just don't have the group with me. I'm struggling. But I've reworked the design, hoping it will be better tomorrow."

She responded, "Well, I think it's just fine."

That night around 3 a.m., I sat straight up in bed, awake with the realization of what I was doing—focusing on one table. The room was full of people at other tables who were doing just fine. With this realization, I jumped out of bed, put the design back into its original form, and said out loud, "I'm going to focus on the faces that are open."

The next morning, that's what I did. I didn't even look at the table where the handsome young man was sitting—until the break, when I sneaked a glance at that corner of the room. To my delight, he was the only one who was frowning. The rest of his colleagues were now with me.

Later in the day, my dinner companion approached. "Now I see what you were talking about last night. It's Peter. Don't pay any attention to him. He frowns all the time."

That's how I learned that what I focus on gets stronger.

Sometimes people ask me, "Do you think it really gets stronger, or is it just your perception?"

My answer is, "That sounds like headwork to me. It doesn't matter."

Many years later, I had the opportunity to apply this lesson in a high stakes personal issue. On an especially dark day emotionally, sitting downstairs in my home, I felt the light change outside. Without hesitation, I sprang to my feet, ran upstairs, and grabbed my camera. Quickly I opened the door that led to a small balcony outside my bedroom on the second floor and started snapping. Fig. 4-1 visually represents what the Voice said to me.

From that moment on, through this crisis that lasted almost a year, I focused on the *light*. I kept telling myself that Love is the strongest force in the universe; nothing can overcome it. I made greeting cards with this photograph. Ultimately, it became the first framing in the Noel Klaus Inspirational series. I kept this photograph in front of me, continuing to work with it in every way that felt right. In the end, things worked out well. Very well.

You might say, "What was it that moved you upstairs so quickly to snatch your camera and start shooting? Intuition?"

I would answer, "I don't care what you call it. To analyze it feels like headwork to me. I only know that my life works better when I listen and respond."

You might say, "You're really talking about God. Why don't you just say so?"

Fig. 4-1: What the Voice Said to Me

My answer is this: In the Old Testament, the word that we now know as *Yahweh* was a collection of consonants that could not be pronounced. God is Mystery. But when we describe God and try to understand how God works, we are reducing Divine Power to fit the boundaries of language. It's not useful to me to frame this work in terms of what I learned as a child in Sunday school, when my brain wasn't fully developed and I certainly didn't understand the power of the human heart and its relationship to the Divine. I still don't understand it. I don't like reductionist or anthropomorphic explanations of God either.

The denomination in which I grew up has a doctrine known as "the priesthood of the believer." That is, each of us has direct access to God. We don't need an interpreter. God speaks every language and is powerful enough to establish a relationship with anyone. Our job is just to open our hearts. The church to which I belong is known as a "grace church." That is, the people who come there find forgiveness and acceptance. We attract the "bruised, battered, broken, and bored." Then, as we learn, we become the blessed.

Someone reminded me that the root word of education is from the Latin word "*educare*," which means "to draw out." So I'm not pushing my story on anyone; rather, I seek to be authentic while supporting and encouraging others to open and then simply say what they learn. In fact, this is another good tool for Wayfinders to use in staying on course. Ask yourself, "Do I feel like I'm pushing?" If so, you're not on course. If you simply feel open to receive and confident to speak as led by your heart, to be drawn out, then you're on course.

If you have made a decision to open to the Voice but, because of patterns developed for safety over the years, you cannot open enough to "hear," then be assured that the Voice will find you even if it has to shake you up to get your attention. The following story happened to someone I know.

What Happened to Her

She left for work early because of a dental appointment. This was a day she had looked forward to, when her dentist would fit a new crown. But when she arrived at his office he said, "I tried to call but couldn't reach you. The new crown was broken in transit from the lab. We have to re-do it. I can't complete the work today."

Disappointed, she decided to go on to work even though it was early. Dismayed by the rush-hour traffic, irritated by the inconvenience, and annoyed that she couldn't complete her dental work as planned, she left the freeway searching for a less-traveled route to work and ended up at an intersection in a part of town she rarely visited. There, stopped at a light, in utter amazement she watched a swan fall out of the sky onto the pavement between her car and the car in front of her. Not fly—drop—out of the sky.

Another driver happened to know a lot about birds and came to its rescue, covering its head with a tee shirt to keep it calm. Another driver explained, "I think I saw it hit a power line. It's probably in shock."

She and the bird expert loaded the swan into her jeep and headed for the animal rescue shelter, with him cradling the bird in the back of her vehicle while she drove.

A Letter from God

That afternoon, as she told me the story, she said, "What can this mean? I was in a part of town where I *never* go. Nothing in my morning was going according to plan. I'm just sitting at a stop light, and a swan *dropped* out of the sky right in front of me. What can it mean?"

This person had been coming out of the fog of denial slowly over the many months I had worked with her. She had followed her father's profession. But she also had inherited a physical condition so severe that every week-end after the week's work, she writhed in pain. Massages and back exercises had largely lost their effectiveness over time and she had to confront something she didn't want to acknowledge—that if she didn't have an operation and drastically change her life and profession, she would be in a wheelchair, unable to walk. Her pain would only increase with time.

Stubbornly, she refused the surgical procedure. But over the months I had known her the severity of her pain had forced her to acknowledge the truth—that her back had disabled her and something had to be done. She hated the word "disabled," hated the idea of surgery, hated her job. Even her marriage, which had been a source of strength, was suffering, and she had begun to grouse about her husband and their relationship. Still, stubbornly, she tried to live her life on her terms, with increasing pain.

But today, with a swan dropping out of the sky right in front of her, she seemed teachable. I remembered a story about a swan in a book I used early in my spiritual journey. The book came with a set of animal cards, accompanied by a story with spiritual insight, using animals metaphorically as inspiration. As a Wayfarer, I had used the cards as part of my morning ritual to help change thought patterns and open new possibilities. I ran upstairs to retrieve the book.

The story I read aloud to her was about leaving illusion, called "dreamtime." As I read, she felt chills all over her body, as if this story were a letter from God. I gave her the book. Obviously, I had saved it for her.

After enough days had passed for her system to assimilate the profound emotional experience, I asked her to tell me which part of the story especially resonated with her. Here's what she said:

> "I truly believe that swan was dropped right in front of me to teach me and remind me to trust God, Great Spirit (I like that) and accept today and what lies ahead.
> "What an incredible gift! The swan, then the story.
> "It's interesting that the swan in the story returns after being changed and has a long neck. I equate that to a straight back, not only in the literal sense, but straight that I can stand tall and accept myself for who I am."

The Voice can even be a swan dropping noiselessly from the sky. Shortly after this experience, she scheduled the dreaded operation and accepted the managerial position that she had previously and steadfastly refused. Whatever we need is the form that the Voice takes. Whatever it takes is what the Voice is willing to give.

> "Whenever one definitely commits oneself, then Providence moves, too… A whole stream of events issues from the decision, raising in one's favor all manner of unforeseen incidents and meetings and material assistance, which no man could have dreamt would have come this way." Goethe

The Third Person

We human beings have an innate need to reach out to something that is beyond us. In the movie *Castaway* (2000), the character played by Tom Hanks is stranded on an island with a few FedEx parcels that survived the airplane crash with him. In one of those boxes is a volleyball, which he soon redesigns and calls "Wilson" after the manufacturer's name embossed on the ball. For the months and years he spent on the island, he carried on constant conversation with Wilson, reminiscent of the ongoing dialogue Tevya had with God in *Fiddler on the Roof.*

"Pray without ceasing" (1 Thessalonians 5:17)

After my father died, I found a book I had never seen before—*Handbook for Judges* (1961) by the American Judicature Society. In it is this story from "The Spiritual Side of Judging" by Judge Harold Medina, who presided over the communist trials during the McCarthy Era. At one point the courtroom erupted, and "several of the defendants started toward the bench.

"In all that excitement, I felt just as calm as I do now when I speak to you; I did not raise my voice over the tone which you hear me use now... I tell you, as I stand here, that my unguided will alone and such self-control as I possess were unequal to this test. If ever a man felt the presence of Someone beside him, strengthening his will and giving him aid and comfort, it was I on that day."

Change That Lasts

Judge Medina's story reminded me of a conversation in the early 1990s with then Texas Commissioner of Education Lionel "Skip" Meno. His mission was to focus Texas educators on the outcomes, or results, of their work. In other words, he said, essentially, "Don't just tell me all of the good things you are doing. Tell me what students are learning. Give me data to show that what you are doing is getting the results we want. Break that data apart to show that what you are doing is working for *every student*, regardless of socioeconomic group." Needless to say, he met with resistance. Some of that resistance came from the superintendents who didn't like it that this New Yorker was Commissioner, a post normally reserved for one of them. Some of the resistance Meno encountered came from pressure groups, especially the Far Right, who were suspicious of the word "outcomes." A significant amount of pressure came from the state legislature. Also, many teachers believed that some groups of students could not learn. In other words, he had pressure from all sides.

After watching one particularly contentious state school board meeting in which Meno performed with his usual calm grace under pressure, I asked him how he did it. His answer? "I have an out-of-body experience, as if I am floating in a corner of the ceiling, simply observing the goings-on."

When I saw the movie *What the Bleep* and heard the term "The Observer" to describe the divine aspect of man, the part that can never be hurt and which knows the truth, I thought of Skip Meno and what he had taught me. The "out-of-body" experience he described truly is a "Higher Power."

Interestingly, the work that Meno began in Texas lives on. Resistance to the notion that superintendents and principals must be accountable for measurable results has mostly dissipated. With an unperturbed heart and soul, Skip Meno put into place a foundation that has outlasted three governors and which Texas educators point to with pride because it has yielded results beyond anyone's expectations. In other words, in only four years he provided leadership that lasts even to today. When we do our work with God, "Wilson", a Higher Power, an "Observer", an out-of-body experience, or just plain intuition—we get favorable, lasting results.

Alternative to Fight or Flight

Psychologist Carl Jung theorized that people have a "conscious mind" (the one we are aware of), a "subconscious mind" (the one that houses memory and emotion), and a "super-conscious mind" (The Third Person) that can transcend all the other layers to bring about our highest good.

When we are not activating our "Third Person," we are limited to "fight or flight" responses, which do not bring about our highest good. But when we acknowledge the fear of flight or the anger of fight and simply make a different choice—a higher choice—to rely on something we do not understand and cannot rationally explain, then good results always come—maybe not in the short term, but always in the long term. We transcend: there is a new third alternative to add to "fight or flight." A fitting analogy is a story from my father's family who lived in an area where the Ku Klux Klan was quite active. Grandpa had neither respect for nor fear of the Klan. One day, my aunt told me, she was in the family wagon with some of the other children. While my grandfather was driving his family to church, he came upon a small group of men in white robes and hoods. As they passed the robed men, my grandfather tipped his hat and said, "Good morning, *Ladies.*"

My aunt said, "I was terrified. Papa had accused the men of being dressed like women. In that era, they were likely to take offense. I crouched down low, fearing they would follow and shoot us. But they didn't." My grandfather, tipping his hat to anger and fear, simply chose to drive by. To live our lives to the fullest, that is the choice each of us must make.

"Fear not; choose faith" is an often-repeated message throughout scripture, from Genesis to Revelations.

> "In conversation between two persons, tacit reference is made, as to a third party, to a common nature. That third party or common nature is not social; it is impersonal; it is God. And so in groups where debate is earnest, and especially on great questions of thought, the company become aware of their unity; aware that the thought rises to an equal height in all bosoms, that all have a spiritual property in what was said, as well as the sayer. They all become wiser than they were."
> Ralph Waldo Emerson, *The Over-Soul,* 1841.

Blinded by our conscious awareness, most of us do not take this Third Person into consideration.

Conclusion

To neuroscientists our "fight or flight" tendency is known as the ergotropic system. When we are stressed, our heart rate increases, as do blood pressure and breathing. But there is another less-well-known system, the trophotropic, which is the system of calm. In it our heart rate decreases, breathing slows, and we feel relaxed. Not only does our brain work best in a state of relaxed alertness (a fact well known to anyone who ever thought of a great solution to an intractable problem while showering or lying on the beach) but when we add awareness of another dimension, detached from yet closely related to us, we achieve a higher state of consciousness and get closer to our peak performance.

Chapter 4 Exercise – Meditation

- In a quiet place, close your eyes. Repeat silently to yourself:

    "Thy will be done. Thy will be done. Thy will be done."

- Take three deep breaths from your navel.

- Count to 3 on the inhale and then count to 3 on the exhale.

- Place your hand over your heart and tune in to its beating.

- Just sit in stillness and listen to the beating of your heart for at least 5 minutes

5 Draw Your Circle

Never in the history of the world have people had more choices.

When Henry Ford rolled out the first "Model T" a hundred years ago, there were only a few manufacturers of automobiles. Today, we can choose from thousands of models from nearly 50 domestic and foreign makes. Within three generations, our choices have expanded to circle the globe and even beyond. We can buy a Japanese-made car, or we can choose not to buy a car and still get anywhere we want to go by mass transit, train, or plane. Today it's even possible for those with great wealth to travel in space.

Transportation isn't the only area in which our choices have expanded. Think about what has happened in education. Today's children are scheduled for gymnastics, dance, soccer, baseball, basketball, football, rowing, swimming, art, instrumental music, voice, drama, manners, and beyond. By the time they finish high school, our children are good at so many things that it is very difficult for them to choose a college major, so they spend not four but seven or more years moving from major to major, trying to find the one that most appeals to them. Then, degree in hand, they choose a profession, career, or line of work from among increasingly numerous options. As they advance into adulthood, they seek fulfillment through career advancement, financial success, family accomplishments, their standing in the community, and the awards and recognitions they receive.

Choices continually expand in every area of our lives. We can shop virtually in shops in any country in the world through the Internet. We can choose any religion; in fact, once we have chosen a religion, we can choose from a wide variety of forms that religion takes. Even within Christian denominations, churches are vastly different in how they practice Christianity. In our cities, choices are greatly expanded, while Americans increasingly are migrating to cities.

People are restless and rarely satisfied.

Making our way through earthly choices—*wayfaring*—does not bring the fulfillment we seek, and we pay a high price for trying to do/get/have everything and do/get/have it faster. Even those who do/get/have the most are often not fulfilled. The National Institute of Mental Health estimates that 1 in 5 adults suffers from some form of mental disorder, be it anxiety, depression, bipolar disorder, attention deficit disorder, schizophrenia, eating disorder, or psychosis. This number has been rising steadily over time. Also, increasing numbers of people turn to alcohol and other drugs to "numb" their mental illness or general malaise and artificially induce "happiness" or some semblance of peace. At least 1 in 10 Americans are alcoholic, and almost half of us have been profoundly influenced by another person's drinking. This influence manifests in the form of syndromes like codependency and workaholism, which are attempts to find ultimate meaning either through another person or through one's work, with more attention to *what we are doing* or *how we relate to other people* than to *who we essentially are.*

An Old Dilemma

Although our trappings appear advanced and sophisticated, the basic dilemma of human existence has not changed. What will bring satisfaction, fulfillment, and contentment in the relatively brief span of our lives so that we die with the peace of mind that we lived as we truly wanted to live—that we found the essence of our own life and lived it well?

In the early 1590s playwright Christopher Marlowe, a contemporary of William Shakespeare, gave life to this dilemma in the form of a tragedy called *Doctor Faustus.* Having completed his education, Faustus contemplates what to do with his life that will bring him the most *satisfaction.* To find the answer, he sorts through his options: Pursue logic? Medicine? Law? Divinity? Discounting each of these because of their limitations, he chooses magic, believing it to be a superior knowledge that will make him like a god. Thus he summons Mephistopheles, an agent of Satan, and makes a pact with the devil to give him twenty-four years of the ability to perform magic in exchange for his soul. During those years, Faustus travels the world, performing tricks for the world's political and spiritual leaders, believing himself superior to all other people.

But is Faustus *satisfied*? Throughout the twenty-four years of the play, he is constantly tormented by misgivings and fears of hell. Each time Mephistopheles medicates Faustus' pain with yet another sensational trick, the last of which is to summon Helen of Troy to be his lover. "Sweet Helen, make me immortal with a kiss. Her lips suck forth my soul, see where it flies!" (Act 12) Thus, Faustus gives his soul to sexual fantasy.

Similarly, we increase our number of espresso shots per day, the noise around us, the number of movies we see or hours of television we watch, the amount of alcohol required to give us a high or the number of pills we take to calm us down, the degree of danger in our adventures. Or, taking the opposite approach, we might develop physical symptoms to attract more sympathy while increasing our own suffering or withdraw further and further into fantasy or oblivion in an attempt to control our lives. Thus, the core addictions of control, sensation, suffering, and security prevail and determine the course of our lives.

What People Truly Want: Wayfinding

What people truly want is peace of mind. We want our mind's chatter to stop. We want to know where our "bottom line" is. We want to feel fulfilled, contented, reasonably free from doubt and worry, assured that we're on the right track. We want to feel confident about our decisions.

The essential difference between *wayfaring* and *wayfinding* is this: Way-farers move from experience to experience, looking for the ultimate answer that will end their restlessness or malaise. Their point of reference is the ego. The irony is that the ego, thus continually fed, becomes so large that it overwhelms the soul, also known as the voice within or the Authentic Self. Doctor Faustus found, at the end of his life, that his pride had grown so large and taken control of his life to such an extent that he could not, even with hell in clear sight, repent.

Wayfinders, on the other hand, begin from a different point of reference. The star pattern of the night sky tells them where they are. Only after they have their bearings do they make decisions that guide the journey. The 1999 PBS film, *Wayfinders: A Pacific Odyssey,* written and directed by Gail Evenari, details the story of modern wayfinder Nainoa Thompson, who learned the ancient art and science of ocean navigation from Mau Piailug, who learned it from his grandfather. After many months as Mau's student, Nainoa tells this story: "As we watched the sun set and the night sky be-come clear, Mau said, 'Can you point in the direction of Tahiti?'"

Following the discipline of months of teaching, Nainoa first looked up into the stars, positioned throughout the dome above him, to find Polaris (the North Star). With Polaris sighted, he knew where he was. Then he pointed, accurately, to Tahiti in the blackness beyond the horizon, 2500 miles away.

"Can you see Tahiti?" his teacher asked.

"I see the island in my mind," responded Nainoa.

"Good. Keep the vision in your mind. Know where you are, and pull Ta-hiti toward you. If you do that, you'll never be lost." These words were the teacher's last lesson with the student Nainoa, who had thus demonstrated his mastery of the art and science of Wayfinding.

Similarly, in this ocean we call brain chemistry, we are navigators. To find our way, we must first memorize the "stars" in the "dome" that sur-rounds us. What do we choose to guide us?

Unlike Nainoa, we place our own "stars" in the dome, or circle, that surrounds us. Do we want to be guided by truth or lies? Do we want love or lust? Is our choice to be guided by the desire of our hearts? Or do we want to please someone else? These are the decisions to ponder as we determine what goes inside our circle and what stays outside.

Fig. 5–1: The Circle

The tool of the circle is amazingly simple; the practice of it is difficult. In the circle above or one that you draw for yourself, write inside the circle what you want in your life. Then write outside the circle what you do not want to experience.

As we make our way through the world, we might hear admonitions to have values, but no one tells us how to change from a self-seeking existence with no boundaries to a focused way of life, with the values we truly want to live by as the dome above us holds us steady while we pull a clear vision for our lives ever toward us. More about discerning the vision that is right for our lives is written in Chapter 8. Getting our bearings—knowing what's in our circle—comes first.

My Experiences with the Circle

My first circle had more words written outside than inside. I wanted no more jealousy, gossip, fear, or getting even—from other people, of course. Inside the circle, I wanted love, a happy marriage, financial serenity. I placed the circle on the nightstand beside my bed, and it was the first thing I looked at every morning. Over time, my focus centered on what was inside the circle. When someone else's fear came toward me, I didn't catch it. Instead, it bounced off and I stayed on course.

My first circle lasted for several years. I placed it on my bedside table and each morning I read it at the beginning of my meditation/contemplation/prayer. Eventually, when it felt right, I cut out the circle with a pair of scissors and threw away the outer scraps containing what I was no longer willing to experience.

Do not rush this process. Do it at a pace that's right for you. Listen to your heart and make changes to your circle in accordance with guidance from your inner voice.

My voice teacher told me that the best singers in the world are classically trained, spending at least three years of their earliest vocal training doing nothing but vocal exercises—no songs. This discipline of rigorous training is what makes them great. My own experience is that when, in the beginning of new learning, I practice a few simple exercises to perfection, not rushing to become "expert," I love the process more and find that ultimately the work speeds up effortlessly, seemingly on its own.

An example is prayer. When I first decided to be conscious of and act on the scripture that says "Ask, and ye shall receive," I noticed answers to my prayers took about two months to materialize. Then that delay shortened to two weeks. Today, it is not unusual for me to see the answer in my next breath. My own resistance feeds the delay time. So skepticism and trying to control the outcome delay my ability to see the answer I seek. Also, having a preconceived idea of what the answer will look like slows the process. But *surrender, acceptance, letting go and letting God* enhance my ability to recognize answers to prayer.

On the other hand, when we try something new without a circle to guide us we may flounder and even fall short of our aim.

At this writing, I have been working with the circle for over ten years. Over time, the words inside and outside my circle have changed somewhat, but there are constants, as well. I've added compassion, forgiveness, courage, grace, and prayer. I continuously use the circle to guide my journey. I also use the circle for specific areas of my life, like marriage, family, home, work, travel, health and fitness. It can even be used for a specific situation within one of these areas.

No longer do I make hasty decisions or develop resentments based on someone else's words or actions. I have assurance that ultimately I will get exactly what my heart desires, and everyone else in my life will love it, too. Also, it might be better than what I thought it would look like. When I willingly surrender, God sculpts the desires of my heart.

Stephen Covey (1994) encourages people to "put the big rocks in first," using the analogy of filling a container with a collection of sand and big rocks. If you try to fill the container by putting the sand in first, then there isn't room for the big rocks. But if you put the big rocks in first and pour the sand in last, everything can fit.To be more true to life, we could extend Covey's metaphor to include stones and pebbles. Still, we would start with the rocks, then add the stones, next pebbles, and finally the sand. To distinguish between what constitutes a rock, a stone, a pebble, or sand—it sometimes helps to ask the question, "How important is it?"

Once a powerful person accused me of speaking words I didn't speak, bringing one of my greatest fears into reality. Instead of shame and self-flagellation (which are outside my circle), I chose courage and compassion (inside my circle). I recalled that Cardinal Bernardin (1997) told the story of being falsely accused of sexual molestation by a former parishioner, a young boy. Although he did initially feel the human emotions of anger and humiliation, Cardinal Bernardin chose to let his actions be guided by faith, truth and the power of prayer. When he responded to media questions, the Cardinal spoke the truth from his heart.

With the controversy still raging, Cardinal Bernardin asked to meet with the young man. In this meeting the full truth emerged. Cardinal Bernardin was able to look into the young man's eyes and say, "I never abused you." These words were not spoken defensively, but simply with truth. The Cardinal's AIDS-stricken accuser was dying. It was a time for truth, which he told. Someone he trusted had planted the idea that Cardinal Bernardin had been his abuser. The Cardinal offered to celebrate Mass with the young man. At first he refused. But when he saw how completely he had been forgiven, he asked to celebrate Mass with Cardinal Bernardin. This story is made even more dramatic by the fact that Cardinal Bernardin himself was dying from cancer. Imagine the scene of two dying men, accuser and accused, now completely reconciled, celebrating Mass together.

Largely because I had read this book and been inspired by this story, I was able, when my accuser launched her public attack, to stay centered in faith, speak the truth, and pray for her. Consequently, regardless of her actions I remained at peace, harboring no resentment.

Isn't it interesting that I read this particular book just before I, myself, would go through a similar difficult experience? Out of all the books that people have given or lent me to read, I chose this one. Why? Wayfinding. My inner voice chose the book I needed to navigate the waters that were ahead.

Wayfinding Loosens Ego's Control

To become a *Wayfinder,* one must slip out of ego's control. By *ego,* I mean the subconscious part of ourselves for which the neuronal patterns and cellular memories were formed in the early years of our lives—the means by which we learned to protect ourselves and get what we wanted and needed. According to Arntz, Chasse, and Vicente (2005):

"All the emotions, memories, concepts and attitudes are en-coded neurologically and interconnect, the result being what has been variously called the ego, the son of man, the lower self, the human, the personality." (p. 151)

Here is the source of manipulation, falsehood, self-centeredness, and the other host of character defects that ironically got us what we thought we needed as children but as adults block us from becoming our authentic selves. The ego convinces us that the problem is outside ourselves.

Wayfinders choose, instead, a more enlightened path, realizing that our very cells are emitting vibrations which are being "read" by the world out-side of us. "Everything 'out there' of the same frequency will respond to it, and they will then be reflected in your reality. By this notion, everything in your life—people, places, things, times and events—are nothing but reflec-tions of your signature vibrations... Everything in your life is *frequency specific* to who you are. So if you want to know 'Who am I?' just look around; the universe is always serving up the answer" (*What the Bleep*, p. 111). This is exactly why we must live by the Golden Rule, being with oth-ers as we would have them be with us. Taking this perspective removes the possibility for blame and judgment, replacing them with higher-order tools of reflection and self- awareness and bringing into realization the truth of Matthew 7:3 "Why do you look at the speck of sawdust in your brother's eye and pay no attention to the plank in your own eye?" (NIV)

Two careers ago, I accepted the invitation of a junior high school teacher to visit her classroom and give her some advice about how to bring more order and help her discipline the students more effectively. At the ap-pointed hour, she met me at the door of the classroom with a seating chart. Under each student's name was his or her "problem." This one was going through parents' divorce; that one had just lost his grandmother; another suffered from chronic allergies. Thus, she had analyzed (I might even say justified) the reasons for the class being out of control. At this time, I was still a Wayfarer, so the best advice I could give her was, "Throw away that chart. You've given every student a reason for not doing the work. From now on, no excuses. Focus on the work."(Read more about this story in Chapter 10.)

There's nothing really wrong with the advice I gave, but as a Wayfinder, I had another opportunity, with a different teacher. This time, I had a monthly telephone conversation with the leadership team of an elementary school. One afternoon a month, they gathered around the speaker phone in the principal's office to tell stories about the progress they were making. In one of these calls, a teacher asked for help with a particular little boy whose behavior was awful. She had tried every option available to her in the school's discipline management plan and had attended special training to get new ideas, but nothing was working. The child's behavior was out of control, and she asked me what she might do to improve the situation.

My response was, "I'm not an expert in discipline or child psychology. I don't know the answer to your question, but since nothing else is working, let's try an experiment. First, tell me what you were *thinking* as you were working with the child today." Predictably, her thoughts were focused on his misbehavior and internal complaints about his unwillingness to obey.

Then I asked, "Is there anything this little boy does well?"

There was a long silence as the teacher sorted through her experiences with this child. Finally, she said, "He is really good in math."

"Good. Let's start there. Tomorrow, when that child walks into the classroom, say something to yourself like, 'I create an environment where this child develops his beautiful math skills to the max.'" I went on. "Write out your intent and stick to it, no matter how he behaves."

The principal told me later that during this conversation there was a point when she saw the "light go on" in this teacher's eyes—the light of re-alization of her part in the behavior issue. With that acceptance, the teacher changed how she thought about this child.

The next month, I asked how the child was doing. The teacher's answer was, "He's fine. No more problems."

When we look outside ourselves for the problem and the solution, we end up frustrated, angry, perhaps disappointed, because what is outside is beyond our control. What is inside, on the other hand, is completely within our control.

In organizations, the human habit of focusing on what's outside of us creates role-playing and dysfunction in the system. One executive told me her analysis of other employees each time we met, how one person in particular was bringing ruin to the organization and hurting other people within it. Steadfastly, she refused to consider any other perspective than her own. The problem was always someone else. The organizational pattern I observed was role-playing and confusion that led from crisis to crisis, yielding perpetual chaos. Moreover, there were scapegoats. I also noticed that mistakes were not forgiven. People variously played roles of favorites, outcasts, or invisible ones, hoping not to be noticed. In such an environment, marked by threat, fear, control and manipulation, people cannot fulfill potential. This is a result of looking outside ourselves for the problem.

In Nobel Peace Prize nominee Thich Nhat Hanh (1992) writes,

> "When you plant lettuce, if it does not grow well, you don't blame the lettuce. You look into the reasons it is not doing well. It may need fertilizer, or more water, or less sun. You never blame the lettuce. Yet if we have problems with our friends or our family, we blame the other person. But if we know how to take care of them, they will grow well, like lettuce... No blame, no reasoning, no argument, just understanding. If you understand, and you show that you understand, you can love, and the situation will change" (p. 78).

Arntz, Chasse, and Vicente (2005) contains this fascinating story: when Jean's husband died, their pet bird began to scream, pluck his feathers, and be very self-destructive. Jean began to realize that the bird might be responding to her own thoughts and feelings:

> "I wondered if I changed my thoughts and actions, prayed for him and believed, it could be different. [The change] started about two weeks ago. He lets me hold him, bathe him, play with him, and he does not bite. This is amazing [because] this bird has always bitten. He is happier. I am amazed that by changing my thoughts and actions, I impacted his. Before, I was desperate because I didn't know what I was going to do with him. Now, he has a brighter future" (p. 195).

Similarly, a while back my husband and I experienced a crisis in our marriage that came perilously close to divorce. I recalled Ponder's (1987) story about a young woman who said she "hated" her husband. She had young children and for various reasons did not want to leave the marriage, so she began praying for her husband every day, at different times of the day. She would imagine that "Jesus Christ is with him." That was her prayer. Over time, their relationship changed, and she became happy in the marriage.

I decided to try it. Within a few weeks, my husband and I had reconciled and renewed our commitment to have a happy marriage. When the crisis was completely over, I asked him what had made the difference for him—what had tipped him in the direction of saving the marriage. He said, "I prayed for you."

What is praying for someone if not holding that person in high regard with the fervent desire for his well being? Not trying to control or change something outside ourselves, but changing our own internal environment with regard to that person.

When I view the world from the perspective of my ego, I blame other people and resist or resent them for what they are doing. When I view the world as a reflection of myself, I look within to identify and accept my own faults and limitations. Then, and only then, do I take action. Here are two contrasting examples: Someone in my life has a lot of physical/medical problems. Without responding, I've listened to stories of illness, medical treatments, and physical problems for years. In other words, I "stuffed" my feelings about it. But feelings won't stay "stuffed" forever, so finally, fed up, my ego said, "If you have a disease that will kill you, certainly I want to know about it. Otherwise, I don't want to hear about any more of your illnesses." Thus with words devoid of kindness or compassion, I sent a harsh message that I didn't care about her suffering.

Since this incident, I've learned a few things about honoring others' feelings, as well as my own. Once, a close friend made a decision to undergo a major operation that involved a long period of recuperation. Over coffee, she told me many details about the nature of her condition. She even said, "I brought my x-ray to show you."

When she finished her explanation, I asked, "What support do you need from me?"

As she described what she wanted, I felt strong resistance rise within me and I decided to be honest about it. I said, "I have to confess that I don't have any tolerance for hearing about physical illness and disability. After the first three sentences of what you just said, I was no longer present." Without justifying it or over-explaining how I acquired it, I simply said, "What I can stay present for is for you to tell me, when I visit, the progress you have made since the last time I saw you."

She understood. "Maybe you could walk with me? I won't be able to go very far—maybe a block."

"Yes. I can walk with you. And I can read to you. But I can't stay present for a lot of medical talk."

As we parted, she thanked me for being honest and real, then said, "I don't think I'll show you my x-ray."

"Oh, God! Please don't." I laughingly responded.

Then she reciprocated my honesty. "I think I make those long explanations and carry my x-ray because I have to *prove* to people that I really need this—that I'm not just a wimp. But in fact I don't have to prove anything to anybody. This is my decision."

Chapter 5 Exercise

In the space below, draw a circle. Inside the circle write what you DO want to experience in your life/work. Outside the circle, write what you do not want. First thing every morning for 40 days, look at what you've written. Take it in. Make notes in a journal when you start to see tiny shifts in what you are experiencing.

6 A Different Kind of Fire:

The Power of Truth with Love

Prelude

A rural county hospital had searched almost two years to find and hire the perfect hospital administrator. A decade and a half later, the community was still happy with him. His wife loved the people there; they loved her; his children were thriving in school. Although no situation is ever *perfect,* this one was as good as it gets.

Then a large local firm hired a new CEO from out of town. He moved with his family into this idyllic place. Within a short time, he was named to the hospital board, as community leaders often are. Next he became the hospital board chairman. Then, something happened. The CEO/hospital board chairman decided the hospital administrator wasn't doing a good job, and the two men couldn't resolve their differences.

Desperately wanting to keep his job and not disrupt his family, the hospital administrator turned to a friend in the community, who tried to help. But the CEO wouldn't return the friend's phone calls. There was nothing he could do. Ultimately, the disgruntled board chairman fired the hospital administrator. Now this rural county hospital has no administrator, and the fired administrator is packing his family to leave.

The mediator who told me this story concluded, "All of this was preventable." What will it cost to search for a new hospital administrator? How much time will it take? What will the hospital lose from lack of leadership? If we put a dollar cost to all of the time and energy expended on this issue—which could have been mediated for $850-$2000—what would it have been?

Many people do not believe that such conflicts can be avoided. They think some people are difficult, and that's just the way things are. This is a strong belief system that "anchors" bad situations. Then they get worse!

The truth is that people—even people who are "old"—can change. The greater truth is that when we speak the truth from our hearts to each other, we increase the possibility for positive change that comes from learning. The fact is that if companies and boards understood this, they could save millions of dollars while making the workplace safer for the human heart, as well as healthier for the rest of the body. Why don't we change the invisible barriers—our own beliefs—that stand between us and the way we truly want to live and work together? Why do we shy away from conflict until it escalates into situations that tear up people's lives—sometimes even our own?

Because, early in our lives, we developed "calluses" to protect our hearts and souls from being wounded. These calluses make us keep repeating patterns we have experienced, even though they aren't working very well for us. In my work as an executive coach specializing in transitions, I see examples every day, both in professional and personal settings.

My friend and her adult daughter had an uncomfortable relationship. They wanted to make the transition to an adult-to-adult relationship, so I offered to facilitate a conversation between the two of them in a conference telephone call. "Think of an uncomfortable conversation the two of you have had," I said. Immediately, the daughter said, "One happened just last week-end. Dad was leaving for a couple of weeks, and Mom invited me to lunch to see him off. I agreed to go because I didn't want to disappoint her. But my schedule is so full right now. I'm balancing a job that requires a lot of energy, plus my own career pursuits, and I'm in a new romantic relationship. At the last minute, I called to cancel. Mom was hurt. I tried to explain by saying, 'I wish I weren't such a people-pleaser.' She responded by saying, 'Well, you're not pleasing us,' and the conversation didn't end well."

The daughter felt that she just couldn't do enough. Her mother, on the other hand, had concluded that she must not be very important to her own child. She felt that her daughter should want to be with her family "...just because we're family. I know she loves us, but I don't feel very high on her list of important things."

Finally, the daughter said, "Even when I do come to visit, the last thing you do as I am leaving is talk about the next time we're going to be together. I can't do enough."

When I heard that, I asked my friend, "Did anyone ever put that guilt trip on you?"

Without hesitation, she answered, "Yes. My mother."

I followed up. "When your mother said things like that to you, how did it make you feel?"

"I used to hate it. Then I got used to it, and now I just ignore it."

A callus had formed to protect my friend's heart. Now decades old, it is invisible to her and she repeats her mother's mistake saying to her own daughter what was said to her—unconsciously, certainly unintentionally. There is a better way.

The daughter's part in damaging the relationship was that when the conversation got tense she walked away. Having experienced this treatment many times, now her mother was afraid of saying the wrong thing and suffering the indignity of having her daughter's back turned on her.

A callus formed to protect this daughter's heart. Instead of leaning into difficult conversations, she walks away from them, not realizing that her choice is not limited anymore to "fight or flight" response. There is a better way.

In the facilitation that followed, we learned that there was far more positive energy going into the relationship than being drained out for both mother and daughter. An example is that when her daughter's poetry was published, my friend said, "You have such a beautiful voice!" The daughter wept when she recalled that moment between them and she also remembered her mother saying, "I'm proud of you." She knew what she meant to her mother.

Also, this daughter loved to hear about what was important to her mother; she recalled good times listening to her mom talk about her piano students or her music. When they talked with each other about their heart's desires in any area of their lives they strengthened the relationship as their understanding of each other grew. Their appreciation for each other also grew. Then this daughter said, "I admire my mom. She is full of warm, radiant life force." At these words, her mother shed a few tears. I sensed that my friend was receiving the information she had needed for a long time. Who wouldn't want to be near a warm, radiant life force? The unspoken, heartfelt energy behind those words told this mother what she needed to hear. Her daughter not only loves her; she values her. She is important to her daughter, whose lack of attendance at family functions is not a lack of caring; she is simply overwhelmed by life's activities. This mother was reassured.

Moreover, my friend recognized the pattern her mother set and realized it was not enhancing her relationship with her daughter. By the end of the conversation, both mother and daughter were laughing. Afterwards I received an e-mail from my friend saying, "Yesterday's phone call made my heart sing."

This reconciliation took one hour and a few important words. Such a simple solution. If it's so simple, why don't more people do it? A more fundamental question is: How do we get into these messes, in the first place?

Failing with "As"

I failed in "works up to ability." There it was—opposite the row of straight A's in reading, writing, arithmetic, and all the other subjects that "really mattered," according to my family's idea of what was important.

There it was—a "U" for "Unsatisfactory"—on the page that didn't even count for anything!

In the midst of Mother's boxes and throwaways from too many years in that house, I found them—my report cards. She had saved them all, first grade through 12th. When I came to the "U," I was astonished. I don't remember it ever being mentioned. And how, I wondered, is it possible to make straight A's and not be working up to ability? Then I realized what I was doing. It's easy to blame a teacher—or a whole school system, for that matter—because the U's were pretty consistent through the elementary grades. But the greater question was—Why was this low performance allowed to go on, unquestioned? What had kept me from going for things that were slightly beyond my reach? What had made me settle for the fruit on the lowest branches, when juicier fruit could be had, if I were only willing to stretch?

I remembered poor attempts at things like basketball. The first time a foul was called on me, I quit, reasoning, "I didn't mean to elbow her. If I didn't mean it, it shouldn't be a foul."

I also remembered my ninth grade choir experience. The teacher conducted solo tryouts for all of us. When it came my turn, I did my best. Surprised, she said I was really good and put me in a small ensemble. But I didn't learn the music, nor did I show up for our first performance. Needless to say, she didn't spend much time with me from then on. (I showed her!) But I think I made an A. This new school didn't have a category called "works up to ability."

Three Love Stories

As I stood in Mother's living room for the last time, my mind wandered back through all my years. Did anyone ever challenge me to change the "U" to an "S"? Immediately, two people came to mind—one, a church youth director who discovered I had natural speaking ability. Although I've heard that most people have a greater fear of public speaking than dying, I had always loved it. Even when I was a child a favorite pastime was reading poetry, out loud, while sitting in my bed with my door closed. Public speaking is to me like water to a fish or a briar patch to Br'er Rabbit. It's safe and satisfying.

Lift Your Voice. But this audacious youth director challenged me to win at it. "To do that," she said, "you have to love your audience." Well, I was only 17 years old. What did I know of love? I didn't understand what she meant, but I could see it was important—so I kept trying. I entered a local contest for which I wrote a fairly decent speech. But it wasn't good enough. She challenged me to revise, revise, revise. Revise until it had power. Then she said I had to memorize it! So the afternoon before I was to give the speech, I worked on it a little—and, that evening, stumbled through it as best I could. To my amazement I won the local contest. (To this day I still think that contest was rigged; one of her friends was the judge!)

Now I had no choice—I had to represent my local community in a contest at the *state* level. I worked on that speech—with my coach—more than I had ever worked on anything else in my life. The day came for the state competition. Truly amazed, I won that contest, too. As a reward I got to do more work on *that same speech.*

Then the day came for me to compete in a Southwest Regional competition. It was the end of the line; there was no national competition to which the winner advanced. The day before the speech the contest director gathered all the contestants so that we could meet each other, taking a little edge off the upcoming event. There I was, two weeks out of high school. The contestant sitting to my left, as she introduced herself, explained, "I am finishing my master's degree *in speech!*"

My heart fell to my waist.

I thought to myself, "How can I compete with that?" I hadn't had my first college course, and she was about to finish her master's degree—*in speech!*

At first I thought I should just go home—but we had come a long way. So my second decision was, "I might as well just see how much I can enjoy this because there's no way in the world I'm going to win." So that's what I did. I gave the speech from my heart, out of love for what was in it and the people who would hear it. Thus, unwittingly I fulfilled my mentor's goal.

To my utter amazement, I won!

But it wasn't until decades later that I even began to understand what had happened: I had experienced the performance-enhancing effect of relaxation and en*joy*ment, which is a positive energy of the heart. When preparation meets relaxation and enjoyment, peak performance occurs. Miracles happen—like an 18-year-old novice winning out over a 24-year-old, experienced, degreed person.

My speech coach was the first person who helped me change the "U" to an "S" in "works up to ability."

Believe You Can. The second was my college philosophy professor. His reputation was legendary. To make an "A" in his class, you had to memorize your notes from his classroom lectures—which meant that first of all, you had to listen to his lectures; second, take good notes, and finally memorize AND REMEMBER them for the test! Before my first day in his class, based on his reputation, I decided I would settle for a "B."

But he tricked me.

Before he gave the first test he gave us an essay assignment, and I love to write. I especially loved what I wrote about: I envisioned three structures, like houses. Standing in the doorway of each was a shadowy figure making decisions. One turned back and went more deeply inside her shelter, forever disappearing. The second just continued to stand there, forever hesitant and uncertain, much like the shadowy blue images who, from the window or doorway, look out at the world in some of Nena Sanchez's paintings (www.NenaSanchez.com). The third figure boldly went forth living a full life—like Sanchez's larger-than-life Blue Goddess, colorfully dressed—boldly taking on the world.

To my amazement, my grade on that paper was an "A."

But it wasn't a test. That came next. Based on the research I had done about this teacher I studied to make a "B"—and that's what I made. But looking through the graded test, my eyes fell on a note from the professor on the last page. I'll never forget what it said. "You have more ability than any other student in this class. From now on, I expect an A from you."

I was astonished.

One of the hardest, most respected professors on campus thought I was one of the smartest students! And he expected an A from me! I didn't think I could do it, but before the next test I studied as if I could. On the second test, and for the course, my grade was "A."

Then, I went back inside my shelter.

After college what I truly wanted to do was go to graduate school at Northwestern University, one of the top communications schools in the country. But I didn't know anyone who could help me do it. I didn't know where to start, and it seemed too difficult. I didn't even ask for help. The easier road was to get married and start teaching school. So that's what I did. I continued the lonely journey of trying to shape myself to other people's expectations.

Come Out of Hiding. Until, after two decades of living in a "safe harbor," a third person challenged me. He was my first husband's uncle—an adventurer with a warm, engaging laugh. Everyone loved him. One of his several careers was as a counselor. He had great compassion for people and had even headed a rescue mission on Bourbon Street trying to help those who most of us would reject. I trusted him because he had helped me through a difficult time many years before. That's how Uncle Wade was—genuinely caring and willing to help, no matter what the situation. A family member whom everyone loved and respected. Someone who lived life with zest and love. Someone who accepted human weakness with grace.

He brought me out of hiding when, in a quiet moment, he asked a calm, simple question, "What are you doing here? You seem out of place." His question shattered my shelter. It knocked down the door of the house and invaded all of the corners. It confronted my soul—in my case blue—not from paint but from lack of air. I didn't have a good answer to his question. He didn't follow up. So I sat with his question for several more years. Then slowly I found the courage to breathe more deeply, leave the security of this safe haven where I had hidden away for more than twenty years, and move out into a frightening world.

A few years later, in my new church in my new home city, a visiting minister preached a sermon based on the story of the bleeding woman who touched the hem of Jesus' garment and was healed. Except this minister gave a twist to the story I had not previously considered. When this woman touched Jesus' hem, he felt the energy go out of him and turned around to see who she was. "Let yourself be found" are the words I still remember from the sermon, even though I had heard them almost 15 years earlier at a time when I had just come out of hiding to live a more authentic life.

These people spoke the truth with love to me. Three voices—church, school, family. The third voice went all the way through my soul, and *I became aware that I was living someone else's life.*

Most people would probably say that they want to be all they can be. For that to happen, someone has to call us out; in fact, "educare," the root from which we get the word "education," means "to lead forth."

> There was a child went forth every day;
> And the first object he look'd upon, that object he became;
> And that object became part of him for the day, or a certain part
> of the day, or for many years, or stretching cycles of years.
> Walt Whitman, Leaves of Grass

Without awareness, we take in and then imitate whatever we experience. What we focus on, whether we love it or hate it, grows within us and becomes part of our essence. Only after we understand our own human limitations are we able to make choices about what influences we choose to be exposed to.

> "When I was a child, I spoke as a child,
> I understood as a child, I thought as a child;
> but when I became [an adult], I put away childish things".
> (1 Corinthians 13:11)

Igniting the Fire

In my work as an executive coach many of my clients are beautiful, well-educated, intelligent, talented women who have never been challenged. Instead, they have been handicapped by preferential treatment, never tested by fire. Some of them get by on good looks, charm, polish, and connections. They are positively reinforced for how they look or dress, not for how closely their effort aligns with their potential. Certainly not for becoming all that they can be—because their appearance is so dazzling that... well, it's enough.

Sometimes referred to as the "halo effect," (see p. 86), this praise "addicts" them to their perfect image. They may even become "trophy wives" with marital relationships that are only, as my mother used to say, "skin deep." When people misbehave toward them, they take a "How-dare-you-do-that–to-me?-Don't-you-know-who-I-am?" approach. This arrogance or egocentrism marks all relationships, which ultimately fail. Also, it limits their effort even though they may appear to be successful. They make A's in the "important" subjects and "U" in "works up to ability."

> "Try not to become a [wo]man of success, but rather try to become a [wo]man of value."
>
> Albert Einstein

These gorgeous women come to me because they are not getting what they want out of life. They want to be authentic—to be all they can be. They want to be happy—to do well—to get good results—to be respected. They want meaningful relationships. One of my first responsibilities is to speak the truth to them with love. If they are able to accept it and do the work that is necessary to move out of arrogance and into humility, they experience a different kind of fire. Here's a story about one of these women:

Sarah's Story

Sarah came to me as she was finishing an advanced degree, after having left her previous executive position in health care under duress. Divorced from a husband she had helped put through school, she and a new male boss had clashed from the very beginning of his tenure. By the time she finally quit she was so angry that she didn't even negotiate a favorable severance for herself—a pattern repeated from her divorce. My job was to help her remove blockages to her future success.

As mentioned earlier, my first task in working with people is to find out who they are at their essence (see Authentic Profile© in Chapter 8), followed by an Energy Analysis® that answers the questions "What is giving you energy?" and "What is depleting your energy?" Sarah's energy was be-low 0. Remember that a healthy energy range is 300-850. Sarah had no energy to make the changes she wanted in her life.

Sarah worked intensely on these issues for about a month, then with-drew from coaching while these new ideas settled.

When clients do the Authentic Profile© and Energy Analysis® they are doing soul work. As author Parker Palmer says, "The soul is very shy." Sometimes, like a wild animal, it comes forward and nibbles for a bit, then retreats into the brush. Like Nena Sanchez's blue woman in the doorway, it doesn't know if it will be safe in a different environment. So it takes its time, fulfilling the lowest levels of Maslow's hierarchy—the need for survival and security (see p. 87). Once the soul is sure that what I am offering is coming from love, then it is willing to hear the truth that will set it free.

What brought Sarah back into the process was a group conversation in which she angrily fired back in response to a comment by another partici-pant. After the meeting, she e-mailed, "What happened to me? I reacted immediately. I was angry. I felt it." Sarah had "flipped her lid," and this is not an idle expression. When it happens the fire starts at the base of the spine. A hot, burning sensation goes rapidly up the spine, through the neck, and out the top of the head. She actually felt her "lid" "flip." Some people even describe this sensation as having their hair on fire.

My answer to Sarah's question was, "Mirror neurons"[2]. "You were re-flecting back to him the energy you felt coming from him." The man who had provoked Sarah was angry. He used that energy to advance his career, as many people do, and about once a year he has a "meltdown" that some-times lands him in the hospital. His anger sparked Sarah's anger, which flared.

Here's how mirror neurons work: When someone performs an action, certain neurons in his/her brain fire. In the brain of someone who is ob-serving the action, corresponding "mirror neurons"[5] also fire, giving the observer the same experience as the person observed. Mirror neurons tie us, in a sense, to other people's feelings. You may have heard the expres-sion "Monkey see, monkey do." Substitute the word "people" for "monkey," and you're talking about mirror neurons.

In a previous career I was assigned responsibility for designing profes-sional development opportunities for teachers. Dismayed at how much time and effort were required to bring about change, I researched effective staff development practices. I was amazed to learn that teachers teach like they were taught, not like they have been *trained* to teach. In other words,

---

[2] www.pbs.org/wgbh/nova/sciencenow/3204/01.html

teachers teach like their college professors taught them, even when they have "learned" better methods in their education courses. At the time, I didn't know about mirror neurons. Now it makes sense.

Training doesn't teach. Neither does telling. Maybe your parents used to say, "If I've told you once, I've told you a thousand times..." They probably meant to be criticizing you for not paying attention. But the truth is they failed to realize that telling doesn't teach.

I received an e-mail from a colleague bemoaning that people do not *apply* what they *know*. We know the approximate ratio of compliments to criticism is twenty-six to one: that is, it takes about twenty-six compliments to balance the negative effect of *one* criticism. Yet managers and colleagues continue to be drawn, like moths to flame, to what other people do wrong and give negative feedback. This approach does not work. It rarely improves anyone and it harms relationships. Yet people continue to do it. Why?

I've spent many years in education watching programs to improve students' character come and go. While all of them documented success by some sort of evaluation, they are actually ineffective. Think about it: if you complete a peace curriculum and then in the hallway observe two teachers in verbal conflict, which is your greater teacher—the curriculum you just completed, or the scene you just witnessed?

You might say, "Well, a student could see that the teachers were wrong and make a different decision." Yes, that's true. But that's not how we learn. We learn our behavior by imitating (mirror neurons), and it's not possible to teach something like conflict resolution from a curriculum without providing powerful visual models of adults living those behaviors. If we want children to learn values, ethics, positive attitudes, conflict resolution—then we must live those ways in front of them.

Levitt and Dubner (2005) capsulized findings from the U.S. government's Early Childhood Longitudinal Study. They were curious to find out what helps young children become smart, as measured by tests. Here are some of the surprising findings about the children who are "smarter":

- Their mothers were 30 or older when they had their first child.
- The child has many books in the home.
- The parents are well educated, speak English in the home, and are involved in PTA at school.

What didn't seem to matter as much were these factors:
- Reading to children, going to museums, and traveling.
- Mother leaving career to stay at home with young children.
- Traditional, intact family; spankings; television viewing.

The conclusion drawn by Levitt and Dubner suggests the power of mirror neurons: "If you are smart, hard-working, well educated, well paid and married to someone equally fortunate, then your children are more likely to succeed. But it isn't a matter of what you do as a parent; it's who you are."

On a completely different topic of great importance, the spectre of mirror neurons again appears. When friends and families of alcoholics decide to become part of the solution, they go to Al-Anon where they learn to keep the focus on themselves—to stop worrying, criticizing, fearing, and covering up for the alcoholic (a form of lying). In what they often describe as miracles, their degree of happiness slowly changes as they achieve serenity through practicing the principles of the program. The power of love overcomes even the addiction of alcohol, and many of the alcoholics they love become sober and begin living the lives they truly want. Moreover, they are encouraged to find someone at meetings who "has what you want" to teach and guide them. Mirror neurons.

An Al-Anon (1992) book of daily readings has many stories about the importance of keeping the focus on oneself. Here's a typical story:

> "My behavior paralleled that of the alcoholic. The only difference was that I did it sober—insane, but sober. I saw how much I blamed other people for the events in my life, how I took everything personally, and how my reactions to the alcoholic were based on my fears... As time went by, when I found myself in [difficult] situations, I noticed that my reactions were less extreme. Some things that had bothered me terribly no longer mattered. That's when I knew I'd begun to change" (p. 50).

Awareness or *consciousness* allows one to slip out of the power of mirror neurons and make a different choice—a choice that brings into reality the life that is truly desired.

For the wise ones Al-Anon becomes a lifetime practice—because the original neuronal patterns are still there and can quickly re-activate, especially in stressful situations. Thus, serenity and love must be continuously and consciously practiced for people to "mirror" the vibrations they want for their loved ones.

Neenah Ellis (2002) uses the term "lymbic resonance" to describe the power of mirror neurons. Ellis' book sheds light on what life as a 100-year-old is like based on interviews with centenarians. As she conducted the interviews, Ellis felt as if she were "falling into" the minds of the centenarians, an experience quite different for her. She became curious about the phenomenon that was occurring within her and sought information from psychologist Dr. Thomas Lewis (2001), He explained to her:

"We're familiar with traditional senses, like your eyes give you information about changes in sound waves. Well there's another sensory system in the brain, which is designed to give you information about the emotional state inside someone else's brain, and that sensory experience is lymbic resonance... You can sense the inside of someone else's brain, they can sense the inside of yours, and each person influences the other. It's a two-way sensory experience of emotion"

Regardless of which branch of science is used to describe this phenomenon, it points to our responsibility for our own state of mind, if our intent is to give the best to ourselves and others.

Finally, at the UCLA Medical Center, dogs are allowed to visit heart patients[3]. The correlation between stress and heart disease is well established and researchers found that after just 12 minutes with a dog, even the sickest patients improved. Anxiety levels fell 24%, stress hormone rates fell 17%, and pulmonary pressures dropped 10%. It may be that humans mirror the nonjudgmental, accepting vibrations from happy canines, thus speeding their recovery. Or maybe it's lymbic resonance. What really matters is that it works.

> "We must be the change we want to see in the world."
> Mahatma Gandhi

Whether they know the term "mirror neurons" or "lymbic resonance" or not, enlightened people realize that without awareness and conscious choice they are susceptible to influence from the outside. Enlightened people go on a journey of self-discovery to discover who they truly are, at their very core, with their egos stripped away. They are comfortable with their souls; therefore, they choose what stimuli from the outside world to let in, including which advisors to trust, which books to read, what media to watch, what activities to be involved in, what to respond to. This series of conscious choices constitutes an invisible boundary beyond which is the sacred, the "holy of holies," which no one, except that person's soul, may enter.

But because we are human we are susceptible to what Joseph LeDoux (1996) calls "emotional hijackings". Someone else's strong emotion seizes our own state of mind and we end up in a different state—a place where we never intended to go.

From the story that Sarah came to me with (p. 76), the angry man's rage captured her state of mind, and together they went to "war."

---

[3] http://www.abcnews.go.com/GMA/HeartHealthy/story?id=1636155

Transcendence

Sarah wanted to learn how to prevent these hijackings in the future, so together we stripped away the arrogance that had wrapped around her ego, replaced it with a humility that accepts character defects in ourselves and others, forgives them with compassion, and moves on—with the soul undisturbed. Some people refer to this process as alchemy. I call it transcendence.

Once a woman (or a man) has confronted, accepted, and transcended the worst within herself, she no longer has to fear any other person's opinion, judgment, or action. She can simply be calm and comfortable with herself.

> "Then you will know the truth, and the truth will set you free." (John 8:32)

The byproduct of this transformation for Sarah was peace of mind. Relaxation. The state in which the human brain works best—the state of relaxed alertness. Here's the difference it made for her.

Sarah went home for a Christmas visit. Her mother, in a rage, told her to "shut up," but Sarah remained perfectly calm. At another time her brother arranged for a family sledding excursion. Both he and Sarah skidded on the ice, with their sleds going out of control. Sarah "went with the flow" and ended up in a soft bed of snow. The next day, she wasn't even sore. Her brother, on the other hand, dislocated a shoulder and broke his collar bone. Sarah made a conscious choice to remain calm and have peace of mind during her Christmas visit, no matter what. Her jealous sister hurled insults at her. Sarah listened with interest but didn't react.

Several weeks after returning home she sent me this e-mail: "Yesterday I had a conversation with my sister around some of the emotionally charged work she and her husband are doing. She reported having a peaceful mind (not her style) around a very big workers comp issue with his business. I believe a peaceful mind is contagious—like emotional hijacking, except in a good way."

Sarah discovered a truth known by the world's religions, but until now, not scientifically verified.

* * * * * *

"Therefore all things whatsoever ye would that men should do to you, do ye even so to them." (Do unto others as you would have them do unto you.)
Christianity. Matthew 7:12 KJV

"Do not do to others what you would not like yourself. Then there will be no resentment against you, either in the family or in the state." Confucianism. Analects 12:2

"Hurt not others in ways that you yourself would find hurtful." ``Buddhism. Udana-Varga 5, 1

"This is the sum of duty; do naught unto others what you would not have them do unto you." Hinduism. Mahabharata 5, 1517

"No one of you is a believer until he desires for his brother that which he desires for himself." Islam. Sunnah

"What is hateful to you, do not do to your fellowman. This is the entire Law; all the rest is commentary."
 Judaism. Talmud, Shabbat 3id

"Regard your neighbor's gain as your gain, and your neighbor's loss as your own loss." Taoism. Tai Shang Kan Yin P'ien

"That nature alone is good which refrains from doing to another whatsoever is not good for itself."
Zoroastrianism. Dadisten-I-dinik, 94,5

Now we know why the great religions of the world converge on this teaching. While not using the language of neuroscience, they are describing the power of mirror neurons.

Putting the Golden Rule to Work

Once I facilitated a group of curriculum experts in a large-scale effort to make connections across the different disciplines of the curriculum. Our challenge was to open the lines of communication and lay open the work the various groups were doing so that the curriculum would be well aligned and congruent. Early on, conflict arose over the issue of technology and how to integrate it throughout the various content areas. One man, a college professor, was especially aggressive in advocating his position. The first time the conflict erupted I sat back and observed for the entire meeting while someone else facilitated.

Prior to the second meeting I thought, "Almost everyone agrees that the Golden Rule is a good guide. How might it work to ease the tension in this situation?" After asking the question, I waited for inspiration. (Some people call this strategy prayer.) As I opened the next meeting I handed everyone an index card. "On it," I said, "write how you want to be treated during this meeting." I allowed silence while everyone wrote. When I could see that all pens were down I said, "Read what you have just written and make a silent commitment to treat every other person in that way." After a moment of silence we began the work.

Out of the corner of my eye I saw the college professor's body react as he disagreed with a comment from someone else in the room. Almost immediately he leaned forward to begin the conflict. Then he hesitated and picked up the index card. As he silently read it his body relaxed, he took a deep breath, and then he said what he truly needed to say in a way that was perfectly acceptable, evoking thoughtful responses instead of defensiveness and argument. Thus, the energy of harmony went into the development of the connections across the curriculum.

Here's a protocol that would make all meetings more powerful, regardless of the agenda:

Leading Meetings That Reduce Stress

- Start the meeting on time, whether everyone is present or not. (creates "safe space" through keeping one's word and honoring those who respected it)

- Begin with a full minute of silence, allowing everyone's brain to settle and "get into the room." ("Be still, and know that I am God.", Psalms 46:10); also brains work best in a state of relaxed alertness.)

- Encourage everyone to take 3 deep breaths, eyes closed, to bring a fresh supply of oxygen into the brain.

- Have water available in the room for drinking.

- Ask each person to "check in" with what they are grateful for, what they appreciate, or what is going especially well. According to HeartMath,

  "When you intentionally shift to a positive emotion such as appreciation, care or compassion, your heart rhythms immediately change, blood pressure drops, stress hormones plummet, the immune system pumps up, anti-aging hormones increase, and you gain clarity, calmness, and control. The effects are both immediate and long-lasting."

> "In every thing, give thanks." (I Thessalonians 5:18)

- Ask each person to write on an index card how he or she wants to be treated during this meeting. Allow silence for writing. Then say, "Make a commitment that this is how you will treat others during this meeting. Refer to it if you feel anxiety rise."

"Do unto others as you would have them do unto you." (Matthew 7:12)

- Insist that people pause between speakers. This avoids the "jump into the fray" mentality, allows the brain time to process information, and gives people opportunity to choose a positive emotional state.

- Ask people not to speak if someone else has already expressed their idea, question, or thought in different words.

- Ask people to speak only if they believe in their hearts that their words will increase understanding. Avoid chatter. Honor silence as time to reflect.

> "Let the prophets speak two or three, and let the other judge. If any thing be revealed to another that sitteth by, let the first hold his peace. For ye may all prophesy one by one, that all may learn, and all may be comforted." (I Corinthians 14:29-31)

- Stop the meeting on time. (Demonstrates respect for people's schedules and other commitments)

I wrote this protocol from the standpoint of the leader. After reading it one of my clients informed me that it would also work well for any participant in the meeting. "I realized I could use it when I was a participant in a meeting even though the leader wasn't leading from that perspective. For example, get to the room a bit early, take three deep breaths (this could be done even if you get there late), bring water to drink, write down a grateful thought, write down how I want to be treated in the meeting, and follow all the other suggestions. When the discussion gets too heated, ask for a time out to allow everyone to sit back and gather their thoughts."

> "The best and most beautiful things in the world cannot be seen or touched... they must be felt with the heart."
>
> Helen Keller

Conclusion

Recently I worked with yet another beautiful, successful, well educated woman who had just left her job in anger. My goal was to help her process what had happened in the last job so that she would not repeat the unpleasant experience. As she opened the door she said, "I want to get rid of this anger." I picked up my pen and began to write what she said in response to the prompt, "I am really furious that..." Then I took her through the process that you'll learn about later in this book, concluding with her reading out loud the statements about forgiveness. After she finished reading she looked up and said, "I believe this. This is what I tell other people to do. Why am I not doing it?" All I could do was shake my head and say, "It's what we do because we're human."

Without intervention, we will do unto others as someone has done to us. But once we understand our own human frailty—that we learn from *imitating*, not from *knowing* or *being told,* we can break free and choose how we want to be. We can also discern more wisely what experiences we want to have—what words we want to hear, what messages, what people, what media.

We learn that, unlike other animals, we are not limited to a fight or flight response. We can learn to transcend. At last we know what shapes our reality. At last we are aware that we have the capacity and freedom to make choices. At last we can create and live the life we are truly meant to live.

* * * * *

"Constant kindness can accomplish much. As the sun makes ice melt, kindness causes misunderstanding, mistrust and hostility to evaporate."

Albert Schweitzer

"You catch more flies with honey than with vinegar."

Folk saying

"To thine own self be true. And it must follow, as the night the day, thou canst not then be false to any man."

William Shakespeare

"For God hath not given us the spirit of fear; but of power, and of love, and of a sound mind." (2 Timothy 1:7)

"Whatsoever things are true, honest, just, pure, lovely, of good report, think on these things." (Philippians 4:8)

"To keep a bad batch of concrete from setting, throw sugar in it."

> An employee at a concrete plant

"I'd rather see a sermon than hear one, any day."

> Emily Dickinson

"Most folks are about as happy as they make up their minds to be."

> Abraham Lincoln

"Everything has its wonders, even darkness and silence, and I learn, whatever state I may be in, therein to be content."

> Helen Keller

"The greatest of these is love." (1 Corinthians 13:13)

Endnotes

Halo Effect—Believing someone is a high performer in all areas because she or he is beautiful, handsome, smart, athletic, etc. When people react favorably to your physical beauty or other outstanding qualities, you "pick up" their feelings through your mirror neurons, and over time, you believe yourself to be without fault because you have been told you are beautiful, handsome, smart, athletic, etc. For example, once I had a student who was such an outstanding writer that I gave her A's on every paper, without revision. Certainly her writing was superior to that of the other students in the class, but it wasn't until the end of the semester that I realized I could have given her a lot of help with style. This is the risk people run when they over-praise children. See also E. L. Thorndike, "A Constant Error on Psychological Rating", *Journal of Applied Psychology*, vol. IV (1920), pp. 25-29.

Maslow's Hierarchy of Needs was first published in the 1940s. With survival at its lowest level, it "topped out" with self-actualization, which is the desire to become all that we can be (see Fig. 6-1).

For over 60 years, Maslow's pyramid was thought reasonably sufficient to describe the levels of motivation for human beings. But somewhere around the year 2000 someone adapted this pyramid from five to eight levels to fit the evolutionary development of modern man. Shortly thereafter, the 8-level pyramid appeared with three additions: knowledge needs, aesthetic needs, and transcendence needs (see Fig. 6-2).

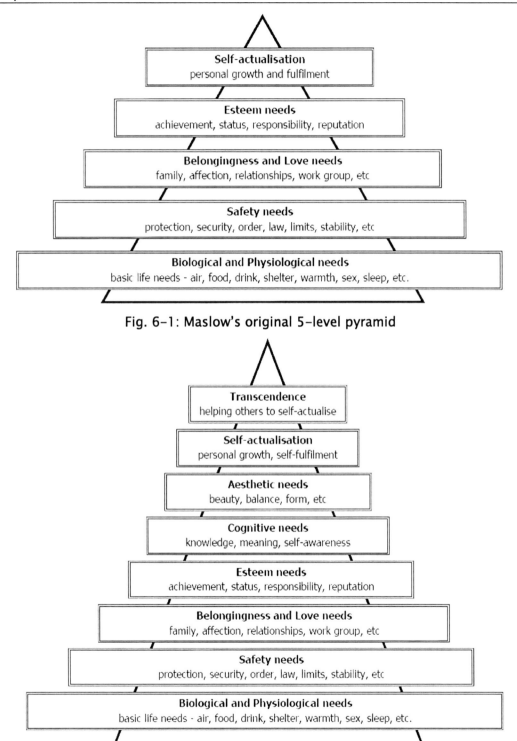

Fig. 6-1: Maslow's original 5-level pyramid

Fig. 6-2: Maslow's new 8-level pyramid

Chapter 6 Exercises

6-1. As a result of what you've read, what will you stop doing?

6-2. What will you start doing?

6-3. What in your life IS working, so you will continue to do it?

7 The Power of Speaking from the Heart

Our world is full of distractions. We are easily pulled in directions we would not have chosen, had we been thinking clearly. What might we do to remain true to ourselves? In metallurgy, a touchstone is a large black stone, usually jasper, that is used as a "streak plate" to test the purity of gold. If the mark left by the gold being tested is bold, we know it is high quality and should be valued. In life, we need a "touchstone" to help us test whether an experience or decision is true for us. For that purpose, I created the Authentic Profile©.

Borrowing an idea from Maria Nemeth (1997), I ask clients to name people they admire and why they admire them, as I listen carefully to the key traits they name. These traits comprise the highest and best of that client who identified them in another person. For example, how would we know what honesty is if we ourselves did not have the trait of honesty? Then I ask them what they have learned from success and failure, followed by favorite quotations that guide their lives, especially in the tough times. Finally, they list their lifetime goals. This Authentic Profile© (see Chapter 8) then becomes a "certificate" as a constant reminder throughout the day. Mine sits just to the left of my computer.

Energy of Love

When I asked one superintendent what quotations or favorite sayings guided his life, he answered, "The path to the head is through the heart." As I worked with his assistant principals—his largest pool of emerging leaders—I was struck by how many of them said, in various ways, that the teachers and administrators "really *care* about these kids." Here's a story from one of those assistant principals about how the energy of love, emanating from the highest level, ripples throughout the district:

"A high school transfer student let everyone know how unhappy he was. He constantly complained about how strict we are, and he was very disrespectful to adults in the building. One day, as we were sitting across from one another in my office, I looked into his eyes and said, 'Do you know what I think the problem is?' His reply was a shrug in my direction. I said, 'I think you're sad about the move you had to make, and you're taking it out on us.' That opened him up. We talked, person to person. This year his grades and attitude have drastically improved. Experiencing these moments is the best part of my job!"

Heartmath.com is an innovative nonprofit organization whose purpose is to help people balance mind and heart energy using scientific research to create tools for sustaining an attentive peace of mind—i.e., relaxed alertness, the state in which the human brain is most powerful. Heartmath's research finds that more nerves go from the heart to the brain than from the brain to the heart. In other words, the energy of our hearts can actually change the chemistry of our brains. Moreover, Heartmath founders Childre and Martin (2000) have discovered:

> "The heart's electromagnetic field is by far the most powerful produced by the body; it's approximately five thousand times greater in strength than the field produced by the brain."

People who have a loving state of mind create safe space for others to learn and change. The "ears of the heart" pick up their loving vibration and people are able to accept the truth about themselves. By contrast, people who judge and gossip about others put *interference* into their messages giving rise to confusion and suspicion. A simple message spoken from the heart, with few words, is powerful.

Words from the Heart

When he was a high school principal, my friend Sean had a problem student—Amy—who referred to every person in authority as "Asshole." Her behavior was rebellious and uncooperative. Once Sean called her father to come in for a conference at which Amy was present. When he heard the problem Amy's father said, "Amy's mother and I fully support whatever action the school decides to take."

Sean turned to Amy. "What do you have to say to that?" he asked.

"My father is an asshole," Amy responded. Predictably, she was expelled from high school.

A few years after her expulsion and after Sean had been promoted to the school district's central office, he received a call from the alternative school principal. "Sean," he said, "Come over. A friend of yours is here."

When Sean walked into the alternative school principal's office there sat Amy. Her first words to him were, "Hello, Asshole."

Sean walked across the room and sat beside Amy on the couch. Without premeditation, he pulled out his wallet, opening it to his driver's license. He pointed to his photograph. "Amy, this is me." Then he pointed to his name. "And this is my name. My parents gave me this name. It's what people call me. Amy, why won't you call me by my name?"

With this simple question, truth broke through Amy's angry walls. She sobbed as self realization flooded over her. Sean spoke out of love for himself and respect for Amy. He told her the truth and believed that she had the capacity to respond respectfully if he kept the space between them free of negative "vibes." He was right; after their conversation, Amy made a decision to finish her high school work in the alternative school. Eventually she earned her high school equivalency diploma.

Amy transcended her anger through the power of truth spoken with love.

Our energy is what other people hear when we communicate—not our words. When we set an intent to speak the truth in love the words flow from our hearts. We don't have to learn a script or say exactly the right words. We don't have to worry about the outcome. Our hearts know what truly needs to be said; all we need to do is give them permission. For those of us who work out of our heads most of the time, this is such a challenge that we need a prompt. So it is sometimes helpful to begin a sentence with "What I truly want to say is..." That's all we need to remember. In fact, when I am in a difficult conversation I often write those words on the back of a business card to hold as I speak.

Divinity of the Heart

Several years ago I became intrigued with brain research, especially what is known about the emotional brain. Then, along the way as I learned more and more, I realized how much the energy of the heart has to do with the brain. Increasingly, I felt myself drawn to the ancient wisdom of the Bible which emphasizes what we "know" with our hearts. People who use only the intellect to come into relationship with God are not getting the whole picture. We can *know about* God with our brains, but God is *experienced* in our hearts.

The book of Deuteronomy, which contains the story of the handing down of the Ten Commandments, contains 44 verses containing the word "heart." The clear message is that the truth that comes from God is embedded in the human heart.

* * * * *

"Acknowledge and take to heart this day that the Lord is God in heaven above and on the earth below. There is no other." (Deuteronomy 4:39 NIV)

"Remember how the Lord your God led you all the way in the desert these forty years, to humble you and to test you in order to know what was in your heart, whether or not you would keep his commands." (Deuteronomy 8:2 NIV)

"Know then in your heart that as a man disciplines his son,
so the Lord your God disciplines you." (Deuteronomy 8:5 NIV)

The other two books of the Old Testament that are weighted with messages about the heart and its relationship to God's truth are the Psalms, with 118 references, and Proverbs, with 77. Here are a few familiar examples.

* * * * *

"I will praise the Lord, who counsels me; even at night my heart instructs me." (Psalm 16:7 NIV)

"The precepts of the Lord are right, giving joy to the heart. The commands of the Lord are radiant, giving light to the eyes. (Psalm 19:8 NIV)

"The law of his God is in his heart; his feet do not slip." (Psalm 37:31 NIV)

"Trust in the Lord with all your heart and lean not on your own understanding." (Proverbs 3:5 NIV)[4]

"A heart at peace gives life to the body." (Proverbs 14:30 NIV)

"I have hidden your word in my heart that I might not sin against you." (Psalm 119:11 NIV)

"As water reflects a face, so a man's heart reflects the man." (Proverbs 27:19 NIV)

What We Learn with Our Hearts, or Not at All

I suspect the reason people take ethics courses and yet behave unethically or values courses and yet behave immorally or courses on truth-telling and yet lie is that they have taken the information into their brains because that is how it was presented. The *heart* is the rightful place for this learning.

Just as the heart is the first organ to form in the human fetus, so in the development of a healthy organization must the heart form first—which

---

[4] A favorite verse of Gerald Ford, 38th President of the United States, this scripture is prominent in his presidential library in Grand Rapids, Michigan. Because he believed that the nation needed healing, he pardoned former President Richard Nixon. Even though he received much criticism and condemnation, he made a decision from his heart.

may be why so many experts emphasize vision, mission, and core values. At the core of a business that is, in the words Collins and Porras (1994), "built to last," are its values and mission. From there develop the "brains" (business processes that assure as much stability with continuous improvement as possible) and finally the "lungs" (environment that enables everyone to "breathe" with creativity and everyone's voice to be appreciated). This progression is consonant with human development as well as the best organizational development models.

Ancient wisdom says, "As [a man] thinketh in his heart, so is he" (Proverbs 23:7). Research conducted by HeartMath over the last ten years has found new evidence that there actually exists a "little brain in the heart" that processes sensory information and then sends information on to the brain, influencing its activity and function (www.HeartMath.com). It is fascinating that scientific research seems to be validating spiritual teachings that are centuries old.

The Heart's Language

The relationship of our hearts to the words we speak bears thoughtful reflection. When people speak from their hearts, differences melt away. We become as one. The "language" of the heart is universal.

For eight years Whole Foods has been listed by *Fortune Magazine* as one of the best places to work; simultaneously, the company's profits have doubled every 3-½ years. C.E.O. John Mackey[5] says, "In the core of my inner being there is endless creativity and there is limitless love." His company lives from the energy of the heart.

Some years ago I was one of three assistant superintendents in a public school system. I always felt edgy with one of the other assistant superintendents. Everyone else felt it, too. When we were both present in a room, the tension in the air escalated. We had never had an outright confrontation; we just didn't like each other, and we strained around that dynamic as best we could. I thought of him as my enemy.

A year after I left that job I returned to the school district for a visit with friends. As I walked down the long hallway of the administration building, I passed my enemy's door. It was closed, but something told me to go in, so I did. He was in. He greeted me with something like, "Hello, Nancy. What trouble can we stir up today?"

But this time I didn't play the game. Somehow he got around to asking me how I had been, and I answered from my heart. I told him the story of struggles I had had with my daughter. He shared similar problems within

---

[5] http://www.libertyunbound.com/archive/2006_06/mackey-winning.html

his own family. We talked earnestly and honestly for about ten minutes. Then I had to leave for an appointment.

As we stood in the doorway he said, "I could just hug you for talking to me like this."

I said, "Well, why don't you, then?" Shedding a few tears, we briefly shared a hug. Then I left.

My enemy-turned-friend sent three letters after that experience to explain that he was a happily married man and the hug was about friendship! But I knew all along what it was: Relief. Reconciliation. Forgiveness. Compassion. These higher emotions are evoked when we speak and listen with our hearts.

Even when we don't speak the truth perfectly, good results occur—maybe not in the short term, but always in the long run. At the heart-soul level, we vibrate at the same frequency; the voice of someone else's soul resonates with our own.

> "Where two or three are gathered together in my name, there am I in the midst of them." (Matthew 18:20)

Children have so much to teach us in this regard. On a trip to Florida with her parents, my four-year-old granddaughter was playing on the beach. My son and daughter-in-law allowed her to stray from where they had set up. She was still in their view, but far enough away that they couldn't hear what she and the playmate she had chosen were saying to each other. "We could hear their chatter," my daughter-in-law said, "but not their words." They played for the longest time—laughing, talking, squealing while chasing and running from the waves, building sand castles, making sand angels. The other little girl's parents were nearby, so my son and his wife felt their daughter was safe. Finally, they decided it was time to go in so they went to collect their daughter. As they neared the two little giggling girls they realized that the other child was speaking *Spanish!* My granddaughter speaks only English. Yet, for over an hour these two little girls had communicated perfectly.

As a further illustration, here's a story told by my friend who took a coaching and counseling course in graduate school at Harvard University from a professor who was profoundly deaf. Although he wore hearing aids he depended on his eyes to "hear," always looking directly at the speaker in order to read lips. According to my friend, "I learned counseling by making audiotapes and bringing them to this professor with whom I was taking the course by independent study. After a couple of weeks I found the courage to ask him how he could critique my coaching if he could not hear the words I was saying. He responded, 'I do not have to hear in order to be able to listen.'" Riding on the energy of her heart, my friend's tone of voice, silences, number of words and duration of speech in proportion to the other person told her professor all he needed to know!

Truth—words spoken from our hearts—must have a frequency that other hearts recognize, regardless of the specific words that are spoken. Truth is what we most desire, not correct words or large numbers of them.

The High Price of Being Nice

By contrast, as our logical/rational brains develop and our minds grow stronger, we unlearn how to speak from our hearts—a language natural to us as a four-year-old on the beach. We replace our native language with the language of the mind—correct, formal language that builds invisible walls between us and the rest of the world for protection and to get what we need. Language that someone has told us we must speak to be "nice." Language designed to create a pleasant outcome. Language thought to *please others*. Here's an extreme example:

When she married Dana thought it was "greedy" to be thinking about gifts, so she decided not to register or give any clues about her preferences. The day after the wedding she and her new husband, in the presence of their families, opened their presents—in her words, "...one weird gift after another." When all the ribbons had been untied she realized, "This was it—this was what I would have for my trousseau. These would be the mementos that I would have wanted to treasure for a lifetime. There weren't any dishes I would ever use. No beautiful platters to use every Thanksgiving. No great candle holders. Plus I would have to write thank-you notes for all of these bizarre things, which I took to Goodwill within days of my wedding, except for a 12-place setting of dishes from my aunt, which I kept in the garage for years and finally donated to my church."

Dancing Between the Cracks

Someone told me, "I'm good at dancing between the cracks of a conversation." Gonzalez (2004) provides a real-life courtroom example of "bumper car words" from a lawyer questioning a witness on the stand:

> "How many complaints about the plaintiff did you hear in a typical week?"
>
> "They were constant... At least 10 times a week I would hear something bad about him from somebody."
>
> "So that would be about 40 complaints a month?... 520 complaints a year?"
>
> "Well, I didn't count them."

> "[Did you say] 10 complaints per week for a 4-1/2 year period?"
>
> "Well, more or less, to the best I can remember."
>
> "So that would be over 2,000 complaints that you heard about the plaintiff during the time that you supervised him?"
>
> Defense Counsel: "Objection. You are badgering the witness"

Everyone who testifies in a courtroom swears on a Bible to tell "the truth, the whole truth, and nothing but the truth." The interchange above suggests that some people don't even know what the truth is. Moreover, the objecting lawyer appears to protect the witness, not to pursue the truth.

The language of the mind is often for protection. The message is basically, "Go away and leave me alone. I know what I know." Its intent is to be right, not to learn and certainly not to appreciate or be truthful.

Think about some of the models from media where we have learned this *communication that doesn't communicate.* From my childhood I remember segments of the 1950s TV sitcom *I Love Lucy.* The main character used humor to deceive, get her way, and get a laugh. What does "love" mean in *I Love Lucy*? How many of us unwittingly might have learned through these episodes how to get our way any way we can?

> Love is patient. Love is kind. Love keeps no record of wrongs. (I Corinthians 13:4-7 NIV)

It's easy to understand that what we eat, drink, and breathe affects our health. It's more difficult to realize that the words and images we allow into our minds and hearts are shaping the reality in which we live.

When theatre was in its infancy, the classical playwrights saw their role as to "...hold... the mirror up to nature" (Shakespeare's *Hamlet*) so that the audience might see the error of their ways and change. Perhaps that intent would be realized if we took the time to reflect, talk through what we just observed, and set an intent to be better, inspired by the bad example we just watched. But most of us don't take the time to process what we have seen or experienced in order to learn from it.

God in Communication

God doesn't care what we call *God.* In the Old Testament, God said, "I am that I am," (Exodus 3:14) and the word from which we derived "Jehovah"[6] was actually a collection of letters that could not be pronounced. But God "calls" people to the experience of something within each of us that connects us with something far greater than we are and simultaneously

---

[6] http://en.wikipedia.org/wiki/Jehovah

connects us with every other soul. Some psychologists say we use only ten percent of our brains; if that is true, we're still using more of the logical/rational portion of our brains and neglecting intuition as well as messages from our hearts. Yet it is with our hearts, not our frontal lobes, that we know God.

Nobre (2004) reports on neurophysiologist Jacob Grinberg-Zylberbaum's experiments in which two people had a 20-minute meditation period together with the intent to feel each other's presence. Then he enclosed them in separate Faraday chambers—which are metallic enclosures that block all electromagnetic signals. A flash of light was shown to one but not the other. In one out of four cases, in the words of consultant Tacito Nobre:

> "…although no electromagnetic signals could have been transmitted between the two subjects, the brain of the person who had not been exposed to the light showed electrical activity quite similar to that displayed in the first subject."

We are more connected than we realize. But most of us are unaware and thus try to force solutions to every problem with logic and reason.

Interference to Truth

In this Information Age, we are often overwhelmed with words. We "chatter" thinking we are relieving stress, when we are actually overworking our brains and creating even more stress.

Just think for a moment about the amount of data coming into our brains, minute-by-minute. First, we have proliferation of print—newspapers, magazines, dailies, weeklies, radio, CD, e-mail, voice-mail, cell-phones with earpieces, pagers, television news shows that split the screen to be in three locations, plus a trail or two of data running along the bottom of the screen. Our eyes move quickly from image to image. Our ears tune to this sound, then that sound, now a different sound! Before we even focus, the noise shifts. Unrelentingly, trails of data are coming into our brain with no quiet time to assimilate anything or reflect on what it means. We think we don't have time to reflect and turn the data into useful information. In *Hamlet* (Act II, Scene 2), Polonius discovers that Hamlet is ignoring him and asks, "What are you reading, my lord?" Hamlet's response: "Words, words, words."

Several months ago I led a workshop on stress reduction for a group of teachers. As they came into the room their chatter was incessant. I felt my own stress level immediately go up. I thought the room might explode! When I finally got their attention I asked first that we have a full minute of silence. Then I showed them how to take three deep breaths, to bring a fresh oxygen supply into the brain. Then and only then could we focus on the topic at hand—relieving stress.

A few weeks later, one of the teachers in that group reported that she had been asked to substitute in a math class. She was nervous because she was rusty on math. Moreover, as she started the class there were several announcements over the intercom and some kind of disturbance in the hallway. So she stopped. She said, "Class, I'm a little nervous anyway because it's been a long time since I taught math. And all these interruptions have unnerved me. So I'm going to take a minute to be silent and just breathe. I'm going to take three long, deep breaths. Please join me if you would like."

About half the students joined her. The others looked puzzled. But all were quiet while she calmed herself. The rest of her time with the class went very well.

What this teacher learned is that we cannot quiet cacophony with more words. The most effective way to bring about calmness is to be quiet.

"Be still, and know that I am God" (Psalm 46:10)

The Wisdom of Silence

In 1952, Max Ehrmann wrote the ever-popular "Desiderata," which begins:

> "Go placidly amid the noise and haste,
> and remember what peace there may be in silence.
> ...
> Speak your truth quietly and clearly;
> and listen to others,
> even the dull and the ignorant;
> they too have their story.
> Avoid loud and aggressive persons,
> they are vexations to the spirit."

In our world there will always be cause for anxiety, but we can always make a choice to be still and connect with a Higher Power—even if we do not know its name. The Institute of Heartmath is committed to reducing stress and anxiety in the interest of greater mental ability and better health. Its research center has found,

> "When you intentionally shift to a positive emotion such as appreciation, care or compassion, your heart rhythms immediately change, blood pressure drops, stress hormones plummet, the immune system pumps up, anti-aging hormones increase,

and you gain clarity, calmness and control. The effects are both immediate and long-lasting"[7]

In the King James version of the Bible, the word "*selah*" often ends a section of scripture. Some say this word means, "Pause and calmly think of that." But in today's world how often does anyone take the time to pause and reflect?

Two hundred years ago Lewis and Clark took the time to reflect. They didn't mean to—they didn't even want to—but their journey to the Pacific ended in December and it was much too dangerous to go back across the Rockies in the dead of winter. So they found themselves stuck on the Oregon coast at Fort Clatsop. They hated it. Fleas in the furs on which they slept were an incessant problem. The cold, rainy weather was oppressive. The natives weren't very friendly, and all they had to do with their time was make salt by boiling sea water, mend their clothing, and prepare to make the trek back to St. Louis. This dull routine went on for *months*.

What did they do? They took time to review what they had written in their journals and reflect on what they had learned as they made the two-year journey from St. Louis to the Oregon coast. Their return trip took *only six months*. Two years going and only six months to return—because they took the time to reflect on what they had learned from their experience and make different choices that shortened their homeward journey.

In other words they had to learn to be content with silence and relative inactivity, and the reward was significant.

As they sat in front of the fire at Fort Clatsop, journals spread out before them, Lewis and Clark must have looked back on their two-year journey in wonder. They had lost only one man. They had not been attacked by Indians. Everything they needed had been provided in some form. Inexplicable coincidences had occurred, such as their encounter with Sacagawea's long-lost brother who supplied them with horses. Surely they knew that Mexican troops were looking for them to put a stop to their mission. The journey, though hard, was without calamity except for one death.

Surely they must have recalled the wonder of finding new species. The vastness of the western prairie. The splendor of sunset in a wide sky. In both cases, a period of intense, rigorous effort was followed by reflection or prayer. What matters is that we honor God and allow ourselves to be awed.

Taking the time for silence, reflection, or meditation actually makes work go faster. Catherine Ponder (1987) relates the story of the creation of a seamless robe for the 1953 motion picture, *The Robe*. A woman and her daughter were given the task of weaving a robe that would be an authentic

---

[7] http://www.ceopartnership.com/heartmath-coaching.htm

reproduction of the one worn by Jesus. After searching out and selecting the materials to be used, the actual task of weaving took 36 hours, and they finished 16 hours before the deadline for delivery. Suddenly,

> "...the daughter's three-year-old son... snipped a piece of cloth from the beautiful seamless robe. It seemed impossible that they could weave another... robe in just 16 hours when it had taken 36 to weave the original one, but when these women got quiet and prayed, affirming that the Christ Mind was showing them what to do, their guidance was to do just that: weave another robe. As they affirmed that the Christ Mind was expressing perfectly through them, they finished their second seamless robe in only nine hours, or one-fourth the time taken on the original robe!"

Two stories from different centuries and different language with similar outcome. God doesn't care what we call God, but it matters greatly that we rely on this great power within and around us.

We Don't Take Time to Solve Our Problems

An expert in international marketing told me that thoughtful, long-term solutions are difficult to market and sell. "People," she said, "think they don't have time to solve their problems." So marriages remain in crisis mode and 60% of them end in divorce. Business partners never reconcile their differences and business suffers. People are content to work "in the business" repeating the same mistakes over and over again, as in the Bill Murray movie *Groundhog Day* (1993), but not "on the business."

At the 2004 Pegasus Conference, MIT professors Bill Isaacs and John Sterman, presented "Lighting the Way: Tipping Points and the Human Side of Collective Transformation" which summarized their emerging ideas on a new theory of change. Their research indicated that the reason organizations don't change is because of behaviors like organizational firefighting, cutting corners, Liar's Club, blame, self-confirming attribution, and Flavor-of-the-Month. Seeming urgencies arise and people move from crisis to crisis not knowing how to stop and solve the root problems. Isaacs and Sterman demonstrated their better model to the assembled group noting that "Every decision we make is governed by feedback processes. No one ever gets credit for fixing problems that never happened."

In other words, what gets rewarded gets done. Therefore, if we reward people for putting out fires, there will be more fires to put out. With more fires to put out, who has time to sit down, reflect on what they have learned, and find better ways to work? The result of this habitual fire-fighting erodes the organization's capability.

When I ask people what depletes their energy, they often say, "Emergencies. I get to work with my day planned, and someone comes in with an emergency." I say, "And are these 'emergencies' really urgent, or are your mirror neurons reflecting someone else's heightened emotions?" After a moment they answer, "They aren't really emergencies." Mirror neurons may be the real culprits here and the place to begin working is with ourselves— to realize that we have a choice. We can let someone else hijack our brain, or we can be in charge of our own state of mind. This is a *simple* concept, but not *easy* to carry out.

Isaacs and Sterman say that people don't know how to work wisely with a sense of having a larger purpose. Instead, we tend to float around like "...fragments that have lost consciousness of the whole."

To experience change, Isaacs and Sterman say three awakenings must occur. We must wake up, first of all, to the physics of the systems in which we live. Yet many people still play a blame game, not realizing that when something goes wrong in a system it's rarely just one person's fault. Usually, it's a way of doing business that has spread, like a virus, over time. Former Enron employee Sherron Watkins (2003) knew that her boss, Jeff Skilling, lacked a moral compass. But she was shocked when she discovered how large the ethics violations had become.

Peter Senge (1993) uses the analogy of the "trim tab," the smallest part of a ship's rudder and the part that turns *first*, to describe the *systemic nature* of human actions within organizations. According to Watkins here's how the message that Enron executives were entitled to the company's largesse might have been communicated. When Ken Lay was president, his sister ran a travel agency that all employees were required to use. The agency was expensive and of dubious quality yet Enron employees were *required* to use her services. Clear message. Not quality. Not value for the dollar. But increasing wealth for those close to the CEO was not only acceptable; it was actually mandated! People who are trained to identify patterns within systems know that they must listen all the way through all the stories to find the *real* problem, which is almost never about just one person but a prevalent *pattern*.

Another thing we must wake up to is the quality of our own character and presence—and learn to express it consistently. When subtle, unspoken pressures are exerted by people close to us, it's easy to drift from our own values and then one day we wake up hating ourselves, hating our work, hating those close to us, and increasingly becoming ill. We sense that issues need to be addressed but we're afraid of the reaction we will trigger.

Sherron Watkins' advice for Enron-type problems is to find or create a group of like-minded people who can support each other in maintaining their own character while not getting drawn into practices that violate your values. Sometimes it's advisable to seek such help from outside the company. Exececutive coach Dr. Nancy Post (2003), tells this story about a rising female executive named "Pam":

> "[My boss] knew I'd handle everything, and I did for a while. As time went on, he was away for weeks, or even months, and I was doing his job." She grimaced when she said this and rubbed one side of her head.
> "How does your head feel now?" [Dr. Post] asked.
> "Funny you should ask," she continued. "Just at that moment, I felt a headache come on."
> "Can you tell me how it feels to you when you do work that you think is really your boss's job?"
> That did it. The cork popped.

Once Pam's true feelings came out, her coach, using an interdisciplinary knowledge base, was able to deliver a multi-faceted intervention for her persistent migraine headaches. This intervention resulted in Pam's eventually—and happily—assuming the position of CEO of that same company.

Finally, Isaacs and Sterman also say we must wake up to the existence of generative action. The movie *Pay It Forward* (2000) depicted how *generative* action works. One good work begets another good work, which in turn begets another good work and so it goes. Conversely, one cruel act can give birth to another cruel act, and so it goes. Most of us have heard the story of the man who gets chewed out by his boss, goes home and chews out his wife, who then chews out one of the kids, who kicks the dog. Or the "different" teenager who is unmercifully teased (which means "to tear the flesh") by his classmates until one day he crashes through the school doors, guns blazing. Generative action.

Importance of the State of Relaxed Alertness

Undeniably, the brain works best in a state of relaxed alertness. Both neuroscience and our own experience verify this fact. When do your best ideas come? During your morning shower? While you are walking through the forest? Lying on the beach, on vacation? Wherever you are, undoubtedly you are in a relaxed state of mind.

Shreeve (2005) reported in *National Geographic* about research by Richard Davidson at the University of Wisconsin-Madison. Davidson and his associates wanted to know the effect of meditation on the brain, so they tracked brain activity in volunteers from a high tech company. The volunteers were divided into two groups, one of which engaged in meditation for eight weeks. Both groups also received flu shots. His findings:

> "By the end of the study, those who had meditated showed a pronounced shift in brain activity toward the left, 'happier,' frontal cortex. The meditators also showed a healthier immune response to the flu shot, suggesting that [meditation] affected the body's health as well as the mind's."

Most employees say their jobs use less brainpower than they have available to give. Part of the problem is that they have insufficient time to reflect and thus get into the underutilized parts of their brains. Another part of the problem is that there is so much "static" in the environment needlessly using the brain's resources: chatter, noise, and elevated emotional states. Employees' brains ricochet from issue to issue and they leave work at the end of the day exhausted. Some are beyond this, working so far into their energy reserves that they may never reach the potential both they and their employers covet. How we speak with each other is also part of the problem.

Our conversations do not generate learning. They are more like reporting, or even game-playing. All our energy goes into the game, not into constructing meaning and receiving learning as a benefit. Here's a typical interchange, a story told by an interior decorator who was hired by an executive's wife to give their home a new look. At her first meeting with the husband he said, "Well, I guess you're the *inferior desecrator*." Having learned how to deal with his type she responded, "Yes. And I guess you're the asshole. I can see we're going to have a *great* time working together."

These word games take energy to maintain; they make relationship-building unnecessarily difficult. My friend, whose work loudly speaks how much she loves it and how good she is at it, reported that by the time the project was finished she had earned his respect. "We became good friends. But the beginning was very rocky." Perhaps watching how she put her heart into her work opened his eyes to her value. But at the outset, how much time and energy was wasted? And how many people, cowed by such aggressive language, might have shrunk back for protection?

Say Only What Truly Needs to Be Said

When we say only what truly needs to be said, we use economy with our words. Our conversations become *generative* in that listeners readily learn and ideas are generated through the interaction. The ski instructor who taught me to traverse a hill actually taught me a great deal more. Our small class of six students rode the ski lift to the top of a gentle hill. The instructor said, "I'm going to ski to the bottom of the hill. One of you start down and do what I say as you ski." The first brave one started down. I heard the instructor shout out, "Look at the tree on your left." Gently, the skier glided to his left. Then, at the right time, our teacher said, "Now look at the post on your right." Thus, one by one, he guided each one of us safely down the hill. One at a time, all of us traversed the hill with no spills. As we gathered successfully around our teacher he said simply, "Remember this. Where your brain goes, your body follows."

I was excited to practice my new skill the next day, but someone close to me—a more experienced skier—said, "You probably need to take another lesson"—and I made the mistake of listening to that advice. The next day I got a different instructor. He started out by explaining in great detail, "To traverse a hill, you must hold your right foot at such-and-such an angle, and your left foot like this—and your big toes do this, etc." Too many words. Too much to think about. (The brain can remember only about 7 plus or minus 3 things at a time, which is why phone numbers are 123-123-1234. And Social Security numbers 123-12-1234.) I had a terrible experience and at the end of the lesson I fell—hard. My tailbone bruised, I wasn't able to ski at all the last day of my trip.

A state of mind that is over-prescriptive—not peaceful—seeking to control things beyond its control—produces words that create interference for others' learning. By contrast, a state of mind that holds unconditional love, acceptance, or nonjudgment is ideal. When we are feeling criticized, judged, analyzed or fixed, we are not relaxed.

Speaking only the words needed to communicate the essence of the message from a nonjudgmental state of mind is what some people call unconditional love. Timothy Gallwey (1974) wrote about the importance of nonjudgment to learning:

> "Letting go of judgments does not mean ignoring errors. It simply means seeing events as they are and not adding anything to them... Judgmental labels usually lead to emotional reactions and then to tightness, trying too hard, self-condemnation, etc... Use descriptive but nonjudgmental words to describe the events you see.
>
> "The rose is a rose from the time it is a seed to the time it dies... At all times, it contains its whole potential. It seems to be constantly in the process of change; yet at each state, at each moment, it is perfectly alright as it is."

Jim Collins (2001), advocates taking "blameless autopsies" when errors have been made. That is, this sound business principle allows even the person who has made the error to relax and learn from it. Blaming, on the other hand, sets up resistance and resentment, both of which create a "noise" or interference in the system.

An executive with an advertising firm told me what she had done to follow Jim Collins' advice. A team had worked very hard to acquire a major account but the prospective client chose a different firm. After a little time for reflection had passed, this executive invited a small sampling of employees from throughout the country to fly to headquarters for the sole purpose of listening to this team tell its story about what happened, asking questions and learning. In a quiet, nonjudgmental way, this executive found an effective way to share learning throughout the company so that people don't repeat each other's mistakes. Most companies do not take the time to learn from their mistakes so they repeat the same mistakes in a *Groundhog Day* (1993) syndrome.

> "A wise man's heart guides his mouth, and his lips promote instruction." (Proverbs 16:23 NIV)

When we speak from our hearts we say what truly needs to be said, with respect for ourselves, as well as respect for the other person—no more, no less.

In other words, when our hearts guide our words we have a "learning conversation." We learn because we don't know exactly what we are going to say—and the other person learns also.

A Growing Movement

The media has made much ado about what it calls the "polarization" of the United States. Beneath their radar, however, is a slowly growing movement, unorganized, that brings together small groups of people for the purpose of having conversations about important—even controversial—topics. These efforts all have different names and slightly different processes. What they have in common is that when one person is speaking, others are only listening to understand. No debate. No discussion. Just speak what you truly want to say with the assurance that you will not be interrupted or judged.

The "rules" for speaking in the early church as spelled out in I Corinthians 14 sound very much like the "rules for dialogue," a process for allowing meaning to "flow through" the people in the group described by physicist David Bohm:

1. Speak one at a time.
2. Speak from your heart.
3. Weigh carefully what others say.
4. Relax and trust the outcome.

A simpler way of saying this is that, in these groups, people speak from their hearts and listen with their hearts. Most reasonable people don't expect to get their way all the time; what they really want is to be heard. The satisfaction derived from dialogue is that we are able to say all that is needed with the assurance that we have been heard. Senge (1993) advocates the use of dialogue to increase the capacity of organizations. My dream is that every organization—even churches, families, and schools—will create unobtrusive processes that work invisibly while exponentially increasing the learning of that organization. Here's an example of a simple process I created for a client:

Employee Conversations that Strengthen Teamwork and the Business

Ground Rules: Sit in a circle—chairs only, no tables. Only one person speaks at a time. No interruptions. Listen to learn.

1. One at a time, tell a story about a recent success with a customer or other group.
2. After everyone has told a story, get customer feedback by passing around feedback forms on which customers have written what they liked and what they think [the company] can do better. Each person read one customer comment from the feedback forms. (No discussion; just read, listen, or reflect).
3. Finally, go around the circle again to answer the questions, "What did I hear that seemed 'on target'? What am I willing to do better?" and "Is this something I can do for myself, or do I need help, and from whom?"

One of the team leaders would be present at every meeting. They decide whether or not the owners need to know anything. The owner will not ask; he will allow these meetings to run completely without him.

To increase self-motivation, people need to be able to have some control over their own work. This format builds self-motivation because team members will have control over how they take in information and make appropriate changes, instead of waiting to be told. I suggest these meetings be held once a week for 3 months; once every other week for the next 6 months, and once a month from then on.

Margaret Wheatley (2002) writes, "We become hopeful when somebody tells the truth... Truly connecting with another human being gives us joy." The energy of joy makes workloads seem lighter. We "work smarter" not harder.

The purpose of much of our conversation is not to tell the truth, but to compete. How this works became clear to me when I participated in a competitive discussion—not a dialogue—with a group of people who were assigned an article to read before we came together. Only two of us actually read the article. The facilitator gave us a set of questions and told us to agree on the answers as a group. Several of the people who had not even read the article argued vociferously that their answers were correct. Even more amazingly, the group often agreed to take their answers which were not accurate! What I learned from this experience is that in teams, committees, and working groups, the opinion of the most persistent or most forceful person is the one that often prevails, whether he knows what he is talking about or not, simply because other people get tired.

But with dialogue, emotions remain quiet. Everyone has an opportunity to speak, without having to fight to be heard. Relaxation prevails so brains may do their best thinking—and it is also safe for the heart to be engaged. After participating in several of these groups, I leave with a feeling of satisfaction and expanded energy derived from feeling that I fully spoke my truth and listened to learn. There's nothing more I need to say; I am complete. If I'm not complete I have learned to say, "Something is still bothering me. I'm not sure what it is. I'll let you know when I get clear on what it is—if it is important."

I've noticed two interesting byproducts of these conversations: I'm not even tempted to talk about the conversation or the people after I have left them—an observation that leads me to believe that gossip is the offspring of dysfunctional conversation. Secondly, I take appropriate personal action in support of my heart's desires. Here's a story about one of those experiences:

On June 8th, 1999, I attended the Visions of a Better World Foundation meeting in New York City. This conversation focused on influencing the media to print or air more positive stories—"Images and Voices of Hope." The following week, I was back home channel surfing one evening. I landed on the community access channel which was showing an Austin School Board meeting. A friend was making a report to the board so I lingered to watch. When her report ended, the camera turned to the director of counseling who reported that Austin students had won over $20 million in scholarship money—a $5 million increase over the previous year. I remembered a recent headline: "Couple Donates $20 Million for a New Arts

Center." If a $20 million donation was front-page news, I figured $20 million in scholarship money to Austin youth was also significant. So the next day I skimmed the newspaper looking for the full story. There was no story. I e-mailed a letter to the editor. It was rejected.

I decided to try something different.

I called the newspaper and asked to speak with the person who makes decisions about what goes into the news. Three days later I reached him. I told this person the channel-surfing story, concluding with, "I think $20 million in scholarship money is newsworthy. Do you?"

"Yes," he said. "It is." He thanked me for calling.

Eight days after our conversation, on the front page of the metro and state section of the newspaper, the following headline[8] appeared with a lengthy story and color photograph of a scholarship student: "Austin Students Amass $23 Million In Scholarships."

I'm not trying to claim responsibility for this headline; someone else may have picked up on this important bit of news independent of me. All I'm saying is that I had a sincere, from-the-heart desire, I took appropriate action, and it materialized.

Conclusion

The power of speaking from the heart is very great. People are listening to hear whether or not we "ring true." If our minds are filled with energy coming from the heart—respect, understanding, and compassion—the words and voice will flow with respect, understanding, and compassion. We will be understood and appreciated. We will say what truly needs to be said.

> "Anyone who wants to know the human psyche... would be better advised to abandon exact science... bid farewell to his study, and wander with human heart throughout the world. There... he would reap richer stores of knowledge than textbooks a foot thick could give him, and he will know how to doctor the sick with a real knowledge of the human soul."
>
> Carl Jung

The smallest things often cause us the greatest anxiety. Upset by her mother's lack of communication, a daughter dropped a simple note in the mail with a photograph of the grandchildren. "When you don't call, it makes me think you don't care." Few Words. True Words. Immediately the

---

8 "Austin students amass $23 million in scholarships" by Erin J. Walker, June 26, 1999. *Austin American-Statesman* (TX) Page: B1.

mother called. She called the next day, too, and sent an e-mail after that. She just didn't know her daughter's feelings. Now that she knows, she will do what is required to keep her daughter's love.

* * * * *

"Something there is that doesn't love a wall—that wants it down."

Robert Frost

"Mr. Gorbachev, tear down this wall."

Ronald Reagan

"I like a look of agony because I know 'tis true. Men do not sham convulsion, nor simulate a throe."

Emily Dickinson

Exercise 7-1:

- Think about a person with whom you are experiencing discomfort or uneasiness.

- Start a sentence with "What I truly need to say or do is... "

- Keep on writing until your heart is completely peaceful.

8   Practice Humility:
Truth and Love Bring Light

My favorite definition of humility is "being neither more than nor less than we truly are." So what is it that we *truly* are? How do we find it? How do we align our decisions, words, and actions with it?

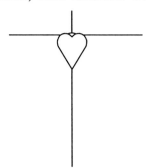

In embryos the first organ to form is the heart, which (we're not sure how) is closely associated with the soul. Throughout history humankind has always acknowledged the heart as the purest, truest part of us.

My teachers say this is the part of us that has never been violated. Sometimes we refer to it as our soul. As we grow up, though, to protect our souls so that we do not get hurt beyond repair, we build defenses, which some people call ego.

How Ego Forms

Because brain development is so rapid when we are young—before the age of 3—we "get" many things wrong because memories are stored and patterns formed before we have the brain capacity[9] to understand them. So these defenses are based on greatly limited brain capacity. Take a look at Fig. 8-3.

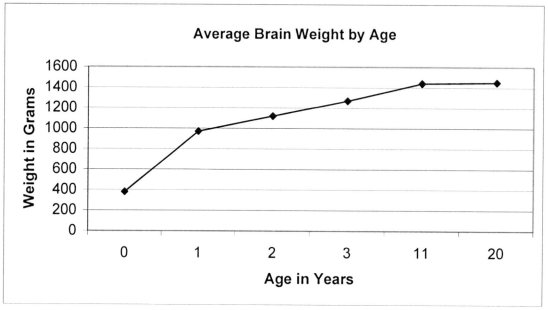

Fig. 8–3: Average Brain Weight by Age

Most of this phenomenal brain browth is due to the lengthening and branching of the dendrites, along with the development of glial cells. The neurons themselves do increase in size to some extent. But primarily our early brain growth comes from making *connections,* building the scaffolding, so to speak, for all future learning. These connections are being made and memories are being stored by a brain that is driven primarily by *emotion without understanding.* Many memories are stored before we even have language to express them.

The brain's frontal lobes—which determine validity of information, assess risk, and make decisions accordingly—do not finish developing until we reach our early twenties. So the emotional part of our brain, which is fully mature when we are born, has more than a 20-year head start on our ability to make sound decisions that are simultaneously good for us and others. Because these early neuronal pathways are so well traveled, we continue to live unaware and out of emotional memories that may have been stored when we were three or nine years old. Unless we go back to the early experiences of our lives and re-interpret them in the light of more reliable information, energy remains trapped. Our "ego" remains in charge

---

[9] Data from Dekaban, A.S. and Sadowsky, D., "Changes in brain weights during the span of human life, *Ann. Neurology,* 4:345-356, 1978

and our soul remains hidden behind protective barriers erected by our ego for protection that is no longer needed.

I became aware of this phenomenon when I read an article in the newspaper about a man who, as a child, survived a fall over Niagara Falls. At the time, he was the only person known to have survived such a catastrophe. A newspaper reporter tracked him down to get his story which involved his going back to Niagara Falls for the first time since the incident. He and his sister had been in a family friend's boat. Misjudging the strength of the current, the friend guided the boat too close to the falls. Somehow someone rescued his sister, but he and the friend cascaded down the falls. The friend was killed. Only the boy survived. From that day forward his family never spoke of the accident. As the boy-now-man told his story to the reporter, he felt a surge of energy from relief. As I read the account my attention focused on the energy he released from simply telling the experience to an appreciative listener. Had the story been retold in his family his state of mind would likely have been full of fear, anger, judgment, guilt, and shame—emotions that "lock us up." But the reporter just wanted to hear and understand the story so he could write it well—a listening state of mind that liberates the storyteller.

Margaret Wheatley (2002) describes this liberation.

> "The practice of 'bearing witness'… is a simple practice of being brave enough to sit with human suffering, to acknowledge it for what it is, to not flee from it. It doesn't make the suffering go away, although it sometimes changes the experience of pain and grief" (p. 82).

In bearing witness, we honor another person's truth telling. The Niagara Falls story and my own experience convinced me that when significant experiences remain unresolved, the heart and brain energies are clogged. It is necessary to release this energy by telling one's story, looking at it from the perspective of a kind, compassionate person, thus releasing the hold it has on us. Ego falls away and friendlier brain chemistry produces the emotions of hope and joy.

"The unexamined life is not worth living."
Socrates

Like a scab on a wound, once that part of our defenses falls away the soul is better able to peek out, stand up, and speak. Some people refer to the process of examining their lives with a now-mature understanding as peeling the onion. Most do not do it unless they are experiencing significant pain.

What does any of this have to do with humility?

Humility as Right Relationship with God and Man

According to Lois, wife of Alcoholics Anonymous co-founder Bill Wilson, "'Humbly'... means seeing myself in true relation to my fellow man and to God." In other words, we must know ourselves well enough to be able to distinguish between an energy that is coming from our ego and an energy that is coming from an inner voice—a Third Person—the voice of our soul—the stirrings of our heart. One of the oldest definitions of sin is that which separates you from God and from your neighbor. And I would add: from yourself.

Until we revisit painful experiences our ego controls us, putting up a no-longer-needed shield of protection. But once we have the courage to re-live a defining experience and assign a name to it, we are no longer controlled by it. We can set aside our pride or indignation and simply accept what happened. A well-known therapeutic model in psychology is talk therapy—encouraging the patient to talk about what happened so that the trauma subsides and truth can emerge. Here are two stories that I have re-lived in my journey to find my soul—my true, authentic self.

The First Story

When I was nine months old my father left to fight in World War II. Mother went to work as a secretary in a city many miles from her parents' home in the country. Since there was no one to care for me, I alternated between my grandparents and an aunt who employed an African-American maid. To this day I have a warm connection with African Americans because I can still feel how that woman—whoever she was—held me in her arms, comforting a child alone. As an adult, when someone once asked me to complete a sentence beginning "Mother is," I finished it with the words "far away."

When I was three years old Dad returned. By that time I had been in the care of older adults who thought I was adorable no matter what I did. But Dad's opinion was that I was "too big for my britches." He thought he had to make up for lost time by "cutting me down to size," which he did in my grandmother's woodshed.

Two of his sisters doted on me. So when my dad headed back into the house with me, limp and chastened, they stood in the doorway blocking his way. They told him if he ever did that to me again he would answer to them.

Dad knew only too well that they would make good on their promise. The twelve children in his family were mostly left to their own devices for coping with each other. On one occasion, after Dad's lips were blistered and parched from working in the fields all day, these two sisters sneaked into where he was sleeping and sprinkled red pepper on his mouth. To this day I thank God for my two aunts and my dad's "red pepper memory." For the rest of my childhood and teen years I remember only one other incident of physical punishment—minor. Mostly Dad didn't touch me.

Only three years old, my only-partially-developed brain could not understand what was happening. But my emotions were greatly aroused. For the rest of his life I was angry with my father—in fact, with all men and women who had authority over me.

> "Ye fathers, provoke not your children to wrath." (Ephesians 6:4)

I had been adequately forewarned not to stray too far from accepted behavior. So I spent the rest of my childhood and teen years vacillating between trying to be and look really good and being very angry. Mostly, I was terrified of my father. His force, perhaps seasoned in the fields of war, had been much too great for an overly-protected three-year-old little girl.

Thus, my ego was born: Be good for protection, and be ready to go to war.

This is how neuronal patterns are formed and connections made. Once I understood what had happened to me, I was free to make a different choice. Only while the experience is unexamined does it have you in its grip.

I have no conscious memory of this woodshed experience. In my forties, as I was collecting family stories, I heard it for the first time. An unresolved experience trapping emotional memory leaving me unconsciously ready to do battle with authority figures who I perceived were trying to control me, while spending whatever was necessary on clothing and accessories to make me look good.

The Second Story

Another ego-created pattern proved more disturbing for me. As the leader of an organization, twice I encountered very painful problems with younger women. Both situations centered around my creative idea. The idea was so big that there was no way I could accomplish it alone so each of these women, in her own way, helped get it off the ground. I was dumbfounded and felt cheated when one of them publicly, before an audience, told people the idea was hers. Instead of confronting the issues as they arose, she and I both vented to other people, developed resentments, and unfortunately handled the situation very badly. This woman ultimately became one of my bosses. By that time we were no longer friends, and our enmity created many difficult situations, both for us and for other people.

In the second instance, I knew I needed a responsible person to carry out the details and implementation. An early volunteer, Beth was bright, well respected, and hard-working with an eye for details that I mostly overlooked. In the beginning she was a contractor. Then I hired her to be project director and handed the whole project to her allowing her to office in a different city. I seem to have been driven by a "program" that compelled me to give up what I love and allow a younger woman to take center stage with it. Although we often met and spoke by telephone, I now believe I failed to provide the support she needed. I just handed the whole project to her and left her with it, yet I continued to inject my opinions about the project. When she resigned several years later, in frustration, she was very angry with me.

After the second ruined relationship failed, I realized that both experiences were similar and felt familiar, so I asked myself "When was the first time I felt like this?" Shortly thereafter the answer came from something that happened when I was nine years old and my younger sister three. My father had a favorite book of poetry which had been autographed by the author, one of his college professors. In it was a beautiful poem called "Level Land" which I loved to read aloud in the privacy of my room, with the door closed. Also in this same book was a bawdy poem with a refrain that went: "And I don't give a damn, said Give-a-Damn-Jones." My three-year-old sister, with Dad's coaching, had learned this refrain.

One evening, my parents had friends over. I remember them gathered in a circle sitting in our living room. Dad called my sister to him to recite with him the poem with the naughty refrain. I turned to my mother eager to read the beautiful poem I had practiced. She said, "No."

The neuronal connection that formed at that moment held information that said, "Stay on the periphery of the circle, not in the spotlight. Give what you want to your little sister." I was only nine years old, too young to understand that when people are partying, they don't want to hear serious poems. My mother understood, though, and saved me from the greater harm of ridicule by saying, "No."

But I didn't understand. For years the incident went unresolved. Three decades later, in answer to my question "Where did this pattern come from?" the memory surfaced.

Then something unexpected happened. A friend and fellow author told me that a local charity—a shelter for abused and neglected children—wanted Austin writers to submit pieces for their newsletter in hopes of attracting donations. He added, knowing my love for poetry, "It doesn't have to be an article. They'll take poetry." Interested, I paid a visit to the children's shelter after which I wrote this poem:

Child

My name is Child;
I have nowhere to go.
May I come in?

I'm tired, confused,
Afraid, and torn.
Will you hold me?

I've lived with frowns,
Disappointment, and want.
Is it warm here?

Sometimes I cry out;
I shout and scream.
Will you still care?

I want to live—
To see the sky—
Can you teach me hope?

My sister is small,
And she is bruised.
Is it safe here?

Our name is Child.
We have nowhere to go.
May we come in?

The executive director printed my poem in their newsletter. A previously reluctant donor sent a check for $1,000. The poem was printed and distributed at their fundraising gala. I sat, head bowed, tears streaming down my face, as I heard the emcee read my poem to the group assembled.

When the shelter opened a new facility, the executive director invited me to read the poem as part of the program. As I sat on the front row waiting for the ceremony to begin, I felt someone slip into the chair beside me. I turned to greet Laura Bush, then the First Lady of Texas, who was the featured speaker for the event! The memory of the circle in my parents' living room was shattered. My brain was no longer nine years old and I had a new memory to replace the old one. I was going to read my poem center stage, and one of the people listening would become First Lady of the United States of America.

What Happens When Ego Shatters

Since that time I have been much more sensitive to my responsibility to prepare people, especially younger women, who are helping me with a project—to give them the support they need—instead of dropping everything and leaving them on their own. I have learned to build partnerships with younger women based on honesty and understanding in order to dismantle dynamics that might create jealousy and resentment. I have learned to speak from my heart and say what I need, as well as listen to what they have to say even when it isn't what I want to hear.

The above stories provide examples of how ego grows to protect and then gradually control our lives to keep us as adults from living the lives we *truly* want. As the theme of the movie *Groundhog Day* indicates, we are doomed to live the same day over and over again until we are willing to examine what's not working for us, revisit memories with a now-mature brain, replace them, and make different choices.

Most people don't do this because they don't know the tool is there or they think they don't have time, and thus the unwelcome pattern gets repeated and then passed down to the next generation.

Another Way Ego Grows and Takes Over

I had learned to withhold anger through some bad, though well-meaning, advice from my grandmother. I remember it well. We were in the garden just north of her house, near the barrel that caught the rainwater Grandmother used to wash her hair. I must have been expressing anger because my grandmother said, "You mustn't be angry. Anger releases a poison that goes through your whole body." The word "poison" got my attention and I made a decision to stop being angry. I didn't know that goal was impossible to achieve. What I actually did was *suppress* my anger.

Sometimes ego grows because we take bad advice. What Grandmother did not know is that there is no "switch" in our brains that allows us to "turn off" anger but "leave on" joy. Rather, if we tell our brains to stop anger, what it "hears" is "stop emotion" or "stop feeling." We find ourselves, as I did decades later, unable to feel pleasure or pain, having forgotten what brings joy—which is the native language of the soul.

Role Models

Another way our ego grows out of control is by watching someone else live life—even watching someone pretend to live life (play a role) as we do through the media. Marshall McLuhan coined the phrase "the medium is the message" in 1964. McLuhan knew the power that visual images have to establish a pattern for our own behavior noting that "we become what we behold," emphasized by the title of his 1967 book, *The Medium is the Message*.

A woman who engaged in verbal sparring with her husband as a matter of course and felt "martyred" by her two sons told me she never misses an episode of the TV show *Everyone Loves Raymond*. Her favorite character is Marie, mother of two grown sons and the quintessential martyr.

Just as we are responsible to be aware of what the food we eat does to our bodies, so must we be vigilant about the words and images that we "let in." They are shaping our lives and our relationships.

Through lack of awareness, as our goals drift and our discipline sags, our hearts absorb energies that are not in our best interest. If we are fortunate, something happens in our lives that brings us to our emotional knees in the realization that other people are not the problem; we ourselves are the problem.

Sophocles' *Oedipus Rex* illustrates such an experience. Blight has come over the country ruled by King Oedipus. People are suffering. Finally, after trying everything else he knew to do, Oedipus summoned a blind prophet who explains that the curse has fallen because someone, though unwittingly, has killed his father and married his mother. Oedipus swears to find the man and take swift action to punish this unnatural, heinous act. Then the blind prophet spoke the truth in love. "You are the man."

> "Clean your finger before you point at my spots."
> Benjamin Franklin
>
> "Why do you look at the speck of sawdust in your brother's eye and pay no attention to the plank in your own eye?"
> (Matthew 7:3)

When we finally stop looking outside of ourselves to find the problem, when we are finally willing to turn our eyes inward and acknowledge our own frailties, mistakes, and shortcomings—we gain humility. We come into right relationship with both God and our fellow man. We don't put ourselves down and someone else above us. We don't put ourselves above and someone else below us. We acknowledge the unlimited power of God. God is truth. God is love. God is light. When we hear the truth, spoken in love, we are enlightened. We become humble.

I remember how this happened for me. I asked for it, but I didn't want to hear what I had to hear. My life pattern of trying to be perfect manifested to other people as a "halo effect." In other words, I came across to them as holier-than-thou or know-it-all. I always had an explanation or justification that made me look good: I'm right, so you must be wrong. Only a few select people saw my heart; the others I kept at arm's length. Because I had been following this pattern for so long, I could not see it. *We don't know what we don't know.* When someone finally had the courage to tell me, my first response was anger; in fact, I was so furious that I picked up an object and *threw* it across the room—not characteristic for a nice girl. But completely understandable for an ego whose cover has been blown. My anger was directed toward the person who delivered the message, and, predictably, I wanted to kill the messenger. Normally I would have done that through gossip—but, in this case, I did not. Instead, I just sat with the message, letting it soak in.

Today when I become angry, that old pattern re-emerges, but now I accept it—so when someone says I'm judgmental and condescending, as someone recently did, I know it's time to step back and let go of something that is irritating me.

Jim Collins (2001) tells the stories of companies that sustain success, over time, says they are headed by "Level 5" leaders who possess "personal humility." They are not superstars. You probably would not recognize their names. In many cases they have had:

> "...significant life experiences that might have sparked or furthered their maturation... A strong religious belief or conversion might also nurture development of Level 5 traits" (p. 37).

> "Speaking the truth in love, we will in all things grow up into him who is the Head, that is, Christ." (Ephesians 4:15)

Not too long ago, I had lunch with an executive in state government. I asked her if she ever had to deal with big problems that, had they been addressed in the beginning, would have been little problems. She said, "All the time!" Then she told me that on that very afternoon mediation would be taking place in her agency. "At the outset," she said, "one person was upset. Now four people are upset. Two of them went home yesterday, sick. I wasn't sure they would even be able to participate in the mediation today."

I noted the cost this escalation had incurred. First, the time and productivity lost by the four participating in the mediation. Second, the expense of the mediation process. Finally, energy and opportunity lost to the organization from the inception of the problem through its escalation.

Then I asked, "What needed to happen in the beginning to prevent all of this?"

Her answer was, "People get promoted to managers' positions because they are very good at something valuable. But they don't always know how to manage people. They just aren't able to do it." I've heard this response from so many different people that I believe it's a "worm" in the system— insidious, invisible, and blocking progress.

The belief that nothing can be done is the reason that nothing gets done. When the bad situation reaches the breaking point, people confront it because they have no choice. By that time, everyone is working out of anger or fear. This is the work of the ego. Words spoken from an angry, fearful state of mind are usually not accepted. But there is a better way— humility. Rudyard Kipling's much-loved poem "If" is about humility.

"If"

> If you can keep your head when all about you
> Are losing theirs and blaming it on you;
> If you can trust yourself when all men doubt you,
> But make allowance for their doubting too;
> If you can wait and not be tired by waiting,
> Or being lied about, don't deal in lies,
> Or being hated, don't give way to hating,
> And yet don't look too good, nor talk too wise:
>
> If you can dream — and not make dreams your master;
> If you can think — and not make thoughts your aim;
> If you can meet with Triumph and Disaster
> And treat those two imposters just the same;
> If you can bear to hear the truth you've spoken
> Twisted by knaves to make a trap for fools,
> Or watch the things you gave your life to, broken,
> And stoop and build 'em up with worn-out tools;
>
> If you can make one heap of all your winnings
> And risk it on one turn of pitch-and-toss,
> And lose, and start again at your beginnings
> And never breathe a word about your loss;
> If you can force your heart and nerve and sinew
> To serve your turn long after they are gone,

And so hold on when there is nothing in you
Except the Will which says to them: "Hold on!"

If you can talk with crowds and keep your virtue,
Or walk with kings — nor lose the common touch,
If neither foes nor loving friends can hurt you,
If all men count with you, but none too much;
If you can fill the unforgiving minute
With sixty seconds' worth of distance run —
Yours is the Earth and everything that's in it,
And — which is more — you'll be a Man, my son!

Transformative Power of Truth in Love

On March 12th, 2005 a young woman in Atlanta, Georgia made headlines. An escaped convict, Brian Nichols, sought refuge in her apartment after a killing spree that included killing a judge who was sitting in his courtroom. Nichols gagged Ashley Smith as he had done to victims before her, and bound her in her bathtub[10]. But instead of raping or killing her, as he had done to others, he set her free and prepared to turn himself in. What happened?

During the seven hours they were together, Ashley did several things. She told Nichols the story of how her young husband had died in her arms of stab wounds. She told him about her young daughter who would have no parents at all if he killed her. She read to him from a book entitled *The Purpose-Driven Life* by Rick Warren. A previous victim pointed out to the media that she, also, had quoted scripture and talked to Nichols about God, to no avail. What made the difference this time?

Only Brian Nichols knows the answer to that question. But my best guess is that Ashley Smith touched his heart. She listened to him. Having experienced violence before she knew her own vulnerability, which is a form of humility. She spoke the truth in love and enlightenment—the fruit of humility—came.

Many people have attributed the outcome of this encounter to the book from which Ashley Smith read. Some have even said she gave him crystal methamphetamine, to subdue him. However, the story is very similar to a situation that happened on November 1st, 2000. A 15-year-old boy in a Dallas suburb came to school with a a loaded 9mm Sig Sauer pistol taken from a locked box belonging to his stepfather[11]. He held a class hostage for

---

[10] http://en.wikipedia.org/wiki/Ashley_Smith

[11] "Teen in school hostage case to stand trial as juvenile - Carrollton boy accused of holding teacher, classmates at gunpoint". *The Dallas Morning News*. 12/19/2000.

25 minutes. He released a few of the hostages and then turned to the teacher, who was four months pregnant with twins. "You can go." he said.

The teacher said, "No." Then she went on. "I'm really scared. I want to live to see these babies. But I also want to help you. What can I do to help you?" Within a few minutes the young man had put down the gun and the crisis was over. This teacher's behavior was truly remarkable. In a situation when she might have been completely focused on herself, she was able to see the young man's needs and speak in a manner that conveyed compassion and forgiveness to him. Truth, spoken in humility, is powerful.

Both of these young women exhibited what many talk about but few have—courage. The root word from which "courage" comes means "heart." To speak from the heart requires courage. To speak from the heart without being self absorbed, keeping one's focus as much on the other person's well being as one's own, is humility. The calmness that comes from humility allows people to walk right through their fears and gives them the state of mind to do their best thinking. Who knows? Maybe the phenomenon of the mirror neurons then works to allow the other person to lay down their fears and do their own best thinking as well.

Your Highest and Best—The Authentic Profile

Most of us would like to be living from our highest and best selves—as these two women were—not just in times of crisis, but as a normal way of being. One way of aligning our daily lives with the highest and best within us is to create an Authentic Profile. Here's how.

The Interview

Choose someone to interview you and make notes as you answer the following questions. Perhaps then you will reciprocate with each of you interviewing the other for the purpose of developing your Authentic Profile:

1. Whom do you admire? Your list may contain real or fictional people of any gender, any nationality, any race, any period in history. These may be famous people or those you actually know. As you call each name, explain what you admire about this person. Make your explanation complete; that is, keep talking until you feel you have said everything you truly need to say. Continue to list as many people as you can think of, until you find yourself repeating what you admire about them.

2. When people tell you why they value you, what do you say?

3. What is your greatest success? Tell the story—everything you truly need to say. What did you learn from that success?

4. What is your greatest failure? Tell the complete story and what you learned from this failure.

5. Do you have any favorite quotations—sayings or verses that guide you, especially in troubled times, and keep you on course? What are they? If you have many favorites, choose only 2 or 3 that first come to mind.

6. What are 3-5 big goals for the rest of your life?

Creating the Profile

What we admire in other people is also present within us. If we didn't have the trait, how would we even know what it is when we see it in others? This is true of others' faults as well as their virtues. But the Authentic Profile is about our highest and best, so we claim the virtues. One dominant characteristic will float to the top of the list and it leads the Authentic Profile. Combine and bullet the answers to questions 1 and 2.

You will see how to place the remaining information into the Authentic Profile from the examples in Figs. 8-4 (a) and (b) by using one of the certificate templates in Microsoft *Publisher.*

Once created, the Authentic Profile becomes a touchstone to keep us on track. It's easy to get lost out there in the world, so it's nice to have something tangible to bring us back to ourselves when we feel pulled toward something that is not authentic for us. Then, we may align our daily lives with the highest and best that is within us—being the "right size."

Tool for Course Correction: Lifeline

You may be saying, "All this is well and good, but where is the *action?* How can I know for sure I am accomplishing my divine purpose?" Try this simple tool. How old do you think you will be when you die? If you have no idea, then think of your own family. How long have your relatives lived, especially those you greatly admire? Factor in advances in modern medicine, adding a few years. Now what is your best guess? Let's say 105 for purposes of discussion.

Now imagine that it is the eve of your death. Your head is clear and you are filled with gratitude for the life you have lived. You have no regrets. You did everything you truly wanted to do. You fulfilled your purpose. Now, write what you did, in list form. Make the list complete.

Now come back to today. How many decades do you have left? Use the timeline in Fig. 8-5 on p. 128 and list under each decade what you will do towards fulfilling your life. This work is not permanent; you can change it as you achieve new understanding of your Authentic Self and what brings you joy. In fact, the very act of writing it puts into motion an internal process that will start moving you toward the life that is most fulfilling for you.

Now you have an Authentic Profile—the highest and best within you—and a plan for action. These tools establish a sort of boundary for living your life, making it manageable and keeping you on course.

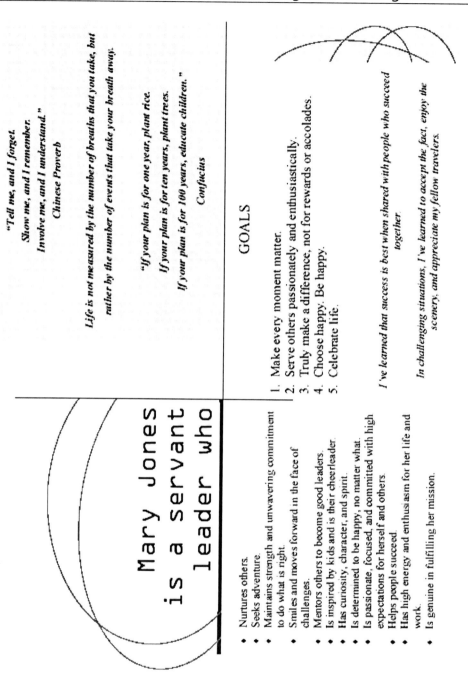

"Tell me, and I forget.
Show me, and I remember.
Involve me, and I understand."
Chinese Proverb

Life is not measured by the number of breaths that you take, but rather by the number of events that take your breath away.

"If your plan is for one year, plant rice.
If your plan is for ten years, plant trees.
If your plan is for 100 years, educate children."
Confucius

GOALS

1. Make every moment matter.
2. Serve others passionately and enthusiastically.
3. Truly make a difference, not for rewards or accolades.
4. Choose happy. Be happy.
5. Celebrate life.

I've learned that success is best when shared with people who succeed together.

In challenging situations, I've learned to accept the fact, enjoy the scenery, and appreciate my fellow travelers.

Mary Jones
is a servant
leader who

- Nurtures others.
- Seeks adventure.
- Maintains strength and unwavering commitment to do what is right.
- Smiles and moves forward in the face of challenges.
- Mentors others to become good leaders.
- Is inspired by kids and is their cheerleader.
- Has curiosity, character, and spirit.
- Is determined to be happy, no matter what.
- Is passionate, focused, and committed with high expectations for herself and others.
- Helps people succeed.
- Has high energy and enthusiasm for her life and work.
- Is genuine in fulfilling her mission.

Fig. 8–4a: Example of an Authentic Profile

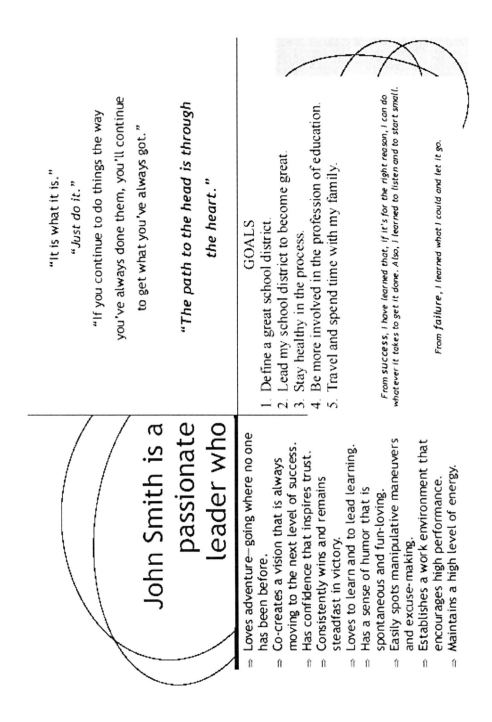

"It is what it is."

"Just do it."

"If you continue to do things the way you've always done them, you'll continue to get what you've always got."

"The path to the head is through the heart."

GOALS

1. Define a great school district.
2. Lead my school district to become great.
3. Stay healthy in the process.
4. Be more involved in the profession of education.
5. Travel and spend time with my family.

From success, I have learned that, if it's for the right reason, I can do whatever it takes to get it done. Also, I learned to listen and to start small.

From failure, I learned what I could and let it go.

John Smith is a passionate leader who

⇑ Loves adventure—going where no one has been before.
⇑ Co-creates a vision that is always moving to the next level of success.
⇑ Has confidence that inspires trust.
⇑ Consistently wins and remains steadfast in victory.
⇑ Loves to learn and to lead learning.
⇑ Has a sense of humor that is spontaneous and fun-loving.
⇑ Easily spots manipulative maneuvers and excuse-making.
⇑ Establishes a work environment that encourages high performance.
⇑ Maintains a high level of energy.

Fig. 8–4b: Example of an Authentic Profile

Decade	What I Accomplished!
95	
85	
75	
65	
55	
45	
35	
25	

Fig. 8-5: Construct the Timeline of Your Life

Exercise 8-1: Reflection

What was happening in the first five years of your life?

What did you love to do?

What were you good at?

What did you do when you didn't get what you wanted?

What did you want that you did not get?

How do these experiences still shape your behaviors and actions today?

9 Thread the Eye of the Needle

Most of us, in spite of our ardent efforts to get more, settle for too little. We resign ourselves to unacceptable situations believing that there are some things we just have to put up with—things that cannot be changed. We look at other people's behaviors as fixed, failing to consider what they and we might be able to learn. While we *say* that we believe people can change, our actions often contradict our words.

Challenging Assumptions

I was invited to a small gathering of business owners who meet regularly to share experiences and help each other through the tough issues that come with owning your own business. The tough issue they wanted help with was confronting unacceptable behavior in their workplace. One of the owners told me about rage attacks of his business partner. The partner would "blow up" at employees, leaving them frightened, confused, or just plain fed up. As he described the problem, this owner said, "I don't want to change his God-given personality." His words took my breath away. For a moment I paused to recover. Then I said, "Rage is not given by God. The personality is not God given but created by the human ego. The attributes God gives are kindness, compassion, truth, and love."

The meeting facilitator, who knew the partner with the problem, intervened. "That's right," he said. "And he is basically a very kind guy." At this the owner nodded, so I knew it was true.

"Well then," I said, "You might say something like, 'When I know how kind you can be, yet I see you raging at people, it makes me very sad. I wish you could choose kindness instead of anger.'"

All around the table the other business owners nodded. Apparently my words rang true for them. I don't know what the business owner with the raging partner decided to do. I had challenged one of his basic assumptions and people cannot be expected to embrace a new way of thinking at once.

The assumption that people won't change prevails in all types of business and industry. Only a few weeks later I heard a similar story from a chief executive in a different industry who was expending a significant amount of emotional energy on one employee who was not performing well. The employee's behavior was gossipy and glum, her words often laced with plenty of sarcasm. Since sarcasm is a symptom of anger, I wondered what this young employee was angry about. The chief executive explained that the employee's previous manager had been dishonest, deceiving the company and using its resources to build his own private business on company time. Because this manager was adept at hiding what he was doing, the chief executive did not catch on for a long time. In fact, she trusted him and confided in him. During that time, the employee-who-was-now-a-problem was witnessing her manager's self-serving behavior. Eventually the truth came out, the errant manager was fired, the employee received a new boss, and the chief executive handled the trauma by simply saying, "Let's put this behind us and move on." Although this dismissal was an attempt to wave away the damage that had been done, months later not even the chief executive had been able to recover fully from the wounds. And by her actions, the young employee revealed she was still suffering as well.

When pressed about why she was *still* willing to tolerate the unacceptable performance of an employee, the chief executive dismissed the young woman's behavior as her *personality*, a set of immutable traits. When I asked what might happen if the chief executive confronted the inappropriate behavior by speaking from her heart she said she wouldn't do it for fear of a lawsuit. Following the example set by the leader, people in the organization walked on eggshells, resentful and hopelessly resigned to the belief that this is just how some people are.

The executive's question to me was, "How can I motivate her to change her attitude?" What this executive really wanted is a workplace where people thrive—one in which employees are safe from venomous gossip about their co-workers, which elevates the possibility that they may be gossiped about as well. She wanted a workplace where people don't play the roles of victim, scapegoat, perpetrator, or favored one—roles that sap energy and prevent people from fulfilling responsibility as completely as they might were they not expending energy to play these roles.

Workplaces Where People Thrive

In workplaces where people thrive, change is learning made manifest. Everyone takes responsibility to learn and change continuously and incrementally. People freely share what they are learning for the purpose of giving information that helps their co-workers understand them. In a previous position I had an attractive, intelligent, energetic assistant who was always eager to produce good results. One day I was contemplating sending a letter to a group of constituents; in fact, I drafted it and gave it to this assistant to improve. When I handed it to her, I said, "I'm not sure I want to send this at all, but see what you can do with it." Later that afternoon, her improved version was on my desk. I read it and decided it would be better not to send this particular letter at all; it wasn't needed. Just before the end of the day I walked into my assistant's office with the letter in my hand. "I've decided not to send this, after all," I said, beginning to tear it in half to discard it.

Just as I had begun to tear, I saw the horror-stricken look on her face. I stopped, placing the letter on the corner of her desk. Thinking the matter was settled, I left her office. When she came in the next morning, this young woman, obviously upset, did not speak to me. I decided to address her behavior immediately, calling her into my office. We sat side by side as I said, "I noticed you didn't speak this morning, and you seem upset. I value the friendly working relationship we have always had and I want it back. If I've done anything to cause this, I hope you'll tell me what it is so that I can correct it."

She told me how insulted she had been that I rejected the letter she had revised for me—that I had even started to tear it.

I apologized. Now that I knew how offensive this action was to her, I wouldn't repeat it. But, because her reaction seemed disproportionate to the offense, I wanted more information so I asked, "Is there a story here? What has led you to have such a strong feeling about this?"

The story was that until she was nine years old she had lived in a different country, the affluent child of prominent parents. She was an outstanding student in an exclusive private school. Then her circumstances changed and she moved to the U.S. with her mother who enrolled her in public school. Because her ability to speak and write English was limited she was assigned to an English-as-a-Second-Language program where she was treated, in her estimation, as if she were stupid. A teacher told her she couldn't write and tore up her work.

With those words I completely understood the enormity of my offense. Also, I now had information that would help me not touch this old wound in any way ever again.

Today, with the benefit of these intervening years, I realize that I could have prevented the whole incident if I had been more judicious in asking her to revise the letter in the first place. When I gave the task to her I wasn't sure I really wanted to do it. A better decision would have been for me to put my draft on the corner of my own desk until I knew for sure what I wanted to do before I wasted the valuable time of another person. However, my imperfection opened the door to a conversation that increased both understanding and trust. In perfection there's no learning.

Some people might say, "But that's personal and inappropriate for the workplace."

To these people I say, "Neurons are connected. Our brains and body memory systems don't have separate compartments labeled business and personal. To our human system it's all the same."

And I have one more point to make about this topic: Our conversation took no more than five minutes, yet the trust it built was greater than if we had spent a whole week-end in teambuilding exercises. This one conversation removed the resistance that had already begun. People must develop the courage to confront these situations as they arise, while they are still relatively simple to resolve. Left alone, resistance builds as one unresolved offense is added to another. Once-good relationships erode and resentment prevails. Work slows. Energy drains. Everybody feels it.

In workplaces where people thrive, *people know the big picture and how they fit into it.* The values and vision of the organization align with their own. When you get on an airplane, you know your destination and stops, if any, along the way. A few times during your flight, the pilot will say something like, "We're approaching Portland. From the right side of the plane, you can see Mt. Hood." People have a basic, innate need to answer the question, "Where am I?" When we don't know, we become edgy or agitated. Like a 5-year-old in the back seat of a car we want to know, "Are we almost there?" This truth holds for any trip we take—geographical or otherwise. Many of the problems I see in the workplace arise because people don't know where they are on the organization's route to success. They become irritable and symptoms of their distress surface in the form of gossip, rumors, tension, and conflict. Confusion reigns and employees' highest and best is not available to serve the organization. In workplaces where people thrive, leaders know who they truly are and continuously align their work with the highest and best within them and within the organization or business plan. The best and highest desired by the organization is a compatible fit for the best and highest within its leaders.

In workplaces where people thrive, *human energy is sacrosanct.* People do nothing to diminish others' energy, and they look for ways to enjoy more energy with less effort. For the last five years I have been collecting data from an Energy Analysis® in which I ask people what gives them energy and what takes it away. Overwhelmingly other people's behavior is the top-rated energy depleter, at least five times stronger than any other factor. What in the world is going on here?

The Principle of Non-locality—In 1964, physicist John Stewart Bell proposed a now-famous theorem showing that the predictions of quantum mechanics are not intuitive. Arntz, Chasse, and Vincente (2005) express Bell's theorem eloquently:

> "...you arrange to have two particles created at the same time, which means they would be entangled, or in superposition. You shoot them off to opposite sides of the universe. You then do something to one particle to change its state; the other particle instantaneously changes to adopt a corresponding state... The idea of something being local, or existing in one place, is incorrect. Everything is non-local. The particles are intimately linked on some level that is *beyond time and space.*" (p. 59)

Mirror Neurons—According to Kenneth L. Thompson (2001):

> "Giacomo Rizzolatti and his partners... have discovered a collection of neurons in higher primates that light up when an action is merely *observed*... Dubbed *mirror neurons,* these cells fire when we watch someone else perform an action, say picking up an apple... If a dozen people are in a room with a single apple, only one person can pick up and taste the fruit, but 11 brains will mimic the action and activate salivary glands to begin digestion... With the discovery of mirror neurons, we now have tangible evidence that one person's emotional state will affect the entire group."

The human brain manifests Bell's theorem through *mirror neurons*. It makes sense, doesn't it? If you can choose to be in the presence of a person who affirms you and others and wants the best for other people, or in the presence of a person who complains, criticizes, gossips, and exudes negative energy, what will your choice be? Unless you have masochistic tendencies, you'll choose the positive. Why? Because you *feel* better in the presence of positive energy as you *mirror* the energy-giving brain chemistry associated with sincere positive emotion. In the presence of negativity, by contrast, your brain actually releases negative, energy-draining chemicals. Your negative thoughts either agree with those being expressed by the other person, or your negative thoughts turn toward that person in judgment and criticism. In either case, the chemistry of negativity is swirling in your brain.

It will be a giant step toward creating workplaces where people thrive when executives and managers understand and share these two bits of information from quantum physics and neuroscience with all employees stressing the necessity of taking responsibility for being aware of one's own state of mind, making positive inner changes, and using tools like the Eye of the Needle, which I'll explain within the next few pages.

From Victims/Victimizers to Learners

Hindus have a term, "Namaste," which means, "The god within me greets the god within you." This concept is not new. Shakespeare wrote,

> "What a piece of work is a man! How noble in reason! How infinite in faculty! In form, in moving, how express and admirable! In action how like an angel! In apprehension how like a god! The beauty of the world! The paragon of animals!" (*Hamlet*, Act ii, Scene 2, Lines 255-58).

Centuries earlier, the Psalmist wrote,

> "When I consider your heavens, the work of your fingers, the moon and the stars, which you have set in place, what is man that you are mindful of him, the son of man that you care for him? You made him a little lower than the heavenly beings and crowned him with glory and honor." (Psalm 8:3-5 NIV)

Human beings are capable of the full range of human emotions from love to hate; we are capable of being godlike in our willingness to forgive and to want the best for others. At the same time we have amazing problem-solving abilities that come out of our forebrains. We are human yet share the mind of the divine. We know all of this about ourselves; we just don't know how to identify these diverse qualities, discipline them, and apply them correctly.

Let's return to the executive with the gossipy, sarcastic employee from earlier in this chapter. This employee's inappropriate behavior drained other people's energy as well as her own and she felt victimized, just as she had been victimized by her former manager. The executive's fear of ending up in court if she confronted the employee kept her stuck with poor morale and it kept the employee stuck in poor performance.

What might change if she called the young employee into her office and said something like, "When your previous boss was here, some things happened that shouldn't have happened, and it took me a long time to catch on. I wish I had paid more careful attention. I know that experience must have been difficult for you. Is there anything you need to hear from me that would make amends to you for enduring that difficult situation?" Then wait for her response accepting whatever she has to say and giving whatever information is truly necessary to come to a common understanding. After some conversation with both executive and employee in a peaceful state of mind the executive might say something like, "I've noticed that you sometimes use sarcasm and tell stories about employees who are not present—stories you probably would not tell if they were present. What I want is a friendly climate in which people don't have to worry about what other people are saying about them. I'd like your help in establishing this climate. Please give some thought to what I've said for a few days. Then let's talk again by the end of the week about what needs to change as we move forward. I'm open to hear whatever you have to say."

Such a conversation is both respectful and truthful. It honors confidentiality and violates no one's rights. Most importantly it opens wide the door for information that might leverage change. Maybe the executive could receive information that changes her own leadership practices.

But such a conversation did not occur. Instead, the executive, worried about a lawsuit, dealt with the matter as prescribed by the human resources department—not person to person, but boss to employee, using the right legal words and phrases. While this approach might appear to be safe, it does nothing to build relationships, nor does it consider that the problem might be systemic in nature; that is, a pattern of behavior that might have become ingrained within the organization and that will continue, changing only the names of the actors as disappointed employees leave and new people take their places.

In this case the executive felt victimized by the employee's behavior, and the employee felt victimized by the employer. In some organizations the victim/perpetrator pattern of behavior has gone on so long that there is *always* a victim or scapegoat. Maybe the original scapegoat got tired and moved on; soon he or she is replaced by the new actor who was already in the organization but wasn't playing the role until the part was available. In other words, some organizations actually make it possible for the same script to be played out even though the players and situations are different. In these instances people are playing roles, not fulfilling their responsibilities to the extent to which they are capable. This is what happens when people remain unaware or unwilling to tell the truth.

Responses based on emotion make most people uncomfortable, especially in the workplace. So we avoid any semblance of an emotional confrontation. Instead, we bypass the emotional morass and pretend that unpleasant energy isn't there forging ahead using only our logical/rational faculties and encouraging others to do the same. In this scenario the leader might be sending the message verbally or non-verbally, "Don't talk to me about feelings. What are the facts? Stick to the facts." Or "I know there are politics. I can't do anything about politics. Neither can you. What is your goal? What is your plan?" Or she can say, "Let's just put this behind us." thus disallowing any intervention in the system, ignoring the energy drain and the toll that stress is taking on productivity, goals and plans, and even affecting individual physical health.

There is a better way. We can learn to have conversations in which we increase the possibility that people will learn from each other and self-correct the behaviors which are detrimental to themselves and others. For this to occur, two qualities must be present.

Acceptance and Willingness

Knowing that we and others are capable of both greatness and smallness, we *accept* that we ourselves are susceptible to being influenced by other people's bad behavior and our own erroneous learning from prior experience. We accept that there are moments when we ourselves are at our worst, especially when we're sick, tired, or anxious. Moreover, we accept that there are some situations beyond our control; for example we cannot control another person's use of alcohol or drugs, threat of legal complaint, or life experiences. The only thing we can control, in fact, is our own response. Knowing how susceptible we are to the phenomenon of the *mirror neurons*, we can observe our own reactions, ask, "Is this how I want to be?" and choose a response that is different from the automatic one usually made.

In addition, we must be *willing*—willing to learn, to apologize when we make mistakes, and to forgive when other people err. A major obstacle to willingness is determination to prove ourselves right or to get our way or to have things turn out the way we want them. These underlying motives are so insidious that most of the time we don't even realize they are driving our thoughts, actions, and words. The first time someone asked me, "Do you think you might be trying to get your way?" I answered without hesitation, "I don't think so." It was months before I realized that was exactly what I was trying to do—get my way—while disguising it as trying to do what was best for the other person.

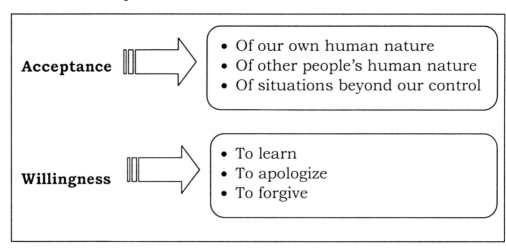

Humility as Prerequisite for Learning Conversations

If humility is being neither more nor less than we are and the root word for education is a Latin word meaning "to draw out," then in order for someone with whom we are speaking to learn something, we must not overpower leaving no space for the other person to be "drawn out." Neither must we under-perform leaving excessive space for the other person to overpower us and thus remain uninformed, reducing the likelihood of learning. Rather, aware of the energy in our own heart and respectful of the heart within the other person, we speak our truth not knowing what the response will be, but knowing we will be improved from participating fully in the conversation. As I speak I'm not angry, sad, judgmental, or critical. Instead, I am accepting of human nature and willing to do my part to improve a situation.

Faith as a Prerequisite for a Learning Conversation

According to a Fox news poll conducted in 2004 by Opinion Dynamics Corporation, 92% of Americans say they believe in God and 69% think religion plays too small a role in people's lives today; in fact, only 15% say they never attend church, synagogue, or other place of worship. Obviously we see and know ourselves to be spiritual creatures; too often, we do not discipline ourselves to align our actions with our beliefs. How well I remember a client who once told me how important her faith was to her—how much energy it gave her. Later in the conversation, as she described to me a problem she was confronting, I asked, "How do you use your faith in helping you deal with this issue?"

Blankly, she looked at me. Then realization dawned. "I don't." she said.

My next question was, "How do you think you *might* use your faith in dealing with this issue and thus reduce your stress?" Immediately she answered. She *knew* what to do; she just wasn't *doing* it.

Mother Theresa was once asked what we should do to bring about world peace. She said, "Go home and love your family." Perhaps Mahatma Gandhi said it best. "We must become the change we want to see in the world." Yet *self-discipline* is something most people are unable or unwilling to attempt or master.

Once I facilitated a conference between a manager and the organization's top executive. The manager's Authentic Profile© disclosed that she "listens well and accepts others and their choices," yet she had just related a story that revealed she wasn't even speaking to the executive because she was so angry. I pointed out the discrepancy and then asked, "So, are you out of alignment with your own profile of how you want to live your life?"

Expressionless, she answered, "Yes." That was it, but she expressed no desire for change; her need to be right in this dispute had overridden the highest and best that was within her.

To live in our highest and best, it's necessary to process through negative emotion because our egos have been forged and are manifested through strong emotion. To get beyond ego, we have to go through it. We can't simply "rise above" without confronting undesirable qualities within ourselves. We must get beyond ego and live more in alignment with the highest and best qualities within us. A very small percentage of the population is "emotionally blind"—that is, unable to access their feelings. It is possible that these processes won't work for them, but for the vast majority of people it works very well.

People don't want to confront unacceptable behavior in other people because they have not yet confronted the unacceptable qualities within themselves. Therefore they feel unworthy or unequipped. They feel guilty themselves and therefore not in a position to confront another person. They feel afraid of the strong emotion that might be released in a confrontation. They are afraid that the other person might leave. Thus, fear is in control.

A young woman confided in me that her boyfriend, with whom she is living, frequently uses illegal drugs. With words, he claims to be a recreational user who uses only about four times a year. But her observation is that he has used for the last three consecutive week-ends. A useful question for drug or alcohol abuse is: Does your drinking or using create a problem for you or someone you love? This young man's use is creating a problem for someone he loves. Their arguments are becoming more frequent and more intense. She dreads the next holiday and isn't sure what to do to take care of herself. I asked her if she thought she could ask her boyfriend to go to counseling with her to work on their relationship and learn a common language for dealing with their problem. She said, "I'm more afraid of asking him that than I am afraid of leaving him." Her own fear, not her boyfriend's drug use, holds her hostage in the relationship. Again, fear is in control.

Ego Forged Through Wayfaring

Following birth we focus on gaining control over our world. We learn to talk, walk, feed ourselves, dress ourselves, bathe ourselves, and get what we want. Later, we learn to write, to read, to run, to play with others, to pass tests, to meet expectations. We get degrees, jobs, promotions. We make a home, have children, and create a family. We find our place in our community. We get what we want based on our view of the world. This is wayfaring, making our way successfully through the challenges of the world, gradually and incrementally gaining mastery of our destiny. Through these worldly experiences, our ego forms. By ego I mean the internal adjustments we make based on our own perceptions of how to get our way in the external world.

At a conference in San Francisco a presenter who coaches executives in leadership development declared that "most leadership problems come from the ego, especially fear of judgment or criticism and the drive to prove one's extraordinary worth to self and others." From the audience a question arose. "You're talking about theory. Are you going to give us tools for getting beyond the ego?" The presenter shirked the question and went on with his *explanation of the problem.* But merely understanding ego's power is not sufficient for getting beyond it. To transcend ego there is work that must be done. The process includes three phases:

- Name the aspects of ego that are most active within you. The simplest way to do this is to identify what is draining your energy and clearly see what part you are playing in that energy depletion.

- Know who you are and what is the highest and best that is within you.

- Make daily decisions that align with your highest and best.

A Tool for Transcending Ego

You can begin to transcend the ego by listening with the ears of your heart, speaking from your heart, and learning to use a tool that I call "The Eye of the Needle."

Chris Argyris and Don Schön (1992) developed a tool called "Right-hand Column, Left-hand Column." To use this tool, you think of a conversation you have had that did not go well. Draw a vertical line down a sheet of paper; in the right-hand column write what the two of you *said* during the conversation. In the left-hand column write what you *thought.*

Next, answer these questions[12]:

- Why didn't you say what's in the left-hand column?

- What might have happened if you had said what's in the left-hand column?

---

[12] Another set of questions is available at http://www.coachingedge.com/12/two-column.htm

What *I* thought	What *we* said

Fig. 9-1: Right-hand Column, Left-hand Column

While this tool is effective in bringing the invisible to the surface, I found when I used it that some people became angry and remained stuck in that anger for days. Other practitioners more highly skilled than I had a similar experience. So for a time I stopped using this tool, although I believed it had value that remained untapped

Later, when I discovered the writing of Candace Pert (1997), I learned that 98% of our memory is emotional, stored outside of our brains, chemically bonded to peptide receptors that are distributed throughout our entire bodies. This emotional memory is lightning fast because it has been part of us for so very long. Our emotional memories begin before birth. Our brains do not finish developing their logical/rational decision-making capacity until about age 23. Along the way, through experience, we learn not to blurt out our first emotional responses to situations. Well, most of us learn this. Occasionally someone will say, "I said what was in my left-hand column!" My next question is, "And did you get good results?" Always, the answer is, "No."

Most of us have learned that what's in the left-hand column, if spoken, will not build positive relationships or serve us well in the long run. So we squelch those emotions and become very logical in our approach. In other words, the logical/rational portions of our brains overwhelm the emotional response, like a big brother or big sister trying to protect or control us. The problem with this strategy is that emotion is very powerful stuff and will not stay squelched forever: it <u>will</u> find a way to express itself. As someone said, "It came out sideways, and we ended up having an argument about something that wasn't the issue at all."

Passive-aggressive behavior is also a way that emotion finds expression. Some women, unable to express their feelings effectively to their husbands, actually use their husbands' toothbrushes to brush the toilet or have extra starch put in their shirts at the laundry. Strong emotion will find a way to express itself, so what are we to do?

First, become aware of the sensations in your body when you get into these difficult conversations. Where in your body do you feel it? Some people say they feel a tightening in their chest; others say their breathing gets shallow. Still others feel something like a fist in the gut or a tightening of the muscles in their necks and shoulders. Some say their jaw tightens; others' faces and necks get splotchy red. All of these are classic stress responses. When they are present, you know you are feeling negative emotion.

Now, think of a time when you were completely at peace—maybe on vacation watching the ocean waves rhythmically come in and go out. Maybe you were tucking the baby in bed for the night, noticing her quiet, steady, peaceful breathing. Everyone can think of such a time. When you are completely in that memory, where in your body do you feel it? Although some people will say they feel it all over, the feeling actually starts with the heart.

The heart was the first organ to form within you, in the third week after you were conceived. Research from the Institute of HeartMath® indicates that the heart has its own "brain" and can actually change the brain's chemistry (see also Chapter 7). The heart is the place where peace begins. It makes sense, doesn't it? The heart that started beating within you in your third week was completely safe, kept at a steady temperature, protected, immersed in the rhythms of its mother's body and attuned to the mother's heart. A place of peace.

With this new information, I revisited the Left-hand Column, Right-hand Column tool and created a hybrid.

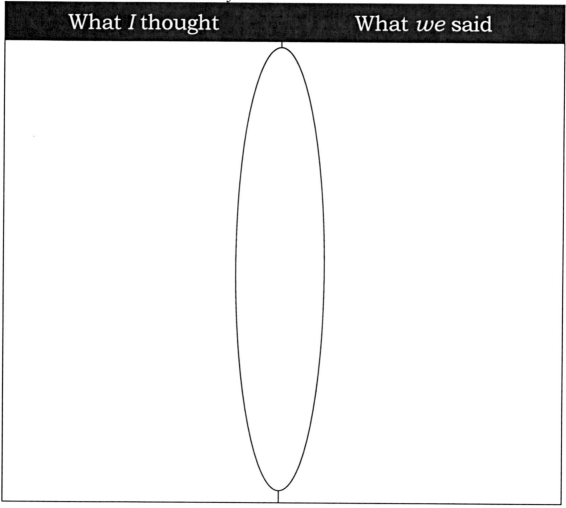

Fig. 9–2: Threading the Needle

As if you are threading a needle within you, come between logic and lower emotions such as fear and anger. Speaking from your heart, say what truly needs to be said. You don't need to worry about the words you say; this internal eye of the needle is holographic; every word that it emits contains the whole, or every possible word that might be spoken from this place. It is the energy of the heart, not the words, that carry its message of acceptance, humility, truth, love, nonjudgment, nondefensiveness, surrender, compassion, courage, willingness to learn. Your words will be completely respectful of you while simultaneously completely respecting the other person. Your intent will not be to prove yourself right or overpower. Your intent will simply be to say what truly needs to be said. This is The Eye of the Needle.

When I've watched people work with this hybrid tool and listened to their stories, I haven't heard a single instance in which the results were not good. People have applied this tool to both personal and professional situations with positive long-term outcomes. Even when the short-term results look dismal, the long-term results are good. A recent story comes from the president of a small company that makes salad dressing. The company's relationship with an important chain of grocery stores had been increasingly strained. In previous visits, the grocery had not been willing to promote the small company's product effectively and sales were declining while the grocer was raising the ante for the product to be placed in their stores.

After she learned to use The Eye of the Needle, the president of a company met with a client and conduit for sales. Calmly, from a peaceful state of mind, she showed him the bottom-line numbers and said, "You are increasing our costs, while our sales in your stores are declining. We can't afford to continue this." The client began to generate some ideas for increasing their sales, including offering free samples of the product to customers while they shopped—which the president of the company had been trying for years to be allowed to do!

The president's peace drew out a peaceful response (*mirror neurons*) from the grocery representative. Because our brains work best in a state of relaxed alertness, the greatest gift we can bring to problem-solving is peace of mind. The Eye of the Needle is a tool that helps us find that peace and increases the likelihood that we will find solutions that benefit everyone.

The Missing Piece of Leadership

Leaders are people who influence others. By that definition everyone is a leader. Starting with my position as a classroom teacher I have been a leader for four decades. In that period I remember only four occasions when people had the courage to say what was truly needed in a way that enabled me to learn and change my leadership practices. All four of the people who spoke the truth to me were men; each was a person I greatly admired.

1. Although I don't recall the specific issue, I well remember the call I took late one afternoon from a trusted colleague who said, "Nancy, every now and then, get off your white horse, walk back to the troops, and ask them how they're doing." His words went straight into my heart; I know I have a tendency to focus on the goal, to be passionate about the cause. I become a zealot, actually repelling people because my energy takes up so much space that they can't find room to participate in the cause. I know I do this, but when I'm in the fray, I can't see what I'm doing. The words of this trusted friend raised my awareness and helped me make a needed adjustment in how I was leading.

2. I do remember the specifics of the second instance when someone had the courage to speak the truth I needed to hear. With the skillful guidance of my associate, I had successfully lobbied for legislation that had passed—with the exception of one minor provision that had been left out. The zealot part of my ego took over and I found myself presenting my case in the office of a well-respected legislative leader who listened patiently for awhile and then said, "Nancy, you've won. It's time to quit." His words hit me right between the eyes. I paused for a moment, then said, "You're right. Thank you." Then I left. To this day I'm grateful that he had enough respect for me to tell me that I had pushed too far.

3. Politics swirled around a major project in which I played a key role. Desiring to be impartial and come out with the best buy-in possible, I listened to a minority voice. Without knowing it, I allowed this voice to manipulate me and unduly influence my leadership. This was the type of public gaffe that makes fodder for the gossip mill. But one of my colleagues, seeing what I was doing while believing I was capable of better, called me. He made no reference whatsoever to anything I had written or spoken; that is, he did not point out what I had done wrong. Instead, he said, "I see you're struggling with _____," naming the faction that I had allowed to manipulate me. "Several years ago, I had a similar experience. Here's what happened." He told me his story. I got the point. I made a correction.

4. The last instance of someone who spoke from the Eye of the Needle within was a conversation I had with my son during a personal cri-

sis. He called me late one evening. I do not remember a single word he said to me, but I'll never forget the love in his voice. I also remember that he said some things about me that were difficult to hear, but I listened. When he finished, I said nothing for a few moments while his message settled within. Finally, I said, "I don't have anything to say, but I want you to know that I heard everything you said." As I hung up the telephone, I was aware that something within me had shifted. Even today, I cannot put words with what happened. All I can say is that, from that moment on, my life changed for the better.

Such is the power of speaking the truth in love—The Eye of the Needle.

Conclusion

This chapter has explained a powerful tool that brings together, within the human heart, two of the most positively powerful energies known to man—truth and love. When we speak the truth in love—life, work, and relationships become easy. Now that you know how the tool works, relax and enjoy reading about different applications of this principle in the chapters that follow. Start using the tool in low-risk situations. Remember that you don't have to do it perfectly. It's not the words you speak or whether or not your voice is quavering when you say them. What people truly hear is the energy that's coming from your heart. Speak the truth in love.

Exercise 9-1: Restoring Communication

Think about someone you love but with whom communication is frequently difficult.

How would your life be different if you spoke the truth in *love*?

What would be the easiest conversation you might have with them from your heart?

By when will you have this conversation from your heart?

10 Throw away the "Chart" and Tune In

Expectations can kill possibility and destroy potential.

One day a junior high language arts teacher asked me to visit her class and make some recommendations about how she could improve discipline. She met me at the door with a seating chart on which she had written the students' names and what was "wrong" with each one of them. This one was going through parents' divorce; that one had a grandmother who just died; another had chronic allergies, etc.

In short, she had figured out a justification for each child's unacceptable behavior. The class was "going wild."

I'm not saying that the teacher was wrong to be aware of or compassionate about her students' personal situations; I am saying that she was adversely affecting their behavior by labeling her students. She was using their unfortunate circumstances to create an excuse for their bad behavior. What seemed to be at work was not *compassion,* which carries the energy of love, but *pity,* which implies the energy of regret. Abraham Lincoln urged Americans to have "malice toward none" and "charity for all." *Charity* is the love of God, which is simultaneously unconditional love and accountability for meeting standards. That is, the highest form of love doesn't allow "anything goes" behavior.

My first suggestion to this teacher was, "Throw away that chart."

What she was doing was human nature—trying to figure the students' behavior out so she could fix it. This strategy works with plumbing—and even with software—but not with human beings.

Why? The human brain has tens of billions of neurons. *Each* dendrite on a single neuron has at least 15,000 connections to other neurons. You think you're going to figure out how someone's actions are connected to their life's experiences? You won't live long enough to untangle the complexity of the electrochemical processor that we know as the human brain.

An employee once related a story about a very difficult situation with the founder-who-sold-the-company-but-stayed-on. People who heard the story immediately began formulating explanations for his behavior. "He can't give up control." etc.

"Stop analyzing," I said. "Let's just focus on what the employee might have said from a calm state of mind, using words that respect everyone involved in this incident—something like, 'What you want to do is against the law. My job is to keep this company out of court with regard to such issues.'"

The most important aspect of these difficult situations is what you are feeling while you are speaking. Be nonjudgmental, non-blaming, and non-analytical. Speak from your heart. Be compassionate and kind. Use few words. If you are thinking, "This man just can't let go." then he is picking up those judgmental vibrations and reacting. Control the only thing you have control over—your own state of mind.

Now think about the people in your world. Do you have a "chart"? Do you think you have figured out why they act the way they do? Do you react accordingly? If so, then throw away the chart. Accept that how other people act is, for the most part, beyond your understanding. Focus on acceptance, compassion, and kindness in your <u>own</u> state of mind.

You might even try a strategy that has worked for many of my clients. Think of someone you know very well with whom you would like to open up new possibilities. Write an intent just before your next encounter with that person. For example, you might write "I greet this person with genuine enthusiasm. I listen with kindness and openness. I speak my truth clearly and respectfully, with no regard for what anyone else thinks. I give my best. I find a way to appreciate and collaborate with this person that is completely comfortable for me." Notice the different results you get.

Intent Changes Attitude

A school superintendent wanted to make some changes in administrator assignments. His motivation was that he wanted to make sure principals and assistant principals were assigned so that their strengths could be used to the maximum, for the highest good of students and the school district as a whole. My assignment was to facilitate conversations that aligned each administrator's Authentic Profile© and Energy Analysis® with the needs of the organization. Simultaneously the superintendent wanted to know the highest aspirations of each administrator and what that person needed from him to achieve full career potential.

In other words the superintendent wanted to discover new possibilities from these conversations. What made the assignment so challenging was that this superintendent was a graduate of the school district he now headed and he had spent his entire career in this place. This was also true of most of the administrators who would be involved in the conversations. I felt I needed a tool with the potential to interrupt the normal expectation developed from years of working together and introduce possibility that perhaps neither had considered before. So I developed a set of intents, typed them on a sheet of paper, and then cut the page into strips with one intent on each strip. I folded the strips and placed them in a box. As each administrator entered the room for the conversation, the superintendent drew a strip which became his intent with that administrator.

Later, he told me that when I first told him about this strategy he thought it was a little weird. But it actually worked. Even though the people involved knew each other very well, these intents opened up new possibilities and at the end of the school year he was able to make new assignments with confidence and very little criticism.

Intents that Encourage Authenticity and Appreciation

Cut these statements into strips. Place the strips in a small box, and draw one out before an important conference or difficult conversation. Read it. Keep it in mind. Let your words flow from that state of mind.

In case you would like to try it, here is the set of intents we used:

- May I see a value in this person I've never seen before.
- I hear a story that opens new possibility.
- I see through the ego to the inner beauty of this person. I speak to the inner person—the authentic one.
- I'm curious about what I might learn from this person.
- With humility and the pure intent to appreciate this person, I simply listen.
- Without judgment, in a state of pure appreciation, I realize the full value of this person.
- Laying aside my past experience with this person, I stay in the present moment, seeing with new eyes.
- Give me eyes to see a small change.
- In a state of unconditional acceptance, I listen with my heart.
- I listen with my heart, and this person tells me what is needed to move to the next level of success.
- What words does this person need to hear from me?
- I simply accept this person for who he/she truly is.
- I celebrate tiny movements. I have microscopic eyes to see tiny movements in this person and celebrate them.
- What words might open the door to possibility?
- What treasure is here?
- How may I celebrate the wonder and accomplishment of this person?

- In a state of nonjudgment, I simply observe.

- Patiently I listen until the full story emerges and truth resonates.

- I find something to admire—one thing for which I can honestly affirm this person.

- I create safe space for the whole truth to come out.

- How may we do this easily and joyfully?

- I speak from my heart, and I listen with my heart.

> "Our premise is that many of the circumstances that seem to block us in our daily lives may only appear to do so based on a framework of assumptions we carry with us."
>
> Zander and Zander (2002)

Assumptions Lead to Expectations

You might have noticed that every intent I just gave as an example is "I-centered," not "you-centered." When we focus on what needs changing in the other person, we get into trouble. Instead, we set the intent for ourselves and give the other person the grace to begin with a clean slate.

Many of us have heard the warning, "When you assume, you make an *ass* out of *u* and *me*." Although crudely put, there's truth here. Assuming objectifies people. We think that, because we've had certain experiences with people exhibiting certain behavior, any other person who reminds us of that behavior will give us a similar experience. Our brains are so adept at making connections that the first hint of similarity activates all the neurons that made connection the first time. Thus, invisibly and silently, assumptions drive us without our conscious awareness and comprise the soil in which prejudice grows.

Someone once said to me, "I can tell by your body language that you are feeling defensive."

I responded, "The next time you notice what you construe as a signal from my body language, I wish you would ask me what I'm thinking." That response opened up conversation and enhanced understanding; a defensive one builds walls.

I'm frankly troubled by all the labels we throw around, as if naming something gives us control over it so that we know how to act around it. At its worst, someone sees one of our character defects and calls us by that name, as if it defines us.

I Know My Name

Dear God, I feel bruised today
From blows delivered in names that are not mine.

Names—labels—roll everything into fists and strike.
I was in the ring without gloves.

Dear God, let Truth be my guide.
I know my name.
Let me not forget.

Even the various assessments that are intended to enhance under-standing among people who work together more often give permission and information for others to predict how someone is going to respond and thus, unintentionally, provide the fodder for manipulation or minimizing potential, sometimes referred to as the "self-fulfilling prophecy." In other words, what we expect to happen, does. This can be negative or positive.

Expectations actually have the power to elicit responses without any-one's conscious awareness of what is going on. Al-Anon, a group for families and friends of alcoholics, stresses consciously keeping the focus on oneself and seeing the best in others. In *One Day at a Time in Al-Anon* (Virginia Beach: Al-Anon Family Group Headquarters, 2000), the reading for September 20 says, "It is vital to my serenity to separate, in my mind, the sickness of alcoholism from the person who suffers from it. I will dignify him with the respect which is everyone's due. This, in turn, will give him back the self-esteem that is an important element in wanting sobriety. In the words of James R. Lowell, 'The surest plan to make a Man is: *Think him so*'" (p. 264).

Zander and Zander (2002) suggest that we think of people in a way that evokes their best. In Taiwan a student ranked 68th in a class of 70. When he entered Benjamin Zander's class Mr. Zander told him he was "an A stu-dent." At first the student was confused, but ultimately he concluded "One day I discover much happier A than Number 68. So I decide I am an A" (p.32).

We must simultaneously hold two truths about people: they are capable of greatness, and they are prone to make human mistakes. But our focus is on their greatness because what we focus on gets stronger. The "needle" that must be "threaded" is that our view of others be neither too rosy nor too jaded. We do not enable people, through our attitude and actions, to remain in behaviors that are harmful to themselves or others. But truth must be spoken with the energy of respect and with intent to bring about the highest good. Benjamin Hoff (1982) writes:

> "The first thing we need to do is recognize and trust our own Inner Nature, and not lose sight of it. For within the Ugly Duckling is the Swan, inside the Bouncy Tigger is the Rescuer who knows the Way, and in each of us is something Special, and that we need to keep"

Our personalities may be altered through conscious choice as we set ourselves free from other people's expectations.

Free To Be Me

What's with these labels?
Bluestocking—zealot—overachiever—liberal

I'm all those things, sometimes.
But none all times, alone.

Don't box me.
I must be free to be me.

Labeling makes no allowance for learning and limits relationships to a narrow range. Thus, possibility is squelched and potential limited. For a time on my spiritual journey I tried to understand this duality—the person other people saw me to be and the person I felt I was. It's an ancient question. In the fifth century B. C. Socrates said, "Let the inner man and the outer man be one." As I began to look for the answer to this question, here's how it seemed:

Gods

There are two gods on this earth.
One is inside,
Permeating, forgiving, encouraging, reaching,
Speaking with our mouths, listening with our hearts.

The other
sits on some people's shoulders, saying,
"Don't." "Stop." "Hear my laws."

"Enforce my rules with vigor, sharpness, tight face, cold eyes,
And haughty, self-righteous acts."

Are there two gods? Or is one an imposter?
Are the voices outside? Or within?

The Authentic Self

Gradually my seeking brought me to the realization that, as a child, I had made adaptations to the person I truly was and that moreover these adaptations came from a brain that was not fully developed and did not yet have the capacity for understanding, compassion, or forgiveness. I found the clearest explanation of what happened to me in Zander and Zander (2002):

> "A child is an exquisite attention-getting device, designed to sound an alarm at the first indication that he will be forgotten or relegated to a position where he does not count... Nature [endows] him with enough fear and aggression... to hold on fiercely to sources of viability... assessing where the power is and learning what he must do to be accepted. A child's ability to control his position and the attention of others is critical... 'Personality' is a strategy for 'getting out of childhood alive." (p. 82).

Even while this process of building the personality through adaptation is being done, the authentic self is still present within the heart of the person. We may find who we truly are through asking ourselves the questions "What gives me joy? What do I love?"

A useful metaphor for the process that must occur in finding our authentic self is the King cake that accompanies Mardi Gras. You keep peeling past the almond paste icing and puff pastry until you find the "prize" that has been baked inside. Then you make this "central self" the "king" or voice that you listen to. The almond paste icing and puff pastry, a combination of air and non-nutritious ingredients, represent the pride that lies underneath the anger, frustration, remorse, guilt, fear, or whatever it was that created our "calculating self," the part of personality that formed to get us out of childhood safely but which is no longer needed (Zander and Zander, 2002.

The challenge is that those neuronal patterns are in place. The connections that have been made do not automatically realize that they are no longer useful. So we must thank them for bringing us to the time when we are ready to let them go and consciously embrace the person we authentically are—the one that has been in our heart since the day it started beating in the third week after conception. Martha DeMille (1956) wrote:

"There is a vitality, a life force, an energy that translates through you into action, and because there is only one of you in all of time, this expression is unique. And if you block it, it will never exist through any other medium and will be lost. The world will never see it. It is not your business to determine how good it is nor how valuable nor how it compares to other expressions. It is your business to keep it yours clearly and directly, to keep the channel open"

The Place Where Truth Lives

Out of the *calculating self* comes pride, perfectionism, people-pleasing, rebellion, stubbornness, and all the other character defects that hinder potential and possibility. Out of the *central self* comes truth. When the central self speaks, it resonates with the central self in others. It's a joyful experience. Thus, we transcend diversity, or the things that separate us, and find commonality. When we hear someone's heart speaking, our own hearts resonate, and we become one, *e pluribus unum* (out of many, one).

Some of the best-loved works of art are actually works of *heart,* with authenticity as their theme. In *The Sound of Music* (1965), Novitiate Maria returns to the convent horrified that she has fallen in love with her employer Colonel von Trapp while serving as governess to his children. She goes into isolation. The distraught children come to the convent looking for her, wanting to speak with her, but she refuses to come out. Upon hearing this, Mother Superior sends for Maria and asks for the truth. Maria tearfully confesses her love for von Trapp, expressing how much she fears not being true to God, not loving God enough, not being faithful to her vows as an initiate into the sisterhood of nuns. Wisely, Mother Superior tells Maria that she must be true to the purpose that created her. Loving Colonel von Trapp and being a mother to his children might be her true calling and by no means implies that she loves God less. Then Mother Superior sings the moving song "Climb every mountain... till you find your dream." That dream is the heart's desire.

Meeting Standards While Developing Potential

Like many educators I have sometimes been confused about how meeting standards figures into the goal of helping students develop their authentic selves, often referred to as their potential. Are standards good or bad? Developing potential has been construed by some as the removal of all external standards—unleashing human creativity. The person who helped me understand the necessity of establishing standards before releasing students to be wildly creative was Madeline Hunter who, as the principal of UCLA's lab school, observed outstanding teaching and wrote what she saw excellent teachers doing in a way that could be understood and replicated by others desiring to be excellent teachers. She told a story once of observing a class of gifted and talented students in small groups discussing how to reduce crime in their city. As she made her way from group to group she asked questions. "Is the crime rate higher in some parts of your city than others?" No one knew. In another group she asked, "What has your city already tried in its effort to reduce crime?" No one knew. To still another group she asked, "What is your city's crime rate?" No one knew. Clearly this teacher had not established the foundation for which these students' creative thinking could be grounded.

You get the picture. Standards are necessary. These students were being encouraged to use their imaginations and creativity, but standards were being completely ignored by the teacher. As Dr. Hunter told the story it was clear that these students were not being well served. By not requiring that data be used, the teacher implied that their opinions, albeit uninformed, were as good as anyone's. But all opinions, in the real world, are not equal.

No one wants to be on an airplane whose pilot does not meet standards. Or be operated on by a physician who does not know how to use the instruments. Or listen to a performance by musicians who cannot read music. Or be taught by a teacher who does not follow best teaching practices. We have to meet standards.

But we must never confuse meeting standards with developing potential, our own or that of others. There's more than one *way* to meet standards. Ideally, way that honors the authenticity in every student. It's not a cookie cutter approach, even though we're all cookies. That doesn't mean some cookies need standards and others don't. The question is: What are the standards that all students need? This question is still being grappled with. What standards comport with those of civilization while honoring the authenticity of the individual?

In Zander's words, a student is given an A just because he is. The teacher acknowledges him or her as a premium person. A grade he makes in a course is no more than how he measures at that moment against a set of standards. Educators must never confuse the two grades. Perhaps teachers could simply say to students something like:

> "Each of you is a unique and special person. I value the person you are. I give you an A as a person. It is also my job to measure how well you achieve a set of standards. The grade you make has nothing to do with the quality of person you are. Never forget that. My promise to you is that I will not forget that. I will

treat you with the respect that a premium person deserves. At the same time I want you to do as well as humanly possible as you demonstrate your mastery of the standards."

A True Story about Ego's Domination

Earlier, I shared the story of my participation in a facilitated group to demonstrate the power ego has to influence groups. That story is, once again, pertinent. The facilitator assigned an article to be read before the group convened—an article that was neither too short nor too long. The group of eight people, once convened, were first asked who had read the article. Two of us raised our hands. Then each person was given the same set of questions and asked to write the answers. Once everyone had written his or her answer the group had to agree on the best answer. What happened was eye-opening for me and changed the way I participate in a group.

The people who were loudest in their defense of their answers were those who had not read the article. Often their voices drowned out the quieter voices of the pair of us who had actually read the assignment. Of course their answers, although accepted by the group, were wrong.

Even though I was one of the two people who had read the assignment, I questioned myself, thinking "Maybe he's right" or "Maybe I misunderstood." I did this even when I knew the person speaking hadn't read the article and had no experience in the topic. Another mistake I made was thinking "We haven't let her have one yet, so it's her turn." A variation of that thinking is "I can't have my way all the time. It's time to let someone else win." My misguided sense of democracy or fairness trumped information and my faith in my own ability to read and understand.

Tune in to What?

The title of this chapter is "Throw Away the Chart and Tune In." Tune in to what? To the emotion that lies underneath your thoughts and words about other people and yourself. It is not useful to quibble over vocabulary—whether "the chart" is about *assumptions or expectations*. What is important is to realize that the ultimate communicator is the feeling behind our words. Think about an inspiring speaker you have heard. Can you remember anything this speaker said? Probably not. What you remember is how you *felt* while the person spoke. Maybe you remember a story with a profound meaning from the speech. Certainly you remember the feelings you experienced while you listened, which have become your overriding impression. Emotion is the "medium" that is the message, to recall the words of Marshall McLuhan.

My friend's father died when she was just a little girl. It was the 1950s and opportunities for her mother were very limited. People in their little town wondered how this fatherless family would survive. My friend remembers, at her father's gravesite following his funeral, that someone approached her standing beside her sister and their mother. This person, in an attempt to be kind, said, "Poor children. What will you do?"

The mother retorted, "Don't you ever talk to my children like that again. We're strong. We will be just fine."

And they were. Her mother started her own business, ultimately remarried, and reared two successful, well educated women.

Tune in to the message.

Chapter 10 Exercises

10-1. Think of a memory or a current situation that is not positive. Write the story in the space below.

10-2. Now, reframe and rewrite the story from a forgiving heart.

11 Set a Boundary and Set Yourself Free

From the time we are in the womb we are affected by our environment. The expectant mother and unborn child share the same cells. A nursing mother eats Mexican food or too many chocolate chip cookies, and she is up with that baby all night. Child psychologists say it isn't until age two, "the terrible twos," that a child begins in earnest the process of pulling away, differentiating himself as an independent creature.

But many of us remain unconsciously dependent. We depend on the opinion of others for our own self-esteem. Or we depend on our wealth, or lack thereof. We depend on our work to give us a sense of worth. Or our degrees. Or how we look. Not many people have been reared so flawlessly by their parents that they don't advance into adulthood without dependence on something for their sense of well being. The NBC home video entitled *Mary: Mother of Jesus* (1999) suggests that Jesus' power was possible because of his mother's rearing. The video jacket says "[Mary] is the quintessential mother figure whose undying strength and love change civilization forever." Jesus, then, only cared what God thought of him and became fully his Authentic Self—the person God created him to be, fulfilling his divine purpose.

But the rest of us have had mothers who were not Mary. So we have some "gaps" in our development that lead us to be shaped by our environment, not our own inner sense of what is right for us. Like fish swimming in water, we are unaware of the water and so *conform* ourselves to *survive*. Our *personalities* thus form, as explained in Chapter 10, "to get us out of childhood alive" (Zander, p. 96).

The Effect of Environment

Perhaps our fascination with genetics has led us to underestimate the effect that environment has on our well being. Frequently people shrug their shoulders and say "It must be genetic" to explain away something about themselves. Similarly we explain inappropriate behavior away with "It's just her personality," i.e. it can't be changed. (See Chapter 9) But through a new science called *epigenetics* we now know that genes are actually controlled by their environment. To extrapolate this finding to human interactions, how we behave is determined by our environment, both within and without, and we *can* change.

Cellular biologist Bruce Lipton (2005) writes:

"Our beliefs control our bodies, our minds and thus our lives... The fully conscious mind trumps both nature and nurture". So our *beliefs*, not our *surroundings,* are our true *environment* and "life is a cooperative journey among powerful individuals who can program themselves to create joy-filled lives" (p. 29).

For most of us this statement sounds reasonable enough. We might remember Dante's words from *The Divine Comedy* "The mind is its own place, and in itself can make a hell of heaven—or a heaven of hell." Or perhaps we've read Viktor Frankl's book *Man's Search for Meaning*—one of whose conclusions is that the ultimate freedom is the freedom to choose one's attitude. Now science is affirming what philosophy and the arts have known all along.

Is This Paradise—Or Not?

Two young women both worked at exactly the same job in a diving company on one of the islands in the Caribbean. They both had grown up in the same European country. One had come to this island out of love for her seven-year-old daughter who had asthma in her native country. She had moved with her daughter to this arid island so that her child could breathe more easily and in my interview with her she frequently expressed gratitude for the air quality. She worked in the dive shop where tourists paid for tee shirts and other souvenirs as well as diving fees and equipment rental. But what she really wanted was to be the captain of the boat that took the divers out to sea. Her dream required certification for which she had little time because she was balancing job and motherhood. So on her day off she came to work—not in the dive shop—but on the boats understudying with certified captains, preparing to make her dream come true.

I was sitting in the outdoor restaurant across the canal from the boat dock on the day she took her maiden voyage. My waitress, thrilled with her friend's accomplishment, told me the rest of the story. This budding captain's first job on the island had been as a waitress in that very restaurant. Day in, day out, she had watched the boats leaving for the open sea. One day she said, "I'm going to become a captain." She quit her job in the restaurant to work for the dive company, beginning in the shop. Today, for the first time, she was at the helm of a boat. My whole body tingled as I realized I was watching a dream come true.

The second young woman who worked in the same dive shop told me quite a different story. She had come to the island to have a good time. Strikingly attractive, she told me through her sobs how disappointed she had been with her relationships on the island, one of which had been especially abusive. "But," she said, "I don't want to go back home. I want to stay here. I like the scenery. I like island life." She went on to say how bitterly disappointed she was with her job. "They make me work in the shop. What I want is to be a captain, but they won't give me time off to learn how."

I asked, remembering how the other young woman with the same dream had managed to learn how to be a captain, "What about your day off?"

Wide-eyed, she looked at me. "That's my time off." she said.

The second young woman was unhappy; the first, almost ecstatic. In fact, the fledgling captain said, "Some people are very unhappy here. I don't understand. Look around us." she said, and my eyes followed the sweep of her hand outward toward blue, blue waters. "We live in Paradise!"

The Consciousness Imperative

One of the challenges of childhood is to distinguish ourselves increasingly from our surroundings and the people in them. Becoming clearer and clearer about who we *truly* are. Learning to listen to an *inner* voice saying what is right for us. Sadly, many people never make the complete transition from childhood to adulthood—from being controlled and defined by circumstances outside ourselves—from saying what other people expect us to say to speaking our own truth—from making choices that conform to a unique authenticity. In the words of Henry David Thoreau (1854) "The mass of men lead lives of quiet desperation." That is, they are unconscious of what they are doing.

We allow our *surroundings* to affect our internal environment. Our stress rises when we encounter a difficult boss. We let an unreasonable person "pull us off our game." We shut the door and shut down, stifling our inner voice. If we were *conscious* that what is happening is only what we *allow*, then perhaps we would make different choices. Therefore *consciousness* is an imperative if we want to live authentic, fulfilling lives. Using Lipton's (2005) words:

> "To fully thrive, we must not only eliminate the stressors but also actively seek joyful, loving, fulfilling lives that stimulate growth processes" (p. 147).

This challenge is easy to meet at a retreat of like-minded people. But how do you do it in the diverse workplace or the troubled home? And how in the world do you do it when you are in the presence of people whose inner environment is awash in the chemistry of addiction?

The Problem of Addiction

Any action we take to thwart our own emotional processing can become addictive. An emotionally healthy adult who feels pain will ask questions like "Where is this pain coming from? Is it actually an old memory that has outlived its usefulness? What am I afraid of? Do I need to forgive someone? Have I accepted forgiveness for myself?" They journal, spend some time in solitude or prayer until they reach understanding and acceptance. Then they let go of the pain and move on with new learning and awareness that will help the next time they feel uneasy.

But many people make the choice, when they feel pain, to make it go away by doing something that brings them *pleasure.* Ironically they don't actually replace pain with pleasure; they simply *overlay* pleasure on top of the pain. Unlike those who recognize the need to process feelings as described above, these people become addicted to all manner of activities—work, religion, internet pornography, eating, drinking alcohol, gambling, exercise, taking drugs, shopping, codependency, sex, spending or hoarding money. The list of things to which people can become addicted seems endless. Experts say that all forms of addiction actually arise from four core addictions: sensation, security, control, and suffering (Eick, 1998).

Addiction to alcohol is by far the most prevalent of all addictions and it is the one I see most often in my work with people and organizations. The jewel of most bars is the array of colorful bottled liquids, usually tiered and lighted to sparkle and reflect against the mirrored wall behind, enhancing the attraction. In the U.S. culture, drinking is a practice that is common. Upscale, it marks one as a person of taste and sophistication. It is a perk of "the good life."

Although potent, ethyl alcohol as a drug does not carry the warnings required of other over-the-counter drugs. While even antihistamines are required to display a printed warning not to operate machinery after taking them, alcohol comes with little on the label besides its exotic name. Yet most child abuse occurs after an adult significant to the child has been drinking, with statistics ranging from 40% to 80%. It is estimated that in two-thirds of cases of violence by a current or former spouse, boyfriend or girlfriend, alcohol is a factor; and the U.S. Department of Justice estimates alcohol is involved in 40% of violent crimes in the U.S.

In the case of children whose adult caregivers abuse alcohol, the damage that is created is tantamount to a "chemical spill" in these children's brains, mirroring the chaos that alcohol creates in the adult brain and adversely affecting them for the rest of their lives. Throughout childhood windows of opportunity for learning open at pivotal times. Through *imitation* children learn not only physically and mentally but also socially and emotionally. If an adult they love is intoxicated, children are likely to experience emotional confusion akin to the chaos in an intoxicated brain. When they are not yet old enough to differentiate between drunkenness and sobriety, the normal learning process is disrupted. They may become confused or angry.

One result is that trust may not develop at the appropriate time with significant adults and might not ever be learned. Another result is that, because they are not yet old enough to *understand and verbally express* the emotion of anger, it simmers within them—maybe even for the rest of their lives. ("[Parents], provoke not your children to wrath." Ephesians 6:4, KJV*)*. Moreover, instead of developing confidence and assurance, willingness to take risks and learn, these children's brains are bathed in the chemistry of anxiety and learn to be unsure and wary. Hypervigilant, these children often exhibit a wide array of disorders including learning disabilities and even the increasingly common malady, attention deficit disorder (ADD). Such disorders may affect other children in the family for years to come. In fact, the family might never recover.

Daniel G. Amen, M.D. (2001) specializes in treating ADD. Using Single Photon Emission Computed Tomography (SPECT), a nuclear technology that tracks blood flow and activity patterns in the brain, he has identified six different types of ADD. His studies reveal that Type 3, Over-focused ADD, is common in children and grandchildren of alcoholics. The anterior cingulate gyrus, the brain's "gearshift," is overactive in these people giving them a "tendency to get stuck or locked into negative thoughts and behaviors" (pp. 101-2). I read Dr. Amen's book after a young man close to me was diagnosed with ADD. From the brief descriptions in the beginning of the book, I identified Type 3 as his malady even before I read about its connection with the family disease of alcoholism. The young man's grandfather was an alcoholic.

In this most advanced of civilizations, we require companies that cause chemical spills in the environment to clean up the mess. Yet we remain completely silent about chemistry in the *brain's environment* that adversely affects *generations*. I wonder if adults would make different decisions if, when they purchased alcohol, the seller were required to hand them a card that said something like this:

> **Warning:** The beverage you are purchasing contains alcohol, which for at least 1 in 10 people is addictive. You know you are addicted if you crave it, can't stop drinking once you've started, experience anxiety or shakiness during periods when you are not drinking, or develop the need for increasing amounts of liquor over time.

> Do not drink too much in the presence of children or other loved ones. Most child abuse and family violence occurs because of loss of control due to excessive use of alcohol. Keep yourself and those you love safe from "chemical spills."

Furthermore, I wonder how the statistics might change if alcohol manufacturers, distributors, and vendors were footing the bill for at least 50% of what it costs to shelter, rehabilitate and educate the victims of abuse by intoxication and paid most of the costs for special learning needs of affected children.

Alcoholism, according to the American Medical Association, is a disease not a moral issue. It distorts the ego or personality to an extreme that makes it very difficult for the person afflicted to get in touch with his or her Authentic Self. Because so many uninformed people think it is shameful to be afflicted with the disease of alcohol, alcoholics "cover up" their symptoms. That's a nice way of saying they lie. In fact, members of AA have a saying: "Do you know how to tell if an alcoholic is lying? His mouth is open." The lie begins with the need to cover up the habit; then lying itself becomes habitual.

Someone afflicted with this disease is not emotionally able to speak the truth and probably is not able to experience love. Alcohol has "medicated" emotion making this person seem distant, unavailable, or even cruel. His or her brain chemistry has been so affected that desirable states of mind and heart are simply too far out of reach. The central tool of this book is the *Eye of the Needle* which is a tool for speaking the truth in love. How does this tool apply in the case of alcoholism which may constitute anywhere from 10% to 25% of the problems in the workplace and home, thus posing challenges for leaders?

The Problem

More than a year ago a human resources director called about a problem with a manager. I agreed to interview the manager and his assistant and determine what course of action, if any, should be taken. In the interview, both the manager and then his assistant expressed a desire for a cohesive, friendly, respectful atmosphere—one that enhances morale. But they were dealing with several problems, the most obvious of which was employee turnover. The manager and assistant described the culture as one of blaming, mistrust, fear, lack of communication, high expectations, low support and scarcity. Emotional and reactive behavior dominated. It was clear to me that people were playing roles, most notably hero and scapegoat, instead of fulfilling responsibilities and communicating with honesty and kindness.

Throughout the interview I observed that the manager's face was flushed and his eyes bloodshot. Moreover, he seemed rigid with comments like "If we make a mistake, we can't correct it." Since these symptoms often accompany alcoholism, I decided in my debriefing with the human resources director, to ask, "Is there a possibility that the manager might be an alcoholic?"

When I asked this question the human resources director almost fell out of her chair. When she recovered she said, "On a recent trip to a conference, he drank so much one evening at dinner that he blacked out."

When I heard that I was able to say with confidence, "The problem is alcoholism, and the problems you are experiencing with the department are not going to go away until that problem is addressed."

I developed a proposal that included an intervention with the manager as well as cleanup for the damage that had been created in the department.

But the organization took no action—until a year later when threats of formal complaints were made and one of the HR assistants conducted a SWOT analysis[13]. So called because it analyzes Strengths, Weaknesses, Opportunities and Threats, the SWOT analysis revealed many of the same issues I had found and reported a year earlier, including rumors about the manager's drinking. Employees suspected he was even drinking on the job. Vendors reported the manager had been verbally abusive to them. Again I submitted a proposal and a meeting with an executive at a higher level than the human resources director was scheduled. When I arrived for the meeting, however, that executive had taken the day off.

The organization wished this problem would go away—or that it was something else. They preferred to wait for incontrovertible evidence. More than a year after the Human Resources director's first call, nothing had changed. No one in the workplace was ready to speak the truth to this manager, a victim of the disease of alcoholism.

Within a few weeks, the manager came to work inxtoxicated. Confronted with the vivid reality, no longer able to avert their eyes, people were fed up. Someone alerted the new CEO, who had experience with alcoholism in the workplace. Also, the Human Resources Director had shared my observations with her. This CEO knew what to do and was prepared to take action. Immediately she removed the manager from his job and made it clear that he would not continue to be employed at all until he had completed a reputable treatment and ongoing recovery program. This CEO used the

---

[13] http://www.netmba.com/strategy/swot/

organization's Employee Assistance Program to provide the financial help that was needed. After completing the treatment program and demonstrating his sobriety, he was reassigned and today is a valued employee.

Setting a Boundary

The challenge of speaking the truth in love to a victim of the disease of addiction is that they are often so angry they are volatile—or so pitiful that they evoke debilitating sympathy and enlist others in *enabling* them to continue drinking, as had happened with this manager and his assistant, who was also removed. Therefore, in preparation, one must be ready for a very difficult experience—more difficult than most people are willing to endure. The most essential preparation for this conversation is to get clear on what your boundary is. That is, what are you no longer willing to accept? Because of her prior experience with alcoholism in the workplace, the CEO in the story knew exactly what needed to happen. With clarity, she dealt with the manager's alcoholism.

Most people do not realize how much love it takes to confront someone afflicted with the disease of alcoholism. It's so much easier to *label* the affliction than to deal effectively with it. Also, the confrontation puts the relationship at risk. The person making the confrontation has to care enough for the alcoholic that he is willing to let the relationship go in order to create conditions that make recovery possible, beginning with truth.

Leaders of organizations have a responsibility to create workplaces where people thrive. Because of the power of mirror neurons to affect the inner environment, it's very difficult for employees to be focused and clear when their leader is a victim of alcoholism. Most people are not that *conscious*. Certainly when supervised by such a person, they are not able to perform at their best. Here's another example:

Two partners owned a $22 million business. One of the partners, an alcoholic, was a super-salesman. He made sales for the sake of making the sale, not considering the bottom line. Often, additional equipment had to be purchased in order to do the work after he had made the sale, negating any profit and sometimes making the bottom line red. The two partners, predictably, had great difficulty working together. Finally, the partner suffering from alcoholism realized that unless something changed the business would not be able to make the next payroll. The other partner had been working with a lawyer, offering a deal to get the problem partner out of the business. The other partner's *boundary* was to assume no more debt as long as the partner with alcoholism was in the business. In the face of not being able to pay their employees, the partner with alcoholism reluctantly accepted the deal, said goodbye to the employees, and signed the agreement to leave. The other partner then borrowed the money to make payroll and invited a consultant with experience in such matters in to listen to the employees and begin to repair the emotional damage (i.e. spill of unwanted chemicals in their brains) that had been done.

A final example of setting a boundary comes from a young mother's personal experience. Expecting her first child, this young woman was the daughter of an alcoholic. She knew that alcoholism is a family disease and that she had been affected. She wanted to stop the cycle of addiction for herself and her child. In preparation for giving birth she worked with a counselor and went to Al-Anon meetings for families and friends of alcoholics. She decided that she did not want her father to have access to his granddaughter when he had been drinking—which, at this time in the progression of his disease, was anytime after 9:00 a.m. This was her boundary. She did not want her daughter to experience her grandfather's drunkenness.

When this young mother communicated her decision to her father, he was resistant and the conversation did not go well. Moreover, the grandmother said that if the grandfather wasn't welcome, she would stay away too. Weeks went by with neither parent visiting her and her firstborn, precious baby girl. Then one day her mother called to say that her father had been admitted to the hospital to undergo detoxification after which he would enter a treatment center for alcoholism.

Often when people who love those who suffer from the disease of alcoholism set a clear boundary and explain from their hearts what that boundary is, the alcoholic decides to tell the truth about his or her disease and get treatment. The courage of this daughter and the love that was required to speak the truth to her father got through to him, but he had to decide to make the change.

Becoming Free

For most people the process of becoming aware and authentic works very slowly. For clients who have achieved a high degree of self understanding through psychological or recovery work, three tools are especially effective: The circle (see Chapter 5), the Energy Analysis®(see Chapter 2), and the Authentic Profile (see Chapter 8). Three years ago I did an Authentic Profile for a client who wanted to experience more success in her business and personal life. We worked together for about three months, then she moved and changed companies. I heard from her once every 6-8 months. Then one day, unexpectedly, she set an appointment for a coaching session. When she arrived one of the first things she said was, "I stopped drinking a week ago."

Surprised I asked, "How much had you been drinking?" Her answer was, "Several glasses of wine, every night." I had no idea she drank so much. Nothing in her behavior suggested that alcohol might be a problem.

Over the next few weeks, as the "fog" of alcohol lifted, her thinking became clearer. Also her emotions, no longer medicated, surfaced and she began to find the courage to say what truly needed to be said, to herself, her business associates and her significant other. I wonder if the truth of her Authentic Profile© had an influence in pulling her slowly toward her Authentic Self. The very act of creating her Authentic Profile© set a boundary for this woman. Inexorably, her inner being was drawn toward it even while she was still unaware.

Setting a boundary is defining the environment we are willing to accept for our lives. This environment isn't outside of us; it's inside. Once we become clear—once we are fully conscious—about the workplace we want to create for our employees or ourselves, the parenting we want to provide, the value we want to give and derive from friendships, the climate of our homes, the quality of our lives, then that vision inexorably draws us toward attaining it.

Another Way of Becoming Free

For clients who have not done the inner work required for self-understanding and acceptance and have not worked with another person to provide accountability, a different method is required in order for them to become free. No matter how many self-help books you have read, if you have not worked with a qualified person to clear the past, you are not free. You might be able to name or explain what your "problem" is, but you are not free from it until you have transformed it and your change has been observed by another human being.

Socrates once said, "The unexamined life is not worth living." The New Testament puts it this way—"When I was a child, I spoke as a child, I understood as a child, I thought as a child: but when I became [an adult], I put away childish things" (1 Corinthians 13:11). Within the last two decades, neuroscience has provided a scientific basis for this wisdom. When we are born our brains weigh about 300 grams. By age 2, our brain's weight has more than tripled to about 1,000 grams. From age two the increase is less dramatic, increasing to about 1,380 grams in a 14-year old.

What accounts for the increase in the brain's weight? It doesn't triple in size from birth to age 2. There is no significant increase in the number of neurons in the brain to account for the weight. When we are born we already have tens of billions of neurons arranged in columns throughout the brain.

What happens is that the dendrites grow longer and branch out to connect with other neurons, thus increasing brain weight. Also, some of the increase is attributable to the thickening of the *glia,* which are cells that surround and nourish the neurons. To give you an idea of how substantial this growth is consider that a single dendrite might have 15,000 or more connections to other dendrites emitting neurotransmitters and other chemicals through the space between the dendrite and axon on the receiving neuron. This space, called a *synapse,* is the connection formed through an electrochemical process (see Fig. 11-1).

Along the way the brain prunes neurons that are not used. We are born with the capacity to make any sound needed for any language. But because no one language utilizes all of the sounds we can make, the ones that are not used are pruned around the age of 9 or 10 causing our ability to learn a foreign language and speak it fluently to decrease sharply. The term "use it or lose it" is true.

The brain is not fully developed until late teens or early twenties when the logical/rational frontal cortex matures. When I say this to parents they often exclaim, "It's true! I couldn't reason with them until their early twenties." Before the frontal cortex finished developing, external discipline was needed. Setting clear expectations and enforcing them consistently with reasonable, nonviolent consequences is a requirement for parenting well. But after the frontal cortex develops the child is what we call "an adult" able to reason out for herself what the consequences of her behavior might be and thus make good choices on her own (self discipline).

How we interpret our experiences shapes the neuronal patterns of our brains. How we experience our caregivers, our siblings, playmates, other people. Books. Movies. Trips. Many of these experiences occurred and were stored in our memory even before we had language to describe them—when we were only hours old, or even in utero. Most of these memories and patterns were formed in the words of one client "...by a child's brain trying to make sense of an adult world."

When Socrates said, "The unexamined life is not worth living," he might have meant that, unless we go back into those childhood and adolescent memories and examine them with adult understanding, the emotions evoked by the original experience continue to drive us without our awareness.

How Neurons Make Connections:
Axon-Synapse-Dendrite Pathways are Electrical to Chemical to Electrical

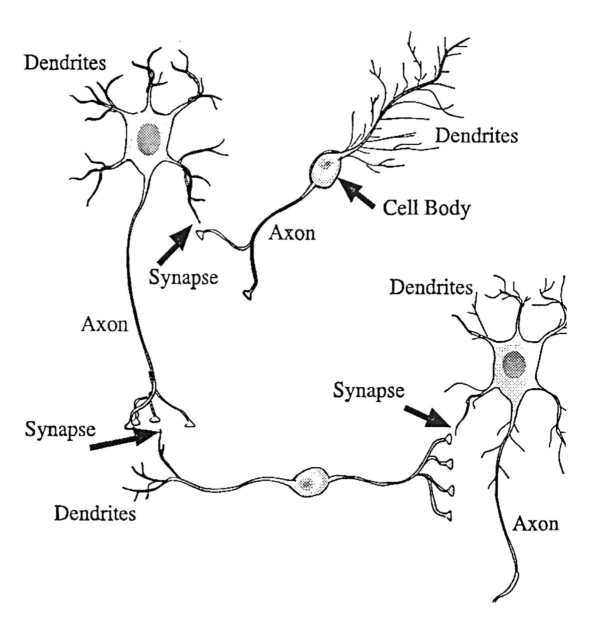

Fig. 11-1: How Neurons Make Connections
Source: Eric Jensen (www.jensenlearning.com)

Dr. Bruce Lipton, cellular biologist at Stanford University in a recent interview for *Science of Mind* magazine, said,

> "The subconscious is the fundamental programs we got from other people in our first six years of life. As you are living your life with your intentions and desires from your conscious mind, 95% of your behavior is coming from your subconscious mind, which was programmed by other people" (*Science of Mind,* October 2005, p. 30).

To transcend this pattern we must summon a force strong enough to overcome 95% of our being. That force is truth. To find it, follow this course:

Find a photograph of yourself at the age of 5 or 6. By now you've probably already looked through all of the family albums and, without looking again, one or two photographs will immediately come to your mind. If all of your family photographs were destroyed by fire or flood—or if you can't remember ever having any—then look at photographs of children in magazines or books until you find one that resonates with you.

Using that child's voice, write your story. You'll know what it is from stories you have heard members of your family tell—or stories that you have heard from any source that strike a familiar chord within you. An example from my own life is the story of *Dumbo* (1940), written by Helen Aberson and popularized by Disney. As a child it was my favorite. When I re-read the story as a grown-up I realized that what struck a chord between the story and me was this: "Dad is angry. Mom is far away. My job is to perform." Maybe there's a story like that for you—a fairy tale or favorite bedtime story or even a childhood song. If there is, reflect on it asking, "Is there a kindred spirit in this art that attracted me to it? If so, what is its commonality with my young life?"

Now consider what was actually happening in your life during your first six years. As I reflected on this time in my life two photographs immediately came to mind. Here they are:

My First Five Years

Someone cares for her, this lonely girl-child standing alone on this barren plot of earth. Someone must care—she wears a warm coat, even a hat. Holding a doll, she smiles for the camera. Someone is holding that camera, taking the photograph. Someone bought the doll for her. Someone cares.

"Child," I say, "Speak to me from the page of the photograph album where you now reside. What have these 5 years of your life on this earth been like? Are you happy here?"

Quickly she answers.

"My life, in a way, has been one of extremes. I was born in a city, with lots of people around. Friends. Both my mother and my daddy. Although I was born sooner than they probably wanted, my parents loved me and were happy to have me. In those earliest days, there was hugging and nuzzling. Play and sunshine. Trips to the zoo. Parties, nourishment and fun.

"But there was a war, and Daddy was a soldier. Before I was even a year old, he left to fight. Mother had to go to work in the City, and there was no one to care for me. So I went to the farm to live with my grandparents. They took delight in me. I gathered eggs with Grandma and sat on Grandpa's knees, on the front porch, at the end of the day. Maybe this is where I learned to love sunsets.

"I thrived on the sugar from Grandma's tea cakes, and I ran the show.

"I especially loved the times when I went to visit Grandma's sister. In her home was what they called a maid—a big woman with a soft bosom whose warmth washed over me like warm chocolate syrup. I loved her.

"My mom and dad both have sisters who have no children. They dote on me, and I love it.

"I'm the darling of both my mother's and my father's families—a beautiful child with bright blond hair and brilliant blue eyes. I love my world.

"Then, when I was three years old, Daddy came home from the war. He has been gone for most of my little life. But he hasn't forgotten me. He has my picture in his wallet. He and Mother come for me, ready to make a home where we are all together.

"I had become accustomed to being the center of attention—the adored one. Everything I did was cute. But Dad, accustomed to the discipline of war, thought my cuteness was disrespect, so he decided to 'show me who was boss' through a trip to the woodshed. What I experienced there was probably not a beating, by child abuse standards, but to my delicate, pampered disposition that had not experienced anything but loving hands, it was a profound shock.

"From that moment on, I believed Daddy was a monster, and I was angry. He could force me to obey because he was bigger and stronger, but he couldn't make me like it. For the rest of his life, at every opportunity, I got even. This poem, written near the beginning of my journey of self-discovery, describes what our relationship was like:

Spears

You've seen them, I'm sure,
On stage or on screen,
Two people fighting with spears.

Not fighting, really,
More like straining,
Both fists clutching the shaft,

Juxtaposed, one against the other,
And pushing with all my might.

Because at the end of his spear is
A mighty point, and if I falter
Or weaken, I disappear—

Massacred.
So I press on, until one day
I'm just—too-tired.

"My anger didn't serve me well. I directed it not only at my father but any man or other authority figure who tried to deny me what I wanted. Thus, much of my behavior was playing out this role instead of focusing on my own faults and correcting them so that I might live in closer alignment with who I truly am.

"My parents, like most young parents of their generation, didn't know the difference between discipline and punishment. What I needed was discipline. What I got was punishment. My three-year-old brain was thus hardwired, and I was angry.

"So here I stand on this barren ground that they say will become my home. It doesn't look like much to me. But next door is a magical place—a spacious, two-story home with a large garden and flowers! A teenaged girl lives there—Marsha. She loves me. I can tell. She wears a locket and pearls, sweaters and saddle oxfords. Her closet is stuffed with satin and tulle—dresses to dance in! I decide to spend as much time as possible in *this* wondrous, warm home, not my own.

"Mother is pregnant with my sister. She is pale and frail. I feel she has gone away and won't come back. But I am strong and healthy. I have a warm, welcoming place to go. I'm ready to explore more of the world."

This is the story that is hardwired within me. I learned to be angry and independent. I didn't believe it was safe for me to express my anger, so I remained quiet and "showed" my dad that I was a worthy human being by making good grades and being attractive. Simultaneously, I begrudgingly obeyed—that's obedience with an attitude. I learned to communicate in a way that obscured my true feelings—with bumper car words.

Bumper Car Words

Bumper car words from
Rubberized tongues
Bang around rinks, avoiding.

Bumper car words belong in
Arcades—not on the
Highways called Life.

This hardwiring was created by a 3-year-old brain. Now that I have not only full brain capacity but also years of experience that have brought some degree of wisdom, understanding, and compassion, I rewrite my story with kinder, more forgiving eyes.

Rewrite of My First Five Years

"Although my arrival into this world was sooner than my parents might have planned, they are delighted I am here. They are very young and they like to play with me and make me laugh. My mother is a great beauty and Daddy is very handsome—as handsome as a movie star! This is a fun family to be in.

"While Dad is away fighting the war I get to stay on the farm with my grandparents. What a great experience! At night I can hear the locusts whirring and other night sounds. It's peaceful out here. Even when there's a storm we have a cellar to go to, and I love to look at all the jars of preserves Grandma has placed on the shelves down there. In fact, there are lots of interesting things to do here—a pond, animals, a barn with a hayloft where I pick the peanuts out of the hay and eat them, a tractor to climb on and pens for the cows. I learn to lift the hens before I put my hand under them to collect the eggs. A snake might be there eating the eggs. Grandmother is very careful to teach me how to keep myself safe. By this I know she cares and I feel loved.

"Dad and I had one bad experience when he returned from the war. He had seen a lot of horrible things and he was pretty angry. He didn't mean to take it out on me, but he did. I was protected by my two aunts, however, who let him know in no uncertain terms that he had been too rough with me and he must never do that again. He never did. But I didn't let it go. Seared into my young memory through the reflection of mirror neurons, my anger remained with me until ten years after my father's death.

"Dad was a good man—well respected by everyone who knew him. He had a great sense of humor and loved to tell stories that made people laugh. He was full of life and wanted to be all that he could be. He provided well for our family my mother always said. I don't remember doing without anything. In fact some people would call my childhood privileged.

"Mother had rheumatic fever when she was a girl so her health was pretty frail—and after my sister was born it was really tough for her. My sister was colicky and got sick a lot. So Mom and I didn't have much of a bond—but she made sure I was well cared for. Also, we had great neighbors. Mrs. McCall lived on one side of our house and I used to sit with her in the swing on the front porch of her house, chattering like a magpie, telling her everything that happened to me that day. I don't remember one word Mrs. McCall ever said to me, so I know I must have been a little chatterbox.

"On the other side was the Klein house. I loved Marsha Klein. She was a teenager and she had dresses to dance in. She let me go into her room and look in her closet. Her mother liked crafts and made all kinds of things that made their home interesting and inviting. They even had a plant in their garden that they called a century plant and they had a neighborhood party when it bloomed.

"Every now and then I get a dress in the mail that my aunt has made. I love pretty clothes and Mother buys nice things for me. I have everything I need. I am loved."

Why We Must Rewrite the Story

Many years later, as a parent I heard the admonition never to speak to my children in anger. For most of my life I didn't understand why. My understanding came when I realized my 3-year-old reaction to Dad's angry treatment. I didn't have the brain capacity to understand or correct what happened within me. Instead, I "caught" my dad's anger and unconsciously let it drive me for most of my life. What was especially deceptive was that I rarely lost my temper. But criticism, sarcasm and gossip were common tools whereby I expressed the seething anger that was always lying just under the surface, mostly directed at men and other people in authority.

If your subconscious was programmed in your first five or six years to be driven by an experience similar to mine, then you are living your life out of a reality that is not authentic for you. To discover the pure essence of who you are, revisit those first six years. Go back through experiences you would rather forget. Relive them. Then re-examine them with your now-mature capacity for compassion, understanding and forgiveness.

Some people want to toss off the importance of early experiences with words like "Get over it!" They don't realize that words alone are not sufficient to undo the damage that might have been done. Instead, a process is required that involves feeling the original experience and going through the pain again in order to get to the other side of it. Then and only then can you get back to the spirit you had before the painful experience changed you. From that renewed state of mind, you rewrite your story just as I did above.

Resistance, avoidance and denial of an experience that brought shame, embarrassment and pain serve the purpose of holding us in the pain and can even keep us in a pattern of repeating similar experiences throughout our entire lives. It seems contradictory that we will find release from pain by going through it, but it is the truth. Just as when driving on ice, you must turn into the direction of the slide, not away from it, in order to straighten the car.

Turn Into the Slide

When the car slips on ice,
Turn into the slide;
Yield to the weakness,
Foot off the brake.

Fighting and conquering
Are not okay
For a slide. Do it,
And you die—perhaps.

The slide leads you,
Though you didn't choose,
To a better place.
And when you follow,

You discover freedom—
And safety—
And surprise—

And warmth—
On ice!

When you're ready—when it seems right for you—write the story your 6-year-old has to tell. What childhood story especially struck a chord within you? What real-life experiences did that story connect for you? Now re-write your story of your first 6 years with the kinder, more understanding eyes you have today, just as I have done above. In the words of Safire Rose, "It may be shocking to realize that we have never been a victim to anyone or anything *but our own thoughts*... It is never too late to have a happy childhood." (*Science of Mind*, July 2003, p. 43).

Freedom

Writing and re-writing the story of the first 6 years of your life is an activity you do only once. But other emotional memories will have been stored from other times in your life. As they come up, write/re-write that story.

Maybe the memory comes as an ache without words. When this happens put your hands over your heart and ask "What is this about?" Then wait for the answer. It might come in a dream or in waking hours in a submerged memory. One such memory for me was a time when, as a child, I awoke to see the walls of my room dancing in red. I was alarmed because my wallpaper was pink with darker pink flowers. The next thing I remember was holding my mother's hand in the backyard watching a neighbor rake a small fire away from the outer wall of my bedroom underneath my window. A fire truck was there, lights flashing, but the hose wasn't needed because the fire was so small. Mother said, "Some children must have been playing with matches." Although I said nothing, inside I was screaming "My friends tried to burn my room!!!!" I was so stuck in that shock that, after recalling it, I could not reframe and re-write this story with understanding so I called a trusted friend. He said, "What I heard is that a lot of people came to help." Thus, he re-told the story for me in a way that made perfect sense and brought healing. I still don't know who started the fire or why but it no longer matters. I am free. The ache around my heart disappeared.

12   Use the Toolbox

Life just isn't a straight, level path. Things happen. People who want to change us come into our lives and exert strong influence. Our own inner thoughts and fears kick up and start working against us, even after we have done the work to create the lives we want.

Just as the software we run in our computers has default settings, so do we. Our defaults are the connections and pathways that were formed before our brains were fully developed. These connections and pathways represent the uninformed decisions we made in the past about who we are and how to be.

Because all of us have these default settings, we need a discipline for staying on track so that we're not pulled once more into a life we do not want to live. The tools described in this section are *daily* maintenance tools. During the day, as issues arise and you feel your anxiety rising, pull out these tools. Decide which one fits the situation, and use it. Right then. Don't let things build up within you.

Ask, Release, and Wait.

Asking a question without expecting an immediate answer takes us away from impulsivity and towards patience, keen listening, and observing. This tool also allows everyone who hears to simply "sit with the question" until the answer appears. Ask for what you truly want—your heart's desire—and wait for the answer. Take no action. Wait. Some people call this prayer.

One young man I worked with has changed jobs a lot. For a while, he was a stay-at-home dad; then he worked for this company, then that one, changing fields each time he made a move. Along the way he wrote a book. Always, his first love was speaking. Clearly he was struggling with making a living and following his heart. Recently I received this email from him: "I have found that using 'Ask, release, wait' has amazing power. Many call this the law of attraction, popularized by the best selling movie and book *The Secret.* While some discredit the thought of asking your higher power for your heart's desire and then waiting for it to appear, it actually works. I recently was at a crossroads in my career and felt like a misfit in my job. It was a good job, but not one that inspired my soul. I prayed for a career opportunity that would support my family and allow me to pursue my dream of being a professional writer and speaker. I was clear in what I wanted and I let the thought of it go into the universe. A week later a friend called and invited me to interview with her company. Not only will they support my speaking and writing as a side effort, but they added a component of training the staff to the job description."

Contemplation. Spend at least 15 minutes a day sitting, with your eyes closed. Repeat, "Thy will be done" until your mind settles (a technique suggested by author Bob Lively). Then sit and listen. Say or write what you are grateful for. Sit and listen. Say or write your requests. Sit and listen. Perhaps open the Bible or an inspirational book and read whatever your eyes fall on. Get up when you feel complete.

A client tells this story about the power of the practice of contemplation:

> I've always loved the job I was doing and, in fact, I was good at it. I had achieved and excelled in every level of skill certification in my job field to be considered a subject matter expert. Unfortunately, it wasn't enough for me to have mastered the technical subject matter. What was needed, my greatest challenge, and what I was lacking was the skill and discipline to help me maneuver and master difficult and negative work situations. Simply paying attention to what I am choosing to think about—contemplation—has been a lifesaver for me.

> I have chosen to start each day as a contributor to my own success using my energy in a positive manner. My mantra is 'This is my life and I choose to be happy and healthy.'

> For me this means a conscious effort to spread a cheerful greeting to all I encounter and to avoid negative situations and people where possible. This might sound too simplistic, but it works for me. I practice speaking with integrity and saying only what is needed. This takes daily commitment!!!

> Whenever I feel that my batteries are low, I stop and mediate on the Lord's prayer. Posted in my office is a "Workplace" Psalm which states:

>> "The Lord is my real boss...
>> HE gives me peace,
>> when chaos is all around me. ......
>> His Presence, His Peace and His Power
>> will see me through."

> What I have learned is that while most of us share a common goal of achievement and success in the workplace, we think of success in very narrow terms – career ladder promotions, techni-

cal expertise, salary increases, and job titles, etc. Consequently, we don't know how to deal with conflicts and negative situations that cause the "bumps in the road." And along the way, we stop learning or putting into practice those skills that make for a positive work-life environment.

"For me, SUCCESS is now defined as personal integrity: aligning my whole being with the positive words I contemplate. I have more positive energy now than ever before!"

Silence is a place of possibility. It is the pause that precedes transformation. Silence is a time for emptying—clearing the circuits—of the brain. When we are empty, we create space for new learning to come in. Silence gives our brains a warm, quiet bath, quite a contrast to the splash of chemicals in our brains when we hear blaring music, voices trying to shout over each other, rooms full of clutter and noise. Our brains need to be "unplugged." This moment of silence is a little oasis for the brain to be refreshed. Note: If you tend not to be able to stay in silence without coughing, giggling, shuffling, it's just lack of practice. Keep doing it. Start with at least 1 minute of silence and work up to 5 minutes. The brain must have time to still itself—and stillness is the place of possibility, where new understanding and breakthrough learning happen.

A client who loves the one-page guide entitled "Leading Meetings to Reduce Stress" (see p. 83) writes,

> "I use silence to begin all meetings where I'm working with a team. It works gloriously. I also use it for me when I'm writing. For example, this morning when I sat down to write this email, I first quieted my mind by stopping and feeling my breath. Then I consciously take a couple of deep breaths. I swear that it slows down time as well. I seem to be able to get things done faster and better.

Love Letter

Write yourself a love letter every day for 40 days. Keep it simple. Example: "I love how you keep trying—how you don't give up. I love that you want to live the fullest life possible. I love you."

One of my guides on this journey suggested that I do this. At the time, my husband and I were separated, and I was very angry. But I was willing to try anything, so I followed her advice. To my amazement, I loved it so much that I continued doing it long after 40 days had ended. I'm not sure how long I kept it up; it might have been as long as two years! This steady dose of love contributed to the reconciliation my husband and I experienced.

At a recent meeting with perfect strangers, a man came up to me and said, "When you speak, the love that is coming from you is so evident." At this same meeting, a couple who haven't been together very long expressed this desire for their relationship: "We want to be like Harlan and Nancy." When we hear comments like this—and we hear them often—my husband and I look at each other and smile. The smile is gratitude that we've come so far. It's also the unspoken question, "I wonder if they have any idea what they're asking for!" Now writing those love letters to myself isn't the only thing I did to heal myself and ultimately my marriage. But it certainly contributed.

Sayings That Steer My Course

To choose these quotations, write out every quotation that you have collected through the years. Then read through them again and again, asking, "Is this essential?" If I lost all the words that have ever had meaning but could keep just 2-3, which ones would they be?

A client who is going through an unwanted divorce handed me a business-card-size quotation that his secretary had laminated for him to get him through the tough times. "It helps," he said. That reminded me of the quotation one of his colleagues had given me when we created her Authentic Profile. This person is unflappable, even in the face of great challenges, including unwanted media attention. Here's the quotation, attributed to Mother Theresa, that steers her course:

Do It Anyway

People are often unreasonable, illogical, and self-centered;
Forgive them anyway.

If you are kind, people may accuse you of selfish, ulterior motives;
Be kind anyway.

If you are successful, you will win some false friends and some true enemies;
Succeed anyway.

If you are honest and frank, people may cheat you;
Be honest and frank anyway.

What you spend years building, someone could destroy overnight;
Build anyway.

If you find serenity and happiness, they may be jealous;
Be happy anyway.

The good you do today, people will often forget tomorrow;
Do good anyway.

Give the world the best you have, and it may never be enough;
Give the world the best you've got anyway.

You see, in the final analysis, it is between you and God;
It never was between you and them anyway.

Bibliography for My Life

You have heard, "You are what you eat." To a very great extent, words and images that we allow into our thoughts, our hearts, and our minds largely influence how we think and feel, how we live our lives, and how we treat ourselves and others. So take some time to think about the quotations, books, movies, and other media that you love. Books, articles, movies have meaning and impact for us. They change the way we think and feel. We learn from them. We change. We become more fully the person we want to be. For you, what are the books, articles, movies that touched your heart and provided meaning? That deepened your human experience? These are probably movies, books, articles that you have read more than once—or that you based a portion of your work from—or that you wrote goals from—or that awakened a passion in you that you did not know existed—or that simply opened the door to how to do something you did not know how to do.

An example for me is a video called *Everyday Creativity* (1999) by former National Geographic photographer Dewitt Jones. In the video, he said that for one National Geographic article, he took as many as 300 *rolls* of film. That statement hit me right between the eyes. I had been self-critical because I couldn't get 24 perfect photographs out of a roll of 24 shots. After hearing Dewitt Jones, a renowned photographer, say this, I gave up trying to get it right every time and just started buying lots of film. Immediately, my enthusiasm improved, and I started getting great shots—not a lot—but great shots. Then I started integrating my photography into my work, and it always lifts my spirits. My clients love my photographs, too. So—that video goes into my list.

Listen

So often, as we listen to people, we are clogging our brain circuits with our own thinking, and we miss important information because we just don't have any neurons available to receive it. We're thinking about whether or not we like the person's hair or clothing. We're remembering what we've heard about them and analyzing what's wrong with them. Contrast that with how my dog listens—with full eye contact, just trying to understand. Focus on what's right with each person and listen so that we learn from their experience. Looking into the eyes of the other person while he or she speaks is essential for effective listening. A mantra I often use when listening is this: "I am open for whatever is here for me to learn."

Listening is a tool I used throughout the writing of this book. In the early stages, I worked with a literary consultant to help me put meat on the bones of the content. At the outset I made a decision to listen and say *yes* to everything she suggested. Then there was a second helper who offered to write a review of the manuscript. To that, also, I said "yes." Most recently, the publisher suggested that I put more stories into this very chapter, the Toolbox. At the time he made this request, my energy was suppressed. I couldn't think of any stories, so I said, "Just skip it."

But he gently persisted. Here's an email I wrote him a moment ago:

> "Victor, you must be an angel. Recently work with two clients came to an end. It was a natural ending with good results, but still I was bummed. Then came the issue of chapter 12. Well, with negative thinking running through my mind, I couldn't think of a single story and thought, 'Just let it go as is.' But you gently suggested putting more stories in. So late yesterday afternoon, in desperation, I went to my database and sent a request to people I have worked with to send me a story. I attached the toolkit chapter for reference. Already I have two stories, with promises of more to come. More importantly, I've heard from people I haven't communicated with in awhile. They were glad to hear from me and even happier to help. One, a client from 7 years ago, said how much I had helped her. I didn't know that. So, thank you. I wouldn't have gone to the well without your prompting."

Or, I might add, without my listening. One of the clients I heard from sent me this story about her experience with listening: "I am a talker, and often jumped ahead of people and was ready with my reply without giving them a chance to finish their thought.

I have employed the act of active listening – slowing my brain down and noticing the body language of the person speaking to me – really listening with full attention and then formulating my responses.

By focusing on being "in the moment" interacting with the other person – and letting them take as much time as they need to get their thoughts out have significantly contributed to my success at work. Employing this, along with other strategies from the toolbox, in less than a year I have gone from one direct report to over 100 employees. Part of my success is that I have received feedback that people feel as if they are the only person in the world when we are talking. I give them my full attention."

Apply the Principle of Matching States

The phenomenon of how human brains wordlessly communicate with each other is little understood. But all of us know the phenomenon is real. We receive "vibes" that we interpret and act upon. Author and consultant on the brain and learning, Eric Jensen says, "All behavior and meaning-making is state dependent. We can only behave in alignment with our states. There is no such thing as an unmotivated person—there are only unmotivated states." As our state changes, the meaning we make also changes. In fact, our reality changes. Penny Heath, principal of Farnsworth Middle School in Guilderland, New York, meditated at the beginning of every school day. Then, as she opened her office door to go into the hall-ways, she silently repeated these words by Nobel Peace Prize nominee Thich Nhat Hahn: "Breathing in, I calm my body. Breathing out, I smile."

Penny says, "I had a stretch of hallway coming out of my office where I could repeat those words before I had to start talking to kids. So this is the 'tape' that would 'play' as I interacted with them. There was a calmness within me. Even though the words and directions coming out of my mouth were the same as before—'Pick up that paper; don't bang your locker'—the children's response was different, more positive." Kenneth L. Thompson (2001) wrote:

> "Giacomo Rizzolatti and his partners at the University of Parma have discovered a collection of neurons in higher primates that light up when an action is merely observed. Shortly after this announcement in the late 1990s, another Italian team confirmed the existence of a similar structure in humans. Dubbed *mirror neurons*, these cells fire when we watch someone else perform an action... With the discovery of mirror neurons, we now have tangible evidence that one person's emotional state will affect the entire group"

The clearest example of the power of our thinking was demonstrated to me by a young woman, a client who had quit her high-tech job because, in her words, "The people I worked with were stupid." Immediately, she started looking for another job, with unsatisfying results. Her resume was outstanding, and she was getting interviews—but she wasn't getting hired. Finally, one day she stormed into my office and threw herself into a chair. "I don't understand it," she said. "Yesterday I went for an interview. I was perfect for the job. But the guy interviewing me didn't do a good job at all in the interview, and I wasn't able to present myself in my best light."

I leaned forward and started writing. "What, again, were you *thinking* when you went into the interview?"

"I had a lot of confidence. I knew I was perfect for the job."

I wrote, "I'm perfect."

And now, tell me again what you were *thinking* about the interviewer?

"Oh, he was awful."

So, you were *thinking,* "I'm perfect, and you're awful."

Realization broke across her face. "You mean I'm doing this to myself?"

I nodded. Then we worked on what she would *think* the next time she had an interview and the importance of aligning *thinking* with *feeling* so that a single, authentic message goes out. A Christian, she decided to use the mantra, "Thy will be done" for her next interview.

She got the job. Mantras are an effective way to create a mental state for positive results. Since thought precedes action, positive thought is a precursor for positive action. What we think directs what we do.

Affirmation

The brain works best in a state of relaxed alertness, free from fear of criticism or condemnation. The work of UCLA psychiatrist Dr. Lewis Baxter proves that kind, affirming words spoken from the heart have a similar effect on the human brain as Prozac, a drug commonly prescribed for depression (Jensen 1995, p. 15). Through the release of serotonin, the brain's own chemical comforter, kind, affirming words provide a sense of well being. In this state, the brain works at its best. When she was in charge of employee recognition programs for the Disney Corporation, Dee Hansford found that improvement occurs in people only 30% of the time after they have been criticized; it occurs 90% of the time after they have been recognized for what they do well. It bears repeating that 90% of the time, after they have been recognized for what they do well, people not only repeat that good behavior, but also improve on their own without being told. Therefore, our focus must be on what people are doing well. When we affirm them, we speak from our hearts, with sincerity and truth and without excessive emotion. Without any other effort on our part, what we focus on gets stronger and elevates everything else. In our own inner self-talk, affirmation gets far better results than self criticism or put-downs.

Gratitude is a form of affirmation, washing our brains with chemistry that lifts our spirits. A client recently wrote,

> "I was recently jilted by a girlfriend (luckily, we weren't seriously involved) who dumped me. Along with all my stress of starting my new job, I moved pretty far away from my center, and what helped me immensely was focusing on what I am grateful for. It seemed that if I was filled with gratitude for what I have, I was unable to harbor negative thoughts of other things."

Still another client tells this story of how she uses affirmation with her employees:

> "A tool I use daily is affirmation. I inherited over 100 employees that worked in areas that were not my area of expertise. The previous director required everything to go through him and he caused unnecessary delays. I believe he had paralysis by analysis. He was so afraid of making a mistake that he made no decisions.
>
> "When I met with my new managers, I told them that I would have to rely on them to give me the correct information because they are the subject matter experts. I trusted them to do their job and involve me when and if they thought it was necessary but I did not have the time or desire to approve every decision that they made. It took a few months before my team began to understand that I was serious and that I was not going to be looking over their shoulder every day.
>
> "I try to catch people in the act of doing things right and acknowledge it as soon as possible. Attitudes and productivity have risen in the 4 months since I have had this new team."

Precision in Language

Sometimes we say, "I don't have time," instead of, "This is not one of my priorities." We think we are sparing people's feelings, but in actuality we are creating stress for ourselves and distrust in others. Neuroscientist Candace Pert (1997) writes,

> "When I am at cross-purposes... going through the motions but not really committed to my goal, saying one thing and doing another, then my emotions are confused, I suffer a lack of integ-

rity, and my physiologic integrity is likewise altered. The result can be a weakened, disturbed psychosomatic network, leading to stress and eventually to illness. Always tell the truth, I have said repeatedly to my children for years, not just that it's the moral thing to do, but because it will keep you on a healthy path and disease-free!" *(p. 295)*

That words have power is the premise Don Miguel Ruiz' (2001) "first agreement":

> "Your word is the power that you have to create… What you dream, what you feel, and what you really are, will all be manifested through the word… The word is a force; it is the power you have to express and communicate, to think, and thereby to create the events in your life… Depending on how it is used, the word can set you free, or it can enslave you even more than you know."

I had not heard from my daughter in a long time. She didn't call, nor did she return my phone calls. I was distraught, angry and frustrated. After I fully expressed my anger and disappointment to my husband and the dam of tears and anguish had burst, I started writing, "What I truly need to say is…" When the sentence finished in a way that pleased my heart, I picked up the phone and called her at work. I said, "I'm feeling left out of your life, and that's not okay with me."

At first, she tried to put me off. "Mom, I can't talk right now. I'll call you back."

To which I replied, "I have a lot of fear about hanging up because in the past you've told me you'll call back, and you don't."

These words, spoken from my heart, set both of us free. She told me later that the conversation brought her to the realization that she had become a slave to her work and her life was shrinking. Very shortly after the call, she quit her job. Very shortly after she quit, she found new work doing something she loves in an environment where she can have much more flexibility and time for her family.

The Circle: a Focusing Tool

To have the life you want, first you must make a decision about what you want in your life and what you do not want. Draw a circle. Write inside the circle what you wish to experience; outside the circle, write what you do not want to come into your life. Look at it every morning before you get out of bed. Spend just a few minutes thinking about the life you want. Do this until, one day, you feel that it's time to cut away those things that are outside of the circle, leaving only the circle. Continue to look at your circle every day, first thing, until you sense that you don't need to do it any more. You don't need to do it because those words are written on your heart. Thereafter, from time to time, you'll think of the circle and get it out, fine tuning it as your life circumstances and tastes change.

A client wrote me this true story about how she has used the Circle in her business and the results she has gotten:

> The circle was a very effective tool for [my partner] and me when we were coming to grips with what we wanted our business to truly be. Inside the circle, we put words like "fun, accomplishment, financial success, focused, positive leaders." Outside the circle, we put internal politics and difficult clients.
>
> We defined the "difficult clients" and what made them difficult by focusing on the clients we liked working with and why. We developed a plan for how we would handle the "difficult clients." We reviewed the circle frequently to reinforce our determination for creating the business that we truly wanted. Quickly, the difficult clients were no longer an issue. They either left and found new service providers or conformed to our definition of good clients because we had articulated to them our business process and procedures.
>
> This strategy is something I continue to use today. Because we have defined the difficult clients, I'm much better at identifying what could be a difficult client during the prospecting/interview stage so they are no longer accepted as clients in the first place.

Where, Within Me, is this Flaw?

As we interact with others, experiencing the effects of their behavior, it is so easy to see their flaws. So that we stay away from judgment, an effective strategy is to realize that we cannot see a fault in someone else that doesn't also exist within ourselves. So if there's any cleanup to be done, it's an inside job. It's a waste of the brain's energy to try to correct—or fixate on—what someone else needs to do to improve, because it's beyond our control. But if we ask our brain and memory system to show us where we are at fault, it will get clear. The brain always answers an unanswered question, especially if we are patient and simply wait for the answer to surface. Once the answer is clear, then we ask for more of the virtue that is the opposite of the character flaw.

For example, if we notice someone's anger, then we ask where anger lives in us. Then we ask for forgiveness—or tolerance—or acceptance of human nature. What we focus on gets stronger. Then, the vibrations we send out into the world are forgiveness—or tolerance—or acceptance of human nature. When our brains are emitting these positive signals, sometimes other people—of their own accord—change. (Remember the mirror neurons?) We don't do it to change other people; that would be manipulation. Rather, our intent is purely to monitor and discipline ourselves, with no investment or regard for the outcome. We do it because it is good for us.

In *The Love That Keeps Us Sane* (New York: Paulist Press, 2000) author Marc Foley tells a story about Thomas Merton, who left a "world that repulsed him" to go into a monastery. After seven years of living the silent, ordered life of a monk, he drove one day with a neighbor of the monastery back into the world he had so happily left, expecting to find the same degeneration that he had left. But, to his surprise,

> "I met the world and I found it no longer so wicked after all. Perhaps the things I had resented about the world when I left it were defects of my own that I had projected upon it. Now on the contrary, I found that everything stirred me with a deep and mute sense of compassion… I went through the city, realizing for the first time in my life how good are all the people in the world and how much value they have in the sight of God" (p. 60).

But this truth is not just for holy people; it is for all of us. A client tells the story in this way: I grew up with parents who were (and still are) very judgmental. As a child, I believed that my parents were always right because they would make comments about others and their lack of manners, inappropriate dress, lack of discipline. My parents always knew what was 'right'… when really they were judging everyone else's behavior. I'm a quick learner… so I have been good at judging for most of my life, too.

Over the years, I have become increasingly short-tempered with my parents when they judge others. Whether it's how the neighbors care for their lawns or what the right way is to put a napkin in your lap in a restaurant, I have been judging my parents for their judging. Ouch!

In August, I was with my mother when she was judging my sister and not being very nice. As she walked away from us, in the heat of the moment, my heart melted and instead of getting angry at my mom, I felt compassion. It was a defining moment, and the first time that I consciously decided to just love my mother and not judge her bad behavior. It was very freeing and empowering. In fact, I have not had a negative, judgmental thought about my mother since then—it's been a month—that's a miracle! I realized that I had the same flaw… and breaking the cycle begins with me.

Goal Setting with Blockage Removal

The most important thing about a goal is the emotion behind it. To "cleanse" a goal, write it.Then write what you think about the goal. Now write how you feel about the goal. From what you think and feel, list the energy depleters that you see in what you wrote. Now ask for the energizers that are the opposite of the depleters. Example: I think I won't be accepted. I feel unworthy. The depleter revealed here is rejection of self. The opposite virtue would be acceptance of self and confidence. So I would ask for more acceptance of self and confidence to accomplish my goal. (Thanks, once more, to Liliane and Gilles Desjardins, www.higherpower.info) At this point, I'm using the tool of *Ask, Release and Wait*. As you set goals, be aware of the emotional energy you are using. When I use the words "easily and joyfully" in a goal, I achieve it faster. But positive emotion has power beyond goal achievement. It may even prolong our lives.

Martin Seligman (2002) reported on studies that followed nuns from their graduation throughout their lives. Upon graduation from college in 1932, they wrote brief autobiographical sketches. One sister used the words "very happy" and "eager joy" to describe her life. Another wrote no positive emotion at all. The study showed that "90 percent of the most cheerful quarter was alive at age eighty-five versus only 34 percent of the least cheerful quarter. Similarly, 54 percent of the most cheerful quarter of the nuns was alive at age ninety-four, as opposed to 11 percent of the least cheerful quarter."

Accountability Partner for Goal Achievement

Meet with a partner weekly, bi-weekly, or monthly, with frequency that feels right for you. Write the answers to these questions and read your answers to your partner. Then your partner tells you what she heard, without judgment and certainly without criticism.

1. What's your goal?
2. How do you feel about this goal? Is your positive emotion conveyed in the way the goal is currently stated? If not, re-word it.
3. How will your life be better when this goal is achieved?
4. What do you know about yourself that gives you confidence that this goal will be accomplished?
5. In the past, what big goal did you accomplish and how did you do it?
6. When making change it's good to re-arrange furniture; freshen artwork; drive a different route to work, home, or errands;

change your screen saver, etc. to remind yourself that things are different around here. What sensory clues are you using to remind you to stay on course toward achieving your goal?

7.   In attaining this goal, what will you do first? Second? Third?

8.   Close your eyes and imagine that this goal has been achieved. What are you saying to yourself? How has achieving this goal improved your life?

9.   What is the most significant habit/practice/way of thinking that you'll change in order to accomplish this goal?

10. What are others telling you that lets you know how you're doing or what progress you are making?

Twice I've worked with an accountability partner. Both times, I took my list of what I was working on—all the different ideas I had—to the first meeting. Both times, my partner said something like, "Wow! Your list leaves me exhausted. How can you possibly do all of that?" What I learned is that I have the entrepreneur's disease of generating ideas without legs. Yes, I could do all of the things on my lists, but what would it get me? The ideas didn't work together; I had no focus. My life's purpose would be thwarted, not furthered. Both times, because of the truth and love given by my accountability partner, I dropped extraneous ideas and focused on what is most important. This book is an outcome of working with an accountability partner. I wrote it only after I put everything else aside and made a decision not to give up because it wasn't easy.

Shred It

All of us have negative thoughts from time to time. We pick up bad habits from others. We revert to how we thought when we were children. When you realize there's judgment, criticism, blaming, feeling like a victim, resenting, holding a grudge, etc. in your mind, write what you are thinking and feeling on paper. Get the emotional energy out of you. Don't mince words. Tell it like it is. Then shred it; don't spread it.

You might say, "Oh, I would never say those things!" But if the *energy* is present within you you spread it. You have no more choice about giving it to others than if you had a contagious disease. I repeat: Don't spread it; shred it.

Here's a story from someone who used this tool:

Almost one year had passed since I made the decision to leave my job. Not only did I choose to leave a high paying position but also the profession. When I left, I felt elated, relieved and ready to move on to whatever was to come next. Only I didn't seem to figure that out. I began to have regret, remorse, embarrassment and all kinds of negative feelings about my decision. Needing an income, I returned to the same back- breaking profession. My mind went to work, with my body and spirit dragging behind.

One day I arrived at my workplace in quite a state. Nobody else had yet arrived. I was cursing myself, the people I was about to work with and even those who I would take care of that day. My gut and my husband had already gotten the brunt of my emotional state. I could not work. I called in sick. And I was sick, sick in my heart.

I walked four miles to get home hoping that the exercise alone would clear the mess from my head. It didn't. I sat down in my favorite chair and knew I had to make a change. The tool of "shred it; don't spread it" came to mind.

As I put my pencil to paper and began to write down all that had built up in me, I started to cry. I wrote things I had only thought in my head. At first I was afraid to write, fearing someone might see my feelings on paper. But emotion overcame my reticence, and my feelings poured out as my heart burst. I cried, I wrote, I cried… The more I wrote, the more I felt. Some of the things I wrote about had been buried deep inside for a long time. Then my mind slowed, my pencil stopped and my heart felt lighter. I went to the garbage and tore those sheets of paper into tiny pieces. Then I cried a little bit more. All the evidence of what I had written was gone. But as I returned to my chair, I realized that not only were the written words gone but the angst in my heart had lifted. I could breathe. My crying was no longer out of desperation.

While I walked home earlier that day, before doing this exercise, my mind was filled with lists upon mental lists of tasks to be done. But once I had finished writing and shredding, a sense of calm came over me. I was able to be still. I took care of myself and was able to speak to my husband in a kind manner.

I know what I will do if I get to that scary place again. Shred it, don't spread it. Because no matter how hard I try to be nice, when I'm full of anger and resentment it oozes out of my pores. Nobody deserves to have those feeling released on them. Not even me.

Conclusion

The traits we cannot see within ourselves are sometimes referred to as blind spots. They arise out of our ego—our adaptations to an adult world when we had a child's mind. Someone asked me, "How can we see what we can't see?" That's what this book is about. Its tools lift the veil. Our part is to be willing to hear what we don't want to hear. Remember that it's only brain chemistry—liquid sloshing around in our heads. To change the chemical, change the story. Make a different choice. Talk to yourself and others with different words. Keep doing it and pay attention to the small, incremental improvements you notice—one day at a time.

The wise ones have told us for centuries what we must do. There is no more to be said. Now we must do.

Afterword

People sometimes ask me if my coaching is for personal or professional issues. I say, "Yes." Then I say, "Our brains are not divided into sections that say 'personal' or 'professional'. Instead, our neurons are connected in ways that might surprise us. Something that is really a professional issue surfaces in a personal way; we don't say what we truly need to say at work, so we're frustrated but trying to disguise the problem by putting our "game face" on. Then we go home and yell at our spouse or our spouse constantly makes disparaging or discouraging remarks. Wanting to preserve some semblance of domestic harmony and living in terror that we might lose our children if we don't, we put up with it not saying what we truly need to say. Then we go to work and wrangle constantly with members of the opposite sex. Our neurons are connected. Personal and professional in the human brain and memory system are not separate."

In the mid-1990s I attended a conference in Hilton Head, SC called The Soul of Business. It was here that I first heard the term "organizational energy from Dr. Nancy Post, a consultant from Philadelphia who had developed an organizational development model based on ancient Chinese medicine. Focused on the interdependent influence of the health of the organization and the health of its people, this simple-but-not-easy model has had a profound influence on me and guided my work ever since.

In Switzerland, the University of St. Gallen has an entire program devoted to organizational energy a book has been written, as well as an article, entitled "Unleashing Organizational Energy" by Heike Bruchand and Sumantra Ghoshal, which has been published in the *MIT Sloan Management Review*. The concept of organizational energy is an idea whose time has come.

Clear Impact, a consulting company in Boulder, CO, has developed an organizational energy audit that reminds me of the work my friend Wendell Jones did during the energy crisis of the 1980s. Noting that the school district he served was "wasting not only a lot of energy, but we were also causing the life of vital, expensive equipment to be shortened by unnecessary use," he installed thermostats that cut off gas and electricity when rooms were not in use. Ultimately the practices he put into place saved the organization more than $200,000 a year and those savings have continued even to today. He presented his work at conferences with disappointing results. Most of the people in his audiences simply didn't want to go to the effort to make such drastic changes even in the face of such dramatic savings.

I worked with a leader in an organization whose employees had been experiencing great difficulty for several years. In a coaching session I handed him the list of character defects that appear earlier in this book and asked him to tell me which ones applied to him. "I don't do any of these things." he said.

This leader does not acknowledge his own failings; how can he possibly deal effectively with those of his employees? In his work group there is no forgiveness because there's no acceptance of responsibility. So the people are stuck, not learning, not moving forward, only creating problems for the larger organization. This dynamic won't change until the leader changes—and the leader refuses to change.

Somewhere in the development of our behavioral DNA we began to believe that it's not okay to admit error or fault. That we had to be right. That everything people do can be explained or justified. That there is no wrong that we must acknowledge, process and change.

It will be an extreme challenge to accept that the new energy crisis, which is brought into organizations by humans, requires us to look within, not outside, ourselves. Jim Collins (2001) notes that a Level 5 leader has attained humility only after a personal crisis or profound spiritual experience. In other words leaders won't be very good at dealing with the shortcomings of their employees until they have faced and accepted their own.

Organizational Alchemy

Spanning 2,500 years, alchemists looked for substances and processes that would turn lead into gold. During the Middle Ages they began to look for a mythical substance called the *philosopher's stone* that would be an essential ingredient for their work.

The philosopher's stone has been there all the time. But the substance can't be extracted and contained. It's in the human heart. It is the human heart. It is Love and everything connected to Love. Truth. Light. Forgiveness. Acceptance. Reconciliation. Nonjudgment. Love is the Wayfinder's ultimate destination. It is what Level 5 Leaders are made of. It's what draws the highest and best from others. It boosts organizational energy without tiring inventories and action plans. It creates climates where people thrive and experience peak performance. It's where we all want to be.

To contact Dr. Oelklaus for personal or group coaching to make the journey from head to heart, go to **www.HeadtoHeart.info**

Guide for Wayfinders' Meetings

Thy Will Be Done on Earth . . . .

This guide is designed for groups of 2-4. If the group grows to 5, split into two groups. The time required is 40-60 minutes.

How We Became Wayfinders

Wayfinding is a metaphor for the spiritual journey that was inspired by the story of how the Hawaiian Islands were settled. The islands arose in the middle of the Pacific Ocean through volcanic activity from the ocean floor. Obviously, when land first appeared and grew, no people were there. Yet, when Captain James Cook and his fellow English explorers arrived there in the early 1700's, after the sextant and compass had been invented as navigational tools, they found people living on the islands—and they had been there for generations. Where did they come from? The islands are not close to any land mass.

The best explanation is that they came from Micronesia, the islands off the east coast of Asia, through the ancient art of Wayfinding. Wayfinders sensed that there was land out there. In boats made of tree trunks, they set out to find it. To guide them, they memorized the star pattern on the day they set out. They learned to "read" and be guided by the winds, the water, and the sea animals. They found land and inhabited it.

Using this metaphor, we believe it is possible for God's will to be done on earth. This is our destination. We believe we get very distracted and even confused through all the activity and pressures of human life. We want more awareness of God's presence and guidance in every aspect of our lives—at home, at work, at school, at church, in family, in friendships, in every corner of our lives. We pray only for knowledge of God's will for us and the power to carry it out.

What We Know and Why We are Here

God is Love. God is Truth. God is Light. When we speak the truth in love, we call God into being present with us. We open ourselves to enlightenment and turn our lives over to God, asking God to live through us and do for us what we cannot do for ourselves. In this meeting, we follow these disciplines:

- We speak from our hearts.
- We listen to each other and to God without interrupting or giving advice.
- We avoid religious language because we don't want to dilute the power of the presence of God with the teaching of a single institution.
- We keep sacred what we hear in this place at this time.

In this way, we create space that is safe and sacred enough for God's presence.

The Process

1. We ask God to be present with us. (Each person, in turn, makes the request.)
2. Truthfully say what is in your heart, both gratitude and depleting energy. (In turn, each speaks this truth.)
3. Tell recent stories of how you have noticed God showing up in your life. (In turn, tell the stories. You are speaking to God.)
4. Ask for what you want out loud and say what you're putting in God's hands. (God wants us to ask for what we need and then acknowledge that, ultimately, what we really want is that God's will be done.) Then visualize the highest and best for yourself and each other. Close with the Lord's Prayer.

References

Introduction

Lerner, M. (2006). *The left hand of god: Taking back our country from the religious right.* San Francisco: Harper.

Lipton, B. (2005). *The biology of belief.* Sant Rosa, CA: Mountain of Love / Elite Books.

Chapter 1

Loehr, J., & Schwartz. T. (2003). *The power of full engagement.* New York: Free Press.

Palmer, P. (2000). *Let your life speak.* San Francisco: Jossey Bass.

Steinbrecher, E. (1988). *Inner guide meditation.* York Beach, Maine: Samuel Weiser, Inc.

(2006, December). *The Systems Thinker.* Waltham, MA: Pegasus Communications.

Chapter 2

Covey, S.R. (2004). *The eighth habit: From effectiveness to greatness.* New York: Simon and Schuster.

Loehr, J., & Schwartz. T. (2003). *The power of full engagement.* New York: Free Press.

Peterson, E.H. (1995). *The message.* Colorado Springs: NavPress. p. 208.

Senge, P. (1990). *The fifth discipline: The art and practice of the learning organization.* New York: Doubleday.

Schulkin, J. (2003). *Rethinking homeostasis.* Cambridge, MA: MIT Press. p .99.

Williamson, M. (1992). *A return to love: Reflections on the principles of a course in miracles.* New York: Harper Collins p. 191).

Chapter 3

Alcoholics Anonymous (1976). *Seventh step prayer.* New York: Alcoholics Anonymous World Services. (p. 76).

Nemeth, M. (1997) *The energy of money.* New York: Ballantine. p. 76

Ruiz, D.M. (1997*). The four agreements.* San Rafael, CA: Amber-Allen Publishing Company. pp. 12-13).

Chapter 4

Childre, D.L. & Martin H. (1999) *The heartmath solution: The institute of heartmath's revolutionary program for engaging the power of the heart's intelligence.* San Francisco: Harper, p. 34

Covey, S.R. (2004). *The eighth habit: From effectiveness to greatness.* New York: Simon and Schuster.

Dossey, L. (1997). *Healing words.* New York: Harper Paperbacks, p. 118

Silf, M. (2005). *The gift of prayer: Embracing the sacred in the everyday.* New York: Bluebridge.

Chapter 5

Arntz, Chasse, and Vicente. *What the bleep do we know!?* Deerfield Beach, Florida: Health Communications, Inc. p. 151

Bernardin, J. *The gift of peace.* New York: Doubleday,.

Covey, S.R., Merrill, A.R. & Merrill, R.R. (1994). *First things first.* New York: Simon & Shuster, 1994, pp. 88-89.

Hahn, T.N. *Peace is every step.* New York: Bantam Books, 1992

Ponder, C. *The dynamic laws of prayer.* Marina Del Rey, CA: DeVorss & Company, p. 178

Chapter 6

Al-Anon. (1992). *The courage to change.* Virginia Beach, VA: Al-Anon Family Group Headquarters,

Ellis. N. (2002). *If i live to be 100: Lessons from the centenarians .* Three Rivers Press.

LeDoux, J. (1996). *The emotional brain.* New York: Simon & Schuster.

Levitt & Dubner. (2005). *Freakonomics: a rogue economist explores the hidden side of everything.* New York: Harper Collins.

Lewis, T., Amini, F., Lannon. R. (2001) *A general theory of love.* Vintage.

Chapter 7

Childre, D.L. & Martin H. (1999) *The heartmath solution: The institute of heartmath's revolutionary program for engaging the power of the heart's intelligence.* San Francisco: Harper, p. 34

Collins, J. & Porras, J.I. (1994). *Built to last: Successful habits of visionary companies.* New York: Harper Business.

Gallwey, T.W. (1974). *The inner game of tennis*, Random House, pp.21-22.

Gonzalez, Richard J., "Putting the techniques to work," *Trial Magazine*. Aug 2004, p. 22.

Nemth, M. (1997). *The energy of money: A spiritual guide to financial and personal fulfillment*. New York: Ballantine Wellspring.

Ponder, C. *The dynamic laws of prayer*. Marina Del Rey, CA: DeVorss & Company, p. 178

Post, N. (2003). "The Headaches of Work Life," *Acupuncture Today*. Aug. 2003.

Senge, P. (1990). *The fifth discipline: The art and practice of the learning organization*. New York: Doubleday.

Shreeve, J. (2005) "What's in Your Mind," *National Geographic*, March 2005, p. 31).

Swartz, M. & Watkins, S. (2003). *Power failure: The inside story of the collapse of enron*. New York: Doubleday.

Tacito, N. (2004). "Giving up your soul is bad business", *The Systems Thinker*, Vol 15, Number 6, August 2004, pp. 8-9.

Chapter 8

Collins, J. (2001). *Good to great: Why some companies make the leap... and others don't*. Collins.

McLuhan, M. (1964). *understanding media: the extensions of man*. New York: Random House.

Wheatley, M. (2002). *Turning to one another: Simple conversations to restore hope to the future*. Berrett-Koehler Publishers, p. 19.

Chapter 9

Arntz, Chasse, and Vicente. *What the bleep do we know!?* Deerfield Beach, Florida: Health Communications, Inc. p. 151.

Argrys, C. & Schön, D.A. (1992*). Theory in practice: Increasing professional effectiveness*. Jossey-Bass

Thompson, K.L. (2001). *The Systems Thinker*, Volume 12, Number 7, September 2001, pp. 2-.

Pert, C.B. (1997). *The molecules of emotion The science behind mind-body medicine*. New York: Scribner.

Chapter 10

DeMille, M. (1956) *The life and work of martha graham,* New York: Random House.

Hoff, B. (1982). The tao of pooh. New York: Penguin Books, p. 65.

Zander, R.S., & Zander, B. (2002). *The art of possibility: Transforming professional and personal life.* London, England: Penguin Books.

Chapter 11

Amen, D.G. (2001). Healing ADD: *The breakthrough program that allows you to see and heal the 6 types of add.* New York: The Berkeley Publishing Group,

Eick, C. (1998) The Core Addictions: The Roots of Addictive Behavior" in *EAPA Exchange,* January-February 1998, pp. 10-11).

Lipton, B. (2005). *The biology of belief.* Sant Rosa, CA: Mountain of Love / Elite Books.

Chapter 12

Jones, Dewitt. *Everyday Creativity.* Star Thrower Video. www.starthrower.com.

Thompson, K.L. (2001). "Learning as a Biological Process". *The System Thinker.* Sep. 2001.

Jensen. E, & Johnson, G. (1995). *The learning brain.* San Diego: Turning Point Publishing, p. 15

Pert, C.B. (1997). *The molecules of emotion The science behind mind-body medicine.* New York: Scribner.

Ruiz, D.M. (1997*). The four agreements.* San Rafael, CA: Amber-Allen Publishing Company. pp. 12-13).

Seligman, M. (2002). Authentic happiness: Using the new positive psychology to realize your potential for lasting fulfillment. New York: Free Press. P.6

AFTERWORD

Collins, J. (2001). *Good to great: Why some companies make the leap... and others don't.* Collins.

Suggestions for Further Reading

Amen, Daniel G. *Healing ADD: The Breakthrough Program That Allows You to See and Heal the 6 Types of ADD.* New York: The Berkley Publishing Group, 2001.

Arntz, William, Betsy Chasse and Mark Vicente. *What the Bleep Do We Know!? Discovering the Endless Possibilities for Altering Your Everyday Reality.* Deerfield Beach, FL: Health Communications, Inc., 2005.

Augsburger, David. *Caring Enough to Confront.* Ventura, California: Regal Books, 1983.

Childre, Doc and Howard Martin with Donna Beech. *The HeartMath Solution.* San Francisco: HarperCollins, 1999.

Collins, Jim. *Good to Great.* New York: Harper Business, 2001.

Covey, Stephen. *The Eighth Habit: From Effectiveness to Greatness.* New York: Free Press, 2004.

Covey, Stephen. *The Seven Habits of Highly Effective People.* New York: Simon and Schuster, 1989.

Desjardins, Liliane and Gilles. Creators of the Desjardins Model of Recovery. www.higherpower.info.

Dyer, Wayne. *Inspiration.* Carlsbad, CA: Hay House, 2006.

Dyer, Wayne. *The Power of Intention: Learning to Co-create Your World Your Way.* Carlsbad, CA: Hay House, 2004.

Ellis, Neenah. *If I Live to Be 100: Lessons from the Centenarians.* New York: Three Rivers Press, 2004.

Emoto, Masaru. *The Hidden Messages in Water.* Hillsboro, Oregon: Beyond Words Publishing, Inc., 2004.

Goleman, Daniel. *Social Intelligence: The New Science of Human Relationships.* New York: Bantam Dell, 2006.

Hansford, Dee. Telephone Interview, 2001.

Hoff, Benjamin. *The Tao of Pooh.* New York: Penguin, 1982.

Isaacs, Bill and John Sterman. "Lighting the Way: Tipping Points and the Human Side of Collective Transformation." 2004 Systems Thinking in Action® Conference, www.pegasuscom.com

Jaworski, Joseph. *Synchronicity: The Inner Path of Leadership.* San Francisco: Berrett-Koehler Publishers, 1996.

Jensen, Eric. *The Learning Brain.* San Diego: Turning Point Publishing, 1995. www.jlcbrain.com

LeDoux, Joseph. *The Emotional Brain: The Mysterious Underpinnings of Emotional Life.* New York: Simon and Schuster, 1996.

Lipton, Bruce. *The Biology of Belief: Unleashing the Power of Consciousness, Matter, and Miracles.* Santa Rosa, CA: Mountain of Love/Elite Books, 2005.

Loehr, Jim and Tony Schwartz. *The Power of Full Engagement: Managing Energy, Not Time, Is the Key to High Performance and Personal Renewal.* New York: Free Press, 2003.

Palmer, Parker. *Let Your Life Speak: Listening for the Voice of Vocation.* San Francisco: Jossey-Bass, 2000.

Payne, James E. *Doorways into Mind: An Introduction to Experiential Psychology.* Xlibris Corporation, 2004.

Pert, Candace. *Molecules of Emotion: Why You Feel the Way You Feel.* New York: Scribner, 1997.

Pink, Daniel H. *A Whole New Mind: Moving from the Information Age to the Conceptual Age.* New York: Riverhead, 2005.

Post, Nancy. *Elements of Organization.* Philadelphia, PA: Post Enterprises.

Ruiz, Don Miguel. *The Four Agreements: A Practical Guide to Personal Freedom.* San Rafael, CA: Amber-Allen Publishing, 1997.

Schulkin, Jay. *Rethinking Homeostasis: Allostatic Regulation in Physiology and Pathophysiology.* Cambridge, MA: A Bradford Book of the MIT Press, 2003.

Senge, Peter. *The Fifth Discipline: The Art and Practice of the Learning Organization.* New York: Doubleday, 1990.

Silf, Margaret. *The Gift of Prayer.* New York: Bluebridge, 2005.

Thich Nhat Hanh. *Peace Is Every Step: The Path of Mindfulness in Everyday Life.* New York: Bantam, 1991.

"A User's Guide to the Brain." Time, 29 January 2007.

Watkins, Sherron and Mimi Swartz. *Power Failure: The Inside Story of the Collapse of Enron.* New York: Doubleday, 2003.

Wheatley, Margaret. *Leadership and the New Science: Learning about Organization from an Orderly Universe.* San Francisco: Berrett-Koehler Publishers, 1992.

Wheatley, Margaret. *Turning to One Another: Simple Conversations to Restore Hope to the Future.* San Francisco: Berrett-Koehler Publishers, 2002.

Zander, Rosamund Stone and Benjamin. *The Art of Possibility: Transforming Professional and Personal Life.* New York: Penguin, 2002.

Zukav, Gary and Linda Francis. *The Mind of the Soul: Responsible Choice.* New York: Free Press, 2003.

Zukav, Gary. *The Seat of the Soul.* New York: Fireside, 1990.

Suggestions for Further Viewing

Contact, a movie. The journey inward is the ultimate journey as science and religion find consilience.

Groundhog Day. An arrogant television reporter is assigned the task of going to Punxsutawney, Pennsylvania, for the annual appearance of Punxsutawney Phil, the famous groundhog who predicts whether there will be more winter. His inconsiderate treatment of people earns him the right to re-live that same day over and over until he slowly starts making some changes and finally allows himself to have love and compassion.

Mother. A writer, experiencing writer's block, becomes convinced that the solution to his problem is to go back home. Surprising his mother, he raids the garage storage to retrieve all his old memorabilia and restore his old room to how it looked when he was a teenager. One day while his mother was out, he discovered hat boxes full of unpublished manuscripts. When she returned, he confronted her. "You're a writer!" he shouted. Prodding her to finish what she had left undone, he found his own blockage gone. As he drives away, his mother is happily at work on her manuscripts.

The Legend of Bagger Vance. About golf and much more. When we align our thinking and feeling with the invisible field before us, we achieve our peak performance and accomplish feats beyond our fondest dreams.

Pay It Forward. About a junior high school student whose social studies teacher assigned his class to come up with an idea that could change the world. This young boy thought if one person would do something kind for three people and ask each of those people to "pay it forward" by doing something kind for three more people, it would eventually change the world.

Tuesdays with Morrie, a movie about love. A young, self-absorbed sports reporter, learning that his beloved college professor is dying, decides to spend Tuesdays interviewing him for a book. Along the way, his old professor teaches him to love. "But what good is it?" he laments near the end of the movie. "Now I love you, and you're just going to die anyway."

"Yes. I am going to die. But after I die, you will still love me," his wise teacher said.

What the Bleep Do We Know!? A movie that is part documentary, part animation, and part drama, the movie explores quantum physics, spirituality, and neuroscience to underscore the truth that we create our own reality, whether we are aware or not.

About the Author

Nancy Oelklaus lives on the rim of a canyon in Austin, Texas, with her husband, Harlan, and Feathers, a curly white lap dog. Nancy lightens the load for leaders and ordinary people by teaching them powerful findings from neuroscience ignited by the scriptural wisdom of the ages. Her professional and personal clients learn to create environments where people thrive, at work and at home. Specializing in helping people make transitions, her knowledge and skills have been learned through more than 30 years of working in education and business to understand how adults learn and change— and how they can do it faster so that they may spend more time in "happily ever after."

Dr. Oelklaus holds a bachelor's degree in communications/theater education from Oklahoma Baptist University, a master's degree in English from the University of North Texas, and a doctorate in educational administration from Texas A&M University in Commerce. Nancy enjoys taking photographs and writing poetry.

> The heart knows its home
> And longs to return
> From long absence,
>
> Devoted to work—or
> The process of living.
> The yearning yet glows
>
> For love and expression
> And honest, plain hope.
> When that longing peaks,
>
> The heart turns its wheel
> To the rutted road bed,
> Old and beloved.
>
> It remembers the way
> And returns.

Index

A

accept, 37, 53, 66, 76, 90, 114, 120, 138,
    151, 168, 170, 200
ADD, 165
addictions
    core, 59
affirmation, 190
Al-Anon, 20, 79, 153, 169
alcoholism, ix, 153, 165, 166, 167, 168, 169
Amen, Daniel G., 165
anger, 6, 22, 33, 39, 55, 62, 77, 85, 91,
    113, 118, 120, 121, 131, 132, 143, 145,
    155, 165, 177, 178, 179, 193
    acting out of, 9
antidepressants, 22, 23, 27
anxiety, 25, 26, 42, 49, 57, 84, 98, 108,
    165, 183
Argyris, Chris, 21, 141
Arntz, William, 63, 65
art, 9
attuning, 29
Authentic Profile, 30, 76, 77, 89, 123, 124,
    125, 139, 150, 169, 170
Authentic Self, 11, 43, 59, 124, 155, 161,
    166, 170
authentic selves, 63, 156

B

Baxter, Lewis, 190
Bernardin, Joseph Cardinal, 62
Biology of Belief, The, 163
bird, xii, 52, 65
blind spots, 22, 198
Bohm, David, 105
brain, xi, 14, 28, 35, 39, 45, 51, 56, 59, 77,
    80, 84, 93, 97, 98, 104, 112, 113, 115,
    118, 135, 144, 149, 155, 164, 165, 166,
    170, 171, 177, 178, 179, 185, 199
    and meditation, 103
    development, 14, 111
    emotional center, 2
    evnironment, 165
    neurons, 36
    oxygen, 83
    relaxed alertness, 19, 81, 90, 102, 190
    research, 91
    state dependent, 189
breakthrough, 185

breath, 61, 83, 131
Bruch, Heike, 199
business, 3, 14, 33, 45, 93, 100, 101, 105,
    131, 134, 156, 159, 169, 170

C

callus, 70, 71
Chasse, Betsy, 63, 65
child, 28, 51, 64, 70, 72, 78, 94, 113, 114,
    133, 149, 155, 161, 170, 171, 173, 176,
    181
child abuse, 164
Childre, Doc, 45, 46
children, 1, 18, 20, 36, 43, 55, 57, 63, 65,
    69, 78, 79, 114, 116, 140, 159, 164, 165,
    166, 173, 176, 179, 181, 189, 192, 196,
    199
    overpraising, 86
Christian, 57, 190
Christina's World, 9
church, x, 1, 4, 36, 51, 55, 72, 75, 95, 105,
    139
Clear Impact, 199
Collins, Jim, 105, 120, 200
communicate, 91, 96, 104, 178, 189, 192
communication, 42, 82, 96, 108, 166
conflict, 21, 33, 34, 70, 78, 82, 83, 134
confront, 52, 75, 81, 93, 115, 121, 131,
    134, 136, 137, 139, 140, 167, 168, 210
Contact, xiii
contemplation, 8, 9, 61
Cook, Captain James, 7
core addictions, 21, 164
cortisol, 26
courage, 7
Covey, Stephen R., 30, 62

D

Dalai Lama, xiv
Dante, 162
daughter, 12, 70, 71, 93, 94, 108, 122
Davidson, Richard, 102
death, 12, 23, 99, 124, 179
Declaration of Independence, 17
depression, 57, 190
Desiderata, 98
Desjardins, Liliane and Gilles, ix, 35, 38,
    195
Dickinson, E., 86, 109

discovery, 13, 14, 80, 135, 177, 189
Divine Comedy, The, 162
Doctor Faustus, 58
Dumbo, 173
Dynamic Laws of Prayer, The, 99

E

education, 29, 45, 51, 57, 58, 75, 78, 139
ego, 18, 21, 23
    domination, 158
    excessive, 22
    external world, 21
Ehrmann, Max, 98
Einstein, Albert, 42
electromagnetic field, 45, 90
Ellis, Neenah, 79
emotion, 2, 35, 36, 40, 55, 80, 83, 98, 112,
    118, 137, 140, 143, 158, 165, 166, 191
    pent-up, 6
    positive, 135, 195
emotional energy, 196
emotional hijacking, 81
energy, 21–29, 30, 43, 69, 70, 71, 73, 75,
    77, 83, 89, 91, 93, 95, 101, 103, 112,
    113, 114, 121, 131, 132, 134, 136, 137,
    139, 141, 145, 146, 147, 149, 154, 156,
    195, 196, 199, 200
    emotional, 34
    from the heart, 108
    healthy level, 33
    human, 22
    lack, 4
    negative, 35–37, 135
    of joy, 107
    sources of, 2
    waste of, 193
Energy Analysis, 21, 22, 24, 25, 27, 30, 33,
    34, 76, 77, 134, 150, 169
energy level, 26
energy of love, xv
Eric Jensen, 189
Evenari, Gail, 59
Everyday Creativity, 187
Exodus 3:14, 96
Eye of the Needle, 135, 141, 145, 146, 147,
    166

F

family, ix, 55, 57, 62, 65, 69, 70, 71, 74, 75,
    79, 82, 94, 113, 114, 115, 124, 139, 140,
    159, 165, 173, 178, 179
Family Ties, 5
Faraday chambers, 97

father, xiii, 48, 52, 53, 55, 90, 114, 115,
    116, 119, 159, 169, 176, 177, 179
Faustus, 59
fear, 13, 23, 26, 37, 39, 49, 55, 61, 65, 72,
    81, 85, 113, 121, 132, 136, 140, 141,
    145, 155, 166, 190
feedback, 11, 78, 100
    receiving, 8
feelings, 2, 29, 43, 46, 65, 66, 77, 86, 102,
    109, 137, 140, 143, 158, 164, 178, 191
firefighting, 100, 101
Flowers, Betty Sue, 40
forgiveness, 38, 39, 40, 46, 51, 61, 85, 123,
    155, 164, 180, 193, 200
forgiveness letter, 40
Fox news poll, 139
Fox, Michael J., 5
Frankl, Viktor, 162
friend, 11, 23, 48, 66, 69, 70, 71, 90, 94,
    103, 107, 113, 116, 146, 181, 199
Frost, Robert, 109

G

Gallwey, W. Timothy, 104
Gandhi, Mahatma, 139
Ghoshal, Sumantra, 199
goal setting, 195
God, ix, xi, xiii, xiv, xv, 13, 19, 21, 36, 38,
    46, 50, 51, 52, 53, 55, 61, 62, 67, 85, 91,
    92, 96, 100, 114, 115, 119, 122, 131,
    139, 149, 153, 156, 161
    crying out to, 12
    knowing, 18
    presence of, 8
Golden Rule, 63, 82, 83
Goodwill, 3, 95
grace, xi, 51, 54, 61, 74, 152
gratitude, 191
grief, 6
Grinberg-Zylberbaum, Jacob, 97
Groundhog Day, 100, 105, 118
guidance system, 8

H

halo effect, x, 76, 120
Halo Effect, 86
Hamlet, 4, 96
Handbook for Judges, 53
Hansford, Dee, 29, 190
happiness, 17, 18, 58, 79
Hawaiian Islands, 7
heart, xiii, xiv, 9, 10, 11, 13, 17, 21, 44, 45,
    46, 48, 51, 54, 56, 61, 62, 69, 70, 71, 73,

80, 83, 89, 90, 91, 92, 93, 94, 95, 96, 97,
    98, 103, 105, 106, 107, 108, 111, 113,
    114, 118, 120, 121, 122, 123, 132, 139,
    141, 144, 145, 146, 147, 150, 151, 152,
    154, 155, 156, 166, 181, 183, 187, 190
    change of, 37
    ears of the, 90
    experience of God, 91
    eyes of, 8
    forgiving, i, 160
    speaking from, 90, 190
heart energy, 90, 91
heart's desire, 156
HeartMath, 45, 46, 83, 90, 93, 144
Heath, P., 189
Hierarchy of Needs, 86
High Flight, xv
Higher Power, 19, 54, 55, 98
Hoff, Benjamin, 154
Holy Spirit, 8
human nature, 194
human system, 2
Hunter, M., 156
husband, ix, 36, 48, 52, 65, 66, 74, 76, 95,
    119, 122

I

I Love Lucy, 96
immune system, 26, 84
inner voice, xiv, 4, 5, 6, 9, 10
intent, x, 11, 13, 18, 36, 64, 80, 91, 96, 97,
    145, 150, 151, 152, 154, 194
intuition, 12
Isaacs, W., 100
iThink, 22, 23

J

Jensen, Eric, 189
Jesus, 18, 66, 75, 100, 161
Jones, Dewitt, 187
Jones, Wendell, 199
Jung, Carl, 55

K

Keaton, Alex P., 5, 11
Keller, H., 86
Keller, Helen, 86

L

lawyer, 95, 96, 168

leadership, 22, 33, 54, 64, 69, 137, 141,
    146
learn, x, xi, 9, 12, 17, 20, 22, 33, 42, 45,
    51, 54, 72, 77, 78, 79, 81, 84, 85, 86, 90,
    91, 96, 99, 101, 103, 105, 107, 123, 131,
    132, 138, 139, 140, 143, 145, 146, 151,
    163, 164, 171, 178, 187, 188
LeDoux, Joseph, 80
Level Land, 116
Levitt and Dubner, 78, 79
Lewis and Clark, 99
Lewis, Thomas, 80
Lipton, Bruce, xiv, 161, 163, 173
Loehr, Jim, 2, 24
love, ix, x, xiii, 4, 11, 18, 22, 38, 46, 48, 60,
    61, 62, 65, 72, 73, 74, 75, 76, 77, 79, 85,
    89, 90, 91, 96, 104, 109, 116, 117, 119,
    120, 122, 131, 136, 139, 140, 145, 147,
    149, 155, 156, 161, 165, 166, 168, 176,
    177, 178, 179, 185, 187, 200
    and alcoholism, 169
    and yearning, 5
    speaking truth, 166
    unconditional, 104
lymbic resonance, 80
    defined, 79

M

Magie, John Gillespie, Jr., xv
Man's Search for Meaning, 162
Marlowe, Christopher, 58
marriage, 52, 61, 65, 66
Martin, Howard, 45, 46
Marvin's Room, 48
Maslow's Hierarchy of Needs, 1
McConaughey, Matthew, xiii
McLuhan, Marshall, 119, 158
Medina, Judge Harold, 53, 54
meditation, 8, 61, 97, 99
Medium is the Massage, The, 119
meetings, 79, 83, 169
memory system, 14
Meno, Lionel "Skip", 54
mental models, 21
migraines, ix, 3, 4
minnows, 12
mirror neurons, 28, 77, 78, 79, 80, 82, 86,
    101, 123, 135, 138, 145, 168, 179, 189,
    194
Molecules of Emotion, The, 192
mother, 43, 70, 71, 72, 76, 78, 90, 108,
    114, 116, 119, 133, 139, 144, 156, 159,
    161, 169, 176, 178, 179, 181
Museum of Modern Art, 9

N

nature, 7, 10, 11, 18, 38, 44, 66, 82, 96,
    101, 137, 139, 149, 154, 155, 162
    solace, 6
Nemeth, Maria, 89
New Testament, 170
New York City, 9
Nobre, Tacito, 97

O

observer, 54, 55, 77
Occam's Razor, xiv
Oedipus Rex, 17, 119
Old Testament, 51, 92, 96
One Day at a Time, 153
organization, 14, 28, 33, 34, 42, 65, 90, 92,
    101, 106, 115, 121, 132, 134, 137, 139,
    150, 167, 168, 199, 200
organizational energy, 199, 200

P

pain, 2, 4, 13, 17, 18, 19, 20, 22, 25, 34,
    35, 37, 52, 58, 113, 118, 164, 180
    avoidance, 2
Palmer, Parker, 13, 77
Pay It Forward, 28, 102, 210
peace, ix, 1, 19, 23, 38, 40, 46, 47, 48, 58,
    59, 63, 78, 81, 84, 90, 92, 98, 139, 143,
    144, 145
peaceful, 8, 11, 104, 136, 144, 145, 178
Pert, Candace, 143, 191
philosopher's stone, 200
Piailug, Mau, 59
Ponder, Catherine, 99
Post, N., 102, 199
prayer, ix, 39, 61, 62, 66, 83, 164, 183
presence, 43, 45, 54, 95, 97, 101, 135
principal, 64, 90, 157, 189
process, xi, 13, 14, 18, 20, 21, 34, 35, 36,
    37, 40, 45, 47, 48, 61, 77, 81, 84, 85, 96,
    105, 106, 113, 121, 125, 140, 141, 155,
    161, 164, 165, 169, 171, 180, 200
Prozac, 190
Purpose-Driven Life, The, 122

R

Reagan, Ronald, 109
receive, 22, 30, 42, 46, 51, 57, 61, 137, 188
Rethinking Homeostasis, 26
Rizzolatti, Giacomo, 135, 189
Robe, The, 99

Robinson, A., 12
Rudyard Kipling, 121
Ruiz, Don Miguel, 36, 192

S

Sagan, Carl, xiii
salvation, 18
school, x, 1, 4, 20, 28, 43, 51, 54, 57, 63,
    64, 69, 72, 73, 74, 75, 76, 78, 89, 90, 91,
    93, 94, 102, 122, 133, 150, 151, 157,
    189, 199
Schulkin, Jay, 26
Schwartz, Tony, 2, 25
Schweitzer, A., 85
Science of Mind, 173, 181
Secret, The, xiv
self-discovery, 5, 8
Seligman, M., 195
Senge, Peter, 21, 101, 106
serotonin, 190
Shakespeare, 4, 58, 85, 96, 136
Socrates, 18, 154, 170, 171
Sophocles, 17, 18, 119
soul, 4, 6, 8, 54, 58, 59, 75, 77, 80, 81, 94,
    97, 111, 113, 114, 118
Sound of Music, The, 156
spirit, 85, 98, 173, 180
spiritual, x, xi, 23, 47, 48, 52, 58, 93, 139,
    154, 200
spiritual beings, xiv
spiritual dimension, xiv
spiritual energy, 25
spiritual life, 4
Spiritual Side of Judging, The, 53
spiritual teachings, 5
Steinbrecher, E., 8
Sterman, J., 100
stress, 12, 23, 25, 26, 28, 56, 79, 80, 83,
    97, 98, 137, 139, 143, 163, 191
swan, 52, 53
SWOT, 167
symbolic marriage, xiv
system, 25, 28, 29, 30, 36, 45, 53, 56, 65,
    69, 72, 80, 93, 98, 101, 105, 121, 134,
    137, 199

T

Tables Turned, The, 44
teach, xi, 44, 53, 77, 78, 79, 94, 117, 178
teacher, x, 28, 35, 43, 59, 61, 63, 64, 72,
    74, 78, 98, 104, 123, 133, 145, 149, 157
Ten Commandments, 91
Thich Nhat Hanh, 65, 189

third person, 53, 55, 74, 114
Thompson, N., 59
Thoreau, Henry David, 163
Thorndike, E. L., 86
Toolbox, 14
tools, 13, 14, 22, 40, 46, 63, 90, 121, 125,
    135, 141, 169, 179, 183
transcendence, xiv, 86
    defined, 81
trust, 9
truth, xiii, xiv, 10, 18, 24, 35, 37, 38, 46,
    52, 54, 60, 62, 63, 69, 75, 76, 77, 78, 81,
    90, 91, 92, 94, 96, 98, 107–9, 113, 114,
    119, 120, 121, 122, 131, 132, 134, 137,
    139, 145, 146, 147, 150, 152, 153, 156,
    163, 166, 168, 170, 173, 180, 190, 192
    in love, 168

U

understanding, 20, 21, 25, 33, 38, 40, 53,
    65, 71, 92, 108, 112, 113, 118, 124, 133,
    136, 141, 150, 152, 153, 155, 164, 169,
    170, 171, 178, 179, 180, 181, 185
Unleashing Organizational Energy, 199

V

Vicente, Mark, 63, 65
voice, 12, 19, 28, 29, 42, 45, 46, 54, 57, 59,
    61, 63, 71, 75, 93, 94, 95, 97, 108, 114,
    146, 147, 155, 163, 173
    of nature, 7
    silent, 9
    small, 8

W

Warren, Rick, 122
water, ix, xiii, 8, 12, 41, 47, 65, 72, 83, 84,
    92, 99, 118, 161
Watkins, S., 101, 102

wayfarer, 1, 7, 21, 52, 59, 64
wayfaring, 1, 57, 59, 140
    vs. wayfinding, 6
wayfinder, 7, 8, 9, 12, 14, 45, 47, 51, 59,
    63, 64, 200
Wayfinders: A Pacific Odyssey, 59
wayfinding, 7, 12, 14, 45, 46, 48, 59, 63
What the Bleep Do We Know!?, 54, 63
Wheatley, Margaret, 107, 113
Whole Foods, 93
whole truth, 152
Whole Truth letter, 35–37, 40
Whole Truth letters, 36
willing, 12, 30, 39, 53, 61, 72, 74, 77, 118,
    119, 132, 138, 139, 145, 170, 198
Wilson, 55
Wilson, Bill, 114
words, xv, 17, 24, 29, 36, 37, 41, 42, 48,
    54, 59, 61, 62, 66, 71, 75, 78, 84, 85, 90,
    91, 93, 94, 95, 96, 97, 98, 99, 103, 104,
    108, 111, 114, 119, 120, 131, 133, 137,
    138, 140, 143, 145, 146, 147, 149, 150,
    151, 153, 157, 158, 162, 163, 171, 178,
    180, 181, 186, 187, 189, 200
    different, 198
    goal setting, 195
    have power, 192
    written on your heart, 193
Wordsworth, William, 43
workaholism, ix, 4, 58
wren, 10
Wyeth, Andrew, 9

Y

Yahweh, 51

Z

Zander, Rosamund Stone and Benjamin,
    153, 155, 157, 161

Printed in the United States
103055LV00003B/1-124/P